FIRE FROM
THE FOREST

FIRE FROM THE FOREST

The SAS Brigade in France, 1944

ROGER FORD

CASSELL

Cassell
Wellington House, 125 Strand
London WC2R 0BB

Copyright © Roger Ford 2003

First published 2003

British Library Cataloguing-in-Publication Data
A catalogue record for this book is available from
the British Library

ISBN 0-304-36335-9

Distributed in the USA by
Sterling Publishing Co Inc
387 Park Avenue South
New York, NY 10016-8810

Printed and bound in Great Britain by
Clays Ltd, St Ives plc

To DSB,
Sunray to a generation

If you go down to the woods today,
You'd better not go alone.
It's lovely down in the woods today,
But safer to stay at home ...

CONTENTS

Contents

LIST OF MAPS

INTRODUCTION

W hen twenty-four-year-old David Stirling, a Scots Guards-turned-commando subaltern, talked General Claude Auchinleck into allowing him to create L Detachment, Special Air Service, in Egypt in July 1941, he had in mind the formation of a 'private army' of like-minded individuals, to operate behind enemy lines, outside the regular chain of command and, not at all incidentally, not to be subject to the sort of formal discipline which manifested itself in monotonous, mindless tasks which involved Blanco, Brasso and boot-blacking. He was not alone in this, of course; others were also trying to side-step reality in a way which, in the words of one senior officer,

> contributed precisely nothing to Allied victory. All [the private armies] did was to offer a too-easy, because romanticised, form of gal-lantry to a few anti-social, irresponsible individualists, who sought a more personal satisfaction from the war than of standing their chance, like proper soldiers, of being bayoneted in a slit trench or burnt alive in a tank.

The main difference between Stirling and the other anti-social, irresponsible individuals lay in the degree of success *his* creation was to achieve in North Africa; and it eventually became clear even to his denigrators that he had taken the first steps towards validating a concept which had never before been much more than an irregular aspiration. However, following his capture, in fairly ignominious circumstances, in January 1943, the unit, by now a regiment, looked set to lose its singular identity. Reduced in numbers, it functioned temporarily in a debased role as the Special Raiding Squadron (SRS), under the command of Stirling's somewhat unlikely successor (despite his being second-in-command, he was not Stirling's choice), the mercurial Robert Blair 'Paddy' Mayne, ably assisted by 'originals' such as Bill

Fraser, Tony Marsh and Harry Poat, who went on to become squadron commanders; Johnny Wiseman, who became a troop commander, and Jim Almonds (who was later commissioned in the field), Bob Bennett, Pat Riley, Reg Seekings and Bob Tait, who all became sergeant-majors, when it was reconstituted as the senior formation of the SAS Brigade.

The SRS saw combat again during the Italian campaign, and was joined there by 2 SAS, raised in Algeria late in 1942 by David Stirling's elder brother, Bill. 2 SAS' core personnel came from another 'private army' known originally as the Small Scale Raiding Force and later as 62 Commando. Like L Detachment, it took some time to get up to strength and reach the standards of training set in Egypt, and during that period many men were to contract malaria and later suffered recurring attacks. 2 SAS became operational in May 1943. The missions in Italy, however, achieved little. Bill Stirling placed the blame firmly at the door of Allied Forces HQ, which, he complained, simply did not understand the concept the SAS had been raised and trained to realise, and insisted on employing it as an assault force. The SRS was withdrawn in the autumn and set sail for Glasgow on Christmas Eve, 1943; 2 SAS was withdrawn from the theatre in its turn, in mid-March 1944, and it too returned home.

It had been the Stirling brothers' aspiration to see 'their' regiments combined into a brigade, and now, in the run-up to the invasion of France, the hope was to be realised, certain senior figures having come to the belated conclusion that there was indeed a need for a rather irregular force to be deployed inside enemy-occupied territory. There was still a considerable amount to be done actually to define its role, even in the broadest sense, and there was still stiff opposition to its very existence in some quarters, the 'private army' tag being a hard one to shift, but at least it had weathered the worst of the storm of threatened disbandment, and had found a home in the British Army's Order of Battle, as part of 1st Airborne Corps. Over the course of the next year and a half, in its training area in Scotland first of all, then in France, the Low Countries and finally in Germany, the SAS Brigade grew to maturity. It was to be an uncomfortable experience in many senses, for it had first, to use a metaphor from a later period, to clear a playing field and then painstakingly level it, against opposition from a variety of different sectors which saw it as an expensive irrelevance, drawing on precious resources which would have been better employed in the main battle.

Until now, the story of the part the SAS Brigade played in the liberation of France in 1944 has been told patchily and, it must be said, very poorly. There is not a single history of the SAS Brigade's service in France which does not contain errors, some great and significant, some small and of little import. Even the official and quasi-official histories produced by Lt-Col TBH. Otway (*Airborne Forces*) and Maj-Gen John Strawson (*A History of the SAS Regiment*) with the approval and assistance of the Ministry of Defence and the SAS Regiment are unreliable. It was the wild disparities in the accounts of its doings which led me to undertake this book, in the belief that history, as well as the Brigade, deserved better. I have, in all cases, gone to the original documentary sources in an effort to avoid the repetition of mistakes, misrepresentations and even downright falsehoods which have appeared in existing works.

The opinions expressed here, and in the work which follows, are, of course, entirely my own, and so too, naturally, are any mistakes. During the course of my researches I received the invaluable help of many men in Britain and France; I thank them all. However, I did not rely on interviews for reports of events which took place more than half a century in the past, but rather on the contemporary accounts of SAS Brigade and Special Forces Headquarters activities filed and preserved for all to see at the Public Record Office in London (PRO), the staff of which were and are unfailingly helpful. They are, how-ever, also artificially constrained, for not all documents were retained, and over the years others have been 'weeded' for one reason or another, and some records seem to be irretrievably lost from the public domain, which is lamentable. In particular, files relating to Operation Loyton proved difficult to locate, but here the Special Air Service Regimental Association's archivist came to the rescue. Other files, especially after-action reports, are not always comprehensive for rather different, and perhaps more understandable reasons: the men charged with writing them were keener to enjoy a brief-enough period of leave than to slave over an unaccustomed typewriter reliving the events of the previous weeks and months, and skimped the task in consequence. Happily, the Brigade's reports were not the only ones compiled; almost all its operations also involved Jedburgh teams, and the records of their doings are generally more complete (and are also duplicated and often augmented in the *Office of Strategic Services' Special Operations Branch War Diary*, henceforward 'SO War Diary', preserved at the National Archives and Records Administration in College Park, Maryland); in consequence there is no case where I have been unable to reconstruct a picture of the events of an operation, though in line with my ambition to write a

comprehensive history of the part the SAS Brigade played in the liberation of France, there are some which I wish were more complete.

Few know the full extent of the hardships the men of the Special Air
Service Brigade underwent that summer, living a precarious existence
on the brink of practicality. In a very real sense, they could not have
been said to have been combat-ready before being committed to action;
so much of what they were expected to do, and so many of the techniques they were to use, were completely untried that officers and other
ranks alike were constantly learning how to put sometimes faulty
theory into practice under very arduous conditions in the field, while
being hunted by an implacable and experienced enemy. The surprise is
not that mistakes were made in the process, but rather that many more
were avoided. In the theatres in which they had previously operated, in
North Africa and in Italy, conditions had been very different. There
they had gone out as a self-contained force to do a specific job, with the
intention, at least, of returning to base when it was over; now they were
to be dropped into the darkness over enemy territory and remain there
for weeks or even months, living in concealed campsites in woods and
forests with no certainty of the quality and reliability of support, depen-
dent on strength of purpose and strength of character to get them
through. They pioneered a new way of waging war in an age-old
fashion, proving the validity of a new concept in the process, and so well
that the model has never since required serious modification.

The SAS Brigade, 1944-pattern, succeeded entirely as a result of
being prepared to gamble heavily on its own abilities, quite literally to
dare in order to win, and amongst that which it won was the grudging
but real respect of its peers. Superficially, the SAS trooper of 1944
seems to have had little in common with his modern counterpart, but
underneath the uniform the two share one hard-earned characteristic –
both could claim to be the best soldier of his type in the world of his
time. Although the modern-day trooper's methods may be much more
sophisticated, his training both more rigorous and more specialised,
and the technology at his command many generations more effective
than that available to his counterpart back then, perhaps he would still
recognise himself if somehow he were transported back to the forests
and the fields of France in the summer of 1944, when the young men
who wore Excalibur on their caps came to help fan to full flame the
spark of resistance which the *maquisards* had kept alive at such cost.

St-Paul-Cap-de-Joux,
July 2002

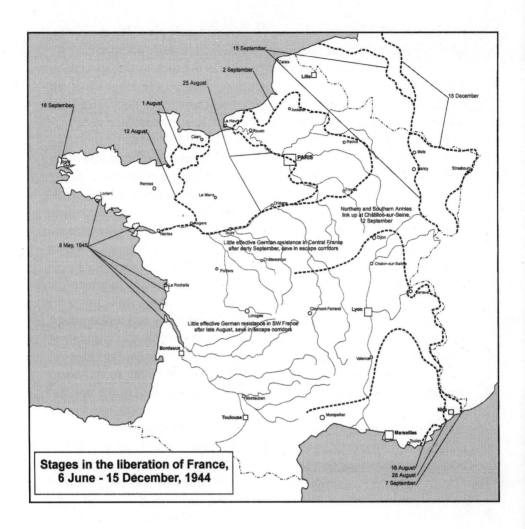

18 September

1 August

25 August

2 September

15 September

12 August

15 December

Calais

Lille

Amiens

Le Havre

Rouen

Caen

Reims

Metz

PARIS

Nancy

Strasbourg

Brest

Rennes

Le Mans

Troyes

Lorient

Orléans

Dijon

Angers

Tours

Chalon-sur-Saône

Nantes

8 May, 1945

Châteauroux

Northern and Southern Armies
link up at Châtillon-sur-Seine,
12 September

Little effective German resistance in Central France
after early September, save in escape corridors

Poitiers

Geneva

Clermont-Ferrand

Lyon

La Rochelle

Limoges

Little effective German resistance in SW France
after late August, save in escape corridors

Valence

Bordeaux

Montauban

Nice

Montpellier

Toulouse

Marseilles

Toulon

18 August
28 August
7 September

**Stages in the liberation of France,
6 June - 15 December, 1944**

Part One
THE SAS BRIGADE

THE SAS BRIGADE

On arriving in the United Kingdom from Italy in the first days of 1944, the first priority for 1 SAS, its identity newly restored, was home leave, and when the men returned to duty it was to the very different environment of the Scottish lowlands. After much dissent at quite exalted levels, plans had been made to give it a formal place within the hierarchy of the British Army as part of a brigade within Lieutenant-General Sir Frederick 'Boy' Browning's 1st Airborne Corps, a part of 21st Army Group. The SAS Brigade was formally authorised in late January, with Brigadier-General (later Major-General Sir) Roderick McLeod as its commanding officer, as an adjunct to the Army Air Corps. The reshuffle meant, amongst other things, that the men had to abandon their sand-coloured berets in favour of the maroon which Airborne Forces wore (although they kept the so-called 'winged dagger' cap badge, actually a representation of the sword Excalibur, which Bob Tait had designed); that particular revision was exceedingly unpopular with 'the originals', and some, notably Paddy Mayne, never complied. The arrangement was actually to be largely an administrative one; in practice, the SAS Brigade (code-named 'Bigot'; those privy to its secrets were said to be bigoted) was entirely self-contained. It 'worked for' 21st Army Group in France within the confines of the area as far south as the Loire and east to the limits of the *départements* immediately east of Paris and along a line parallel to the Somme north of there, and elsewhere was under the direct command of Supreme Headquarters, Allied Expeditionary Force (SHAEF); both were to exercise control over it via Airborne Forces HQ.

The appointment of Rory McLeod, whose career service had been with the Royal Artillery, as the Brigade's commanding officer was to cause considerable disquiet, particularly in the ranks of 1 SAS. Many of its men had served with the regiment since its formation, and some dated their service back to the earliest days of L Detachment. To the veterans of North Africa and Italy, McLeod was, and always remained, an outsider, although there is a considerable body of evidence to suggest that he was fully committed from the beginning to maintaining the identity and integrity of the Special Air Service and worked tirelessly to that end. That was certainly no easy task in the context of a superior command which did not understand the strategic role of the SAS (or even, perhaps, that it *had* one), and was ever ready to employ it as 'just' another commando or shock brigade, as had been the case in Italy. This uncomfortable situation was exacerbated by the appointment of more 'outsiders' to Brigade Headquarters, some of whom, it was soon suggested, were not up to the task at hand and showed a lack of understanding of the operational philosophy 1 SAS had developed, a lack which was later to be blamed for several operational failures. Brigade Tactical HQ was co-located with Airborne Forces HQ at Moor Park, and the newcomers to the former may have fallen under the latter's influence; at least one officer, Major Roy Farran, a 2 SAS squadron commander, was later to say that he felt that there was an element within Airborne Forces' command structure which resented the SAS.

Farran, writing just three years after the events, did not go so far as to suggest deliberate mishandling of the Brigade, but the implication is there, and this is perhaps an appropriate point at which to insert a caveat regarding the nature of the first-person accounts of the SAS's involvement in the liberation of France. Not surprisingly, all are extremely partisan; for their authors, the Special Air Service could do no wrong, then or later, and one must treat their testimonies with due regard. This is not to say that there was deliberate misrepresentation in their accounts, though sadly that is not universally true, but they did (and do; even almost sixty years on, survivors were quite likely to 'check with HQ' before speaking, and then guardedly, with a researcher) follow the 'party line'. We should not forget that the 'private army' was essentially one which was closed to outsiders, nor that the SAS Brigade, for all its new-found respectability, *was* very much a private army still, in a real sense, especially to the likes of Paddy Mayne, a social misfit incapable of surviving in any other environment. Some, notably Rory McLeod, tried to shake off this image, but it clung, and was eventually to contribute to the Brigade being disbanded shortly after the war's end despite the efforts of his short-lived successor, Brigadier-General Mike Calvert; it is a tribute to the quality of David Stirling's original concept, as remodelled by McLeod; to a lesser degree by Calvert, and perhaps rather more so by those who followed in their footsteps, that the Special Air Service, when reconstituted, developed into the prototype for a new and valuable military force.

The first problem facing the SAS Brigade was that of getting itself up to strength. There are difficulties in establishing the source(s) of potential new recruits, and it is by no means clear how they were identified, though that most commonly quoted is 'volunteers for service with the parachute battalions'. One thing is clear: a substantial number of these volunteers had previously served with the British Resistance Organisation's Auxiliary Units. The AUs were small operational groups trained and equipped for the task of harassing an invading enemy and sabotaging his lines of communication and supply; they have no direct relevance to the subject at hand, but they were to become a fertile ground, via the regular Army into which many of their members were later drafted, for the SAS Brigade. The Auxiliary Units were the brainchild of Colin Gubbins, latterly the head of the Special Operations Executive (SOE), and his assistants Peter Wilkinson and Bill Beyts, a specialist in mountain warfare. These three, aided by the likes of Peter Fleming, who was to be an early area commander, and Mike Calvert, McLeod's successor, established their *modus operandi*, generally gave form to what was still a fairly broad notion as to how irregular resistance units were to be organised and operate, and first formalised the sort of level of achievement which could be expected of them. Their experience with the Auxiliary Units was to condition Gubbins's and Wilkinson's thinking in a later period, and one might say that they served, in one respect, as the prototype for the Jedburgh teams; as such they perhaps take on a greater importance than has hitherto been accorded them.

The Auxiliary Units were ostensibly and nominally part of the Local Defence Volunteers and later the Home Guard, but that was little more than subterfuge to allow the men to explain their nocturnal absences from home. The majority of 'Auxiliers' were men who knew the countryside intimately – farmers and agricultural workers, gamekeepers, poachers and the like, although they counted all sorts, especially men with specific skills, such as a knowledge of explosives and demolition techniques, in their ranks – but were chosen as much for their ability to keep their mouths shut as for their innate knowledge of fieldcraft. Each region had regular army personnel forming a small leadership cadre (and it is here that the Jedburgh concept was perhaps born: the three-man Jedburgh teams were what we would now call 'military advisers', parachuted into enemy-held territory to work with resistance groups), and not unnaturally, when the threat of invasion was deemed to have passed, many of them were allowed to volunteer for other duties. Ian Fenwick, who was the north and east Somerset Auxiliary Units' Intelligence Officer, was one who joined 1 SAS Regiment, and his counterpart in Devon and Cornwall, Roy Bradford, was another; both were to die in roughly similar circumstances in occupied France in 1944, the former while commanding Operation Gain, the latter as a troop commander during Operation Houndsworth. Another Somerset AU officer, Victor Gough, was to become a Jedburgh team leader; he was captured, taken to a concentration camp and executed by firing squad at Gaggenau, near Baden-Baden, on 25 November 1944, together with a number of SAS men from Operation Loyton.

The official history of airborne forces speaks of 'nearly 300' recruits to the SAS Brigade coming from 'a special auxiliary force being disbanded at the time', and that is almost certainly a direct reference (although the AUs were not finally stood down until November 1944, volunteers below the rank of sergeant had their *de facto* exemption from call-up to the regular services – and indeed, an informal prohibition on their volunteering – lifted in 1943 and 1944). In fact, the number of ex-Auxiliers who joined the SAS in 1944 may well have exceeded the figure quoted above, and they perhaps accounted for as much as fifty per cent of new recruits to the two British regiments after the Brigade was formed.

It seems that SAS recruiting from the Auxiliary Units followed four paths. One was informal: a small number of officers returned to their parent units, learned through the 'grapevine' of the military old boy network that 'an interesting show' was looking for people, and stepped forward. Paddy Mayne tried to give this process a helping hand when he visited the AU training establishment at Coleshill, near Swindon in Wiltshire, early in 1944, hoping to recruit officers for 'special service overseas'; at least two (Peter Forbes and Dick Bond) volunteered. Colonel Frank Douglas, at that time Commanding Officer '201-203 GHQ Special Reserve Battalions – Home Guard', as the Auxiliary Units were properly known, was on leave at the time of Mayne's visit, and exploded when he learned of this attempt to poach his key men. He was successful in dissuading Forbes, who was his GSO 2 (Signals), largely, it is said, because one of Forbes's arms was immobilised with the elbow bent, as a result of a pre-war car crash. In the case of Bond, who had come to HQ as GSO 2 (Operations) after earlier service as Intelligence Officer with the Sussex AUs, Douglas was only temporarily successful. Bond soon returned to his parent unit (The Wiltshire Regiment), and joined 1 SAS from there; he was killed in Germany in the final weeks of the war while commanding B Squadron, in the course of the engagement in which Paddy Mayne won his fourth DSO.

The other three paths were more or less formal: junior officers who had been posted to the AUs as either Intelligence Officers or Scout Section leaders were returned to their parent units early in 1944, and were subsequently invited to a meeting which took place at the Curzon Cinema in London's Mayfair in March. Here Paddy Mayne first described the role of the SAS to them, and then invited them to stand if they wished to be part of it; the vast majority of men got to their feet, and 'it would have taken real guts to have remained seated, I think', one of those who volunteered was to say, many years later.

The 'regular army' component of the AUs' Other Ranks, the men who made up the Scout Sections, were treated in much the same way; having returned to their parent units early in 1944, they were soon ordered to attend what proved to be a selection board, which was convened at the (long requisitioned) Grosvenor House Hotel in London's Park Lane under Mayne's chairmanship, and a substantial proportion were subsequently 'invited' to join the regiment. Many did; of the twelve men who made up the East Dorset Scouting Section, for example, six joined 1 SAS. One might postulate that having been away from their parent formations for so long, the men in question found little attraction in returning to them.

As for the third component, the volunteer members of the Auxiliary Units, many of whom were being called up for regular service at around the same time, most found themselves posted to a camp in Northamptonshire, ostensibly for basic military training. An historian of the Auxiliary Units cites one ex-Auxilier's recollection of 'a hundred or so' assembled there, while another who also subsequently joined the SAS affirmed that as many as four hundred veterans of the AUs were present. Each man, he maintained, had an Army serial number which was at least a year old (numbers were 'issued' upon induction; these men had been called up only weeks before). Once this was over, and assessments of their capabilities as guerrilla soldiers made, they were posted to various units and some were later invited to join the SAS. That, and the Curzon Cinema and the Grosvenor House Hotel convocations, argues for a systemised approach to the recruitment of SAS personnel from the Auxiliary Units, though no record of such a system being in place has ever been discovered. After more than a half-century, during which it seems that all the documents in question have been destroyed, and memories have dimmed, it is impossible to be entirely sure of the facts, but it seems quite fitting that the men who would have formed the core of the British resistance should have gone on to fight alongside their brothers-in-arms in France and the Low Countries.

Bill Stirling was to experience even more profound problems in bringing 2 SAS up to strength (although he was able to exploit some of the channels opened up by Mayne), for by the time he started to recruit, most of the most likely candidates had been swept up and he had to look further and harder to find suitable men; in consequence, 2 SAS was not up to full strength until well into the summer. Some men from 2 SAS believed that their comrades-in-arms in the 'senior' regiment looked down on them; Roy Farran, during a prolonged drinking session marking the successful conclusion of Operation Wallace (q.v.), asked Paddy Mayne if that was so, and Mayne's reply was characteristically arrogant: 'No we don't,' he said. 'We never think about you at all.'

Rather unusually, McLeod was also to have two battalions of French paratroopers and a company of Belgians under his command. A somewhat irregular unit of French parachutists, *1er Compagnie de Chasseurs Parachutistes*, operated alongside David Stirling's men under the command of Captain George Bergé, whom Stirling later described as a co-founder of the SAS. Returned to Free French control in March 1943, with its original designation, *1er Compagnie d'Infanterie de l'Air* (1CIA), restored and combined with 2CIA to form *1er Batallion d'Infanterie de l'Air* (1BIA), it transferred to the United Kingdom, to be based at Old Dean Camp, near Camberley under the one-armed *Commandant* Pierre Bourgoin. It was redesignated the *4e Batallion* (4BIA) to avoid confusion with *1er Batallion de Chasseurs Parachutistes* (1BCP), and at the beginning of November transferred to Scotland, to a base at Largo, in Fife, across the Firth of Forth from Edinburgh, and later moved to Galston, some five miles west of Darvel, when it became 4 Battalion, SAS Brigade. 3 Battalion was composed chiefly of men recruited from the French army in North Africa which had been loyal to Vichy, notably from the élite *Corps Franc d'Afrique*, who were assembled at Algiers under *Commandant* O'Cottereau and constituted as *3e Batallion d'Infanterie de l'Air* (3BIA), some of whom were to operate with 2 SAS. It is said that the relationship between the two French formations, one Free French through-and-through and the other composed of men who had originally opted to follow Pétain, was always somewhat strained, to put it mildly. 3BIA arrived in the United Kingdom on 6 November and took over Old Dean Camp from 4BIA, under a new (and perhaps more acceptably Gaullist) commanding officer, *Commandant* Pierre Château-Jobert, who took 'Yves Conan' as his *nom de guerre*. It, too, subsequently transferred to Scotland for training and later also moved to the area east of Kilmarnock, to Auchinleck, some twenty miles south of Darvel. The small Belgian detachment, under the command of (then) Captain Eddie Blondeel, was known originally as the Independent Parachute Company; it was eventually enlarged and reconstituted as 5 Battalion, SAS; while the Belgian detachment not unnaturally did its most valuable work when it was on its own ground, so to speak, it also operated in France, and made an important contribution to the British battalions' operations too, by supplying interpreters and signallers. The two French battalions were formed into a *Demi-Brigade* under the command of Lt-Col R Durand, though by May 1944 he had been recognised as 'not suitable' to command troops such as these, and had been gently marginalised. A small liaison section, twelve men in total, known as 20 Liaison HQ, was established under Major Oswald Carey-Elwes, and acted as the link between the Brigade and Free French headquarters, now renamed *Etats-Majeur des Forces Françaises de l'Interieur* (EMFFI). Lt-Col Ian Collins, scion of the publishing family and a veteran of 8 Commando and Layforce, was appointed as Liaison Officer between the brigade and 1st Airborne Corps HQ, which was located at Moor Park near Rickmansworth on the outskirts of London, and four officers under Lt Col Broad were allocated to liaison duties with Special Forces Head-quarters (SFHQ). SAS Brigade HQ was completed by three officers and 154 other ranks from the Royal Army Service Corps' Air Despatch Group (which included fifteen men from the Royal Army Ordnance Corps) and an officer and twenty-three ORs from the Pioneer Corps.

McLeod was formally appointed to command, with Esmond Baring as his Brigade Major, on 7 February, and the next day established head-quarters at Sorn Castle in Ayrshire where, over the next seven weeks, he was joined by the men who would staff Brigade HQ. 1 SAS, when it returned from leave in February, assembled at Darvel, some ten miles away, the men housed in disused industrial premises and the officers billeted in private homes and with their mess in the Turf Hotel. The location, east of the town of Kilmarnock, was chosen for its proximity both to an empty area of the Cunninghame Hills which was to become the Brigade's battle training ground, and the aerodrome at Prestwick where parachute training, begun at Number 1 Parachute Training School at Ringway, Manchester, continued. Bill Stirling's 2 SAS joined the Brigade in the United Kingdom in the early spring of 1944 and was established at Monkton, adjacent to Prestwick. Brigade Main HQ was to remain at Sorn until August (though the Tactical HQ had long moved to Moor Park to co-locate with HQ Airborne Troops), when it shifted to Oare House near Pewsey, in Wiltshire; it later moved again, to Sloe House, Halstead, near Chelmsford, in Essex, when 38 Group RAF began to transfer its operations from airfields in the Wiltshire/Gloucestershire area to be nearer to the Allied forces on the ground as they moved north and eastward into the Netherlands and Germany. 1 SAS HQ moved around that time to Nettlebed, in Oxfordshire, where it remained, while 2 SAS HQ moved to Shipton Bellinger near Tidworth on Salisbury Plain and later to Wivenhoe Park near Colchester. The headquarters of the French battalions were transferred to Fairford (4 Para in May, 3 Para early in August) and then to locations in liberated France, and that of the Independent Belgian Company went first to Fairford and then near to Brussels.

In the context of the Brigade's Table of Organisation we should note that the terms 'regiment' and 'battalion' are, as usual, interchangeable; and that the cavalry designations 'squadron' and 'troop', used by the SAS, equate to the infantry formations 'company' and 'platoon'. (As for French ranks, most are self-explanatory, but *commandant* equates to major, while an *aspirant* was an officer-candidate, reckoned as equal in rank to a *sergeant-chef* or sergeant-major.) British SAS regiments were made up of four squadrons under a major, each with its HQ section, and three troops, under a captain, each of four ten-man sections under a lieutenant (the French and Belgian battalions sometimes provided men to act as translators for 1 and 2 SAS, and that brought the number in a section up to eleven or twelve). Each regiment thus totalled around 500 men including headquarters staff. 4 French Para, which originally had three squadrons (known as companies) was brought up to this strength by means of local recruiting at the start of Operation Spenser, in late August, but many of its sections were commanded by *Aspirants* or senior NCOs. 3 French Para was originally organised as an HQ company, a motorised company and an assault company but was later reformed to conform. 5 SAS, when it was brought up to full strength, adopted that more compact table of organisation. The total manpower of the SAS Brigade in mid-1944 stood at around 2,500, some 2,000 of whom were combatants. Most of the remainder, who made up HQ Squadron, were required to staff the Brigade's stores depot which became known as Station 1090 and was established initially at Williamstrip Park near the village of Down Ampney, some five miles from the main airfield site and transit camp at Fairford, in Gloucestershire. When the Brigade later transferred to Essex, following 38 Group, RAF, Station 1090 moved to Wethersfield.

As the men of 2 SAS were enjoying their own well-deserved period of home leave, the first definition of the Brigade's role in the invasion of France was being formulated at SHAEF. One might wonder why almost two months elapsed between the Brigade being formed and a task for it being formally defined; this has long been presented as firm evidence of the Supreme Headquarters' lack of both foresight and flexibility, and that would seem to be a perfectly accurate assumption, though one might also postulate that there were still elements within SHAEF (and even within the Brigade's parent 1st Airborne Corps) which did not accept that it *had* a worthwhile role to play, given the fairly complex nature of the function it saw itself fulfilling and the degree of support it would require, particularly from the hard-pressed Royal Air Force, and were delaying progress for the sake of it.

When the first plan for the employment of the SAS Brigade in the invasion of France, Operation Instruction No. 2, *was* finally issued (specifically to 1 SAS) on 29 March, it was poorly thought-out, and bore no relationship to the role David Stirling had envisaged for the unit, though to be fair to those who drafted it, it was made clear that the document was for outline planning purposes only. There were no strategic goals, and instead the regiment was to be committed piecemeal on the night of D-2/D-1 (that is, twenty-four to thirty-six hours before the main landings were scheduled to take place), largely to the area immediately behind the coastal strip between the base of the Cotentin Peninsula and Dieppe, with the main objective of establishing a meagre *cordon sanitaire* to delay massive German reinforcements sure to be heading into the invasion area.

It is worth listing the tasks 1 SAS was supposed to undertake: preventing 10. SS-Panzer Division *Frundsberg* from moving towards Caen from Lisieux (this was based on mistaken intelligence; the *Frundsberg* division had been ordered to the Eastern Front before Operation Instruction No. 2 was drafted, and the formation positioned near Lisieux was actually 12. SS-Panzer Division *Hitlerjugend*); preventing elements of 17. SS-Panzer Grenadier Division *Götz von Berlichingen* from moving towards Caen from Alençon (that division was actually south of the Loire, around Châtellerault, with its headquarters at Thouars) and containing 21. Panzer Division at Mantes, down the Seine valley from Paris (it was actually well to the west, south of Bayeux; the division near Mantes was 116. Panzer Division). No mention was made of restricting the movement of the most powerful formation in the region, the *Panzer-Lehr* Division, which was located between Le Mans and Orléans. The regiment was also to provide ten five-man teams for 'special operations' and hold ten jeep patrols in readiness for use after D-Day, as well as establishing resupply areas near Le Mans, Orléans, Nevers and Poitiers. The instruction went on to say that 4 French Para would carry out similar tasks west of a line St Lô–Domfront–Mayenne–Angers (i.e., in Brittany) and that 3 French Para or 2 SAS would carry out similar tasks east of a line Dieppe–Beauvais–Paris.

This was just preposterous, of course. Even without the benefit of hindsight, it must have been clear that such an undertaking was entirely unrealistic; that it would have been a death sentence for the men involved, and worse, that it would have risked giving a clear signal to the German High Command of the site of the impending invasion, twenty-four hours before it was launched. It is worth noting 21st Army Group's policy position, promulgated at around the same time – that no commando-style forces were to be inserted before D-Day, for reasons of security – and that a decision had been taken at SFHQ that no Jedburgh teams were to be inserted before the invasion had taken place.

The reaction to the instruction within the SAS itself was both immediate and extreme, although the focus of it came from a somewhat unexpected quarter: Bill Stirling. It may be pertinent to enquire why it was he and not Paddy Mayne, as Commanding Officer, 1 SAS (to whom Operation Instruction No. 2 was actually issued, after all), or even the Brigade's commanding officer himself who took issue with SHAEF over this. It may well have been that McLeod felt Stirling was better qualified. He *was* certainly better qualified than Paddy Mayne to take on such a task; Mayne had little if any political sense, and his idea of constructive criticism consisted largely of sarcasm laid on very thickly indeed. He was to be praised to the skies by historians of the SAS, but whereas there is no doubting his courage, his tactical skill and his prowess as a fighting man, he was a poor diplomat, despite his legal training.

While Bill Stirling was somewhat less prone to explosions of temper than his brother, he was no less determined, and presented with what he saw as a total mis-statement of the purposes of the Special Air Service (not to mention the likelihood of the Brigade being decimated if it were actually to be so employed), he dug in his heels and demanded a return to the first principles of strategic employment: that parties should be inserted deep in enemy-held territory where they would establish combat bases from which they could operate against lines of communication and high-value targets-of-opportunity, and where possible organise and arm the local partisan bands. In fact, of four 'resupply areas' identified in the instruction, three became such combat bases; this was the only major element of it to survive, but see below. The fact that he had been drawn into the self-same argument in Italy the previous year, had effectively been overruled and yet had been shown to be right, at least by his own lights, only made the situation clearer, as far as he was concerned. Stirling was far from alone in his opposition, and within days there was something close to mutiny in the air in the mess. As Roy Farran, who was personally close to Stirling, was to point out, when he published his own autobiographical account, *Winged Dagger – Adventures on Special Service*, in 1948, the plan put forward by headquarters 'proved such lack of understanding of our role that our confidence in the new command was severely shaken', and seemed like prima facie evidence that the precious freedom of action which the SAS had enjoyed in the early days, and which had been eroded away since late 1942, had now disappeared entirely.

It was time, Stirling felt, to take a stand, and he drafted a letter stating in the clearest terms that he had no confidence in the 'new' command structure and operational philosophy. Eventually he was persuaded, by Farran and others, to delay sending the letter until every possibility of the plan being amended had been explored, and in fact, it *was* subsequently amended, along lines Browning suggested in a letter he wrote to 21st Army Group's Chief of Staff on 8 May, though in it he stated that 'The delay in formation, mobilisation, providing reinforcement, equipping and training of SAS troops and the shortage of intelligence, signal and other specialised personnel' was the reason for the modification, not any representation Stirling or anyone else had made. The new version, which substituted harassing enemy lines of communication and assisting Resistance groups for delaying enemy Panzer divisions, was deemed to be acceptable by most of Stirling's supporters. Once that compromise was achieved, however, Bill Stirling submitted the critical letter anyway. Clearly, such a stance was incompatible with command of the Regiment; he was asked to withdraw the offending criticism, refused (he was convinced, according to Farran, that his taking a firm stand would place his successor in a strengthened position), and was subsequently replaced by Lt-Col Brian Franks, who had served with Layforce in the Mediterranean, commanded a Phantom squadron and had latterly been a brigade major with the Army Commandos in Italy. Franks was nominally an outsider like McLeod, of course, but he commanded the respect of everyone who had served alongside him, and his appointment was widely welcomed, even though, in the words of one observer, he 'ran the Regiment like the Household Cavalry' and there were to be questions asked about some of his operational decisions.

In fact, although Stirling seemed to have achieved his objective, the manner in which SAS troops would actually be deployed was still not decided. On 19 May a memorandum entitled *Strategic Use of SAS Troops* was circulated and seems to have formed the agenda for a basic policy discussion. It offered three possible courses of action:

I Establish safe bases which will be boosted up in the appropriate areas as Resistance develops in order to create 'free' areas.

II Drop a large number of SAS in penny packets along principal enemy reinforcement routes as soon after D-Day as possible, with the object of delaying the enemy reinforcements moving up from the strategic back areas by sabotaging railways.

III Establish safe bases in proximity to main German lines of communication and strengthen them with the object of by, say D plus 25, undertaking a programme of sabotage which will enable SAS to inflict crippling damage on enemy lines of communication.

Advantages and disadvantages were proffered for each of the courses, and were summed up as follows: the first course was deemed to employ SAS 'in a semi-political role for which they are not suited by training or temperament. They can only help create the "free" areas, but they will not be in sufficient numbers to turn these areas into a threat to the Germans.' The second was 'the short-term strategic course. It employs SAS early in large numbers at a time when reception [i.e. by parties already on the ground] is impossible. It is justifiable if it actually achieves significant delaying results.' The third course 'envisages long-term dislocation of enemy communications. It is for consideration whether their efforts can be maintained long enough to achieve this purpose.' Parties to the discussion were asked to come to a rapid decision and they clearly did, for on 24 May McLeod was writing to Baring, his Brigade Major, telling him to amend the Operations Instructions file broadly in line with the provisions of the third course, and four days later Browning issued formal orders to that effect in Operation Instruction No. 1 (why the sequence number was reset is unclear). These were amended, though only in detail, on 1 June, and at that point the basis on which the SAS Brigade would operate during the first phase of the liberation of France can be said to have been decided. And not, some would say, before time.

The Stirling Principle, as we may call it, was thus applied, though not in its entirety: a small number of SAS men were still to be dropped close behind the invasion beaches in the very early hours of D-Day to mount Operation Titanic, a venture of very dubious value, and were lucky to escape with their lives. However, the main focus of operations shifted to the areas deeper inside France which had originally been earmarked as the location of resupply dumps: the forest of Orléans, south-west of Paris (Operation Gain); the wooded hills of the Morvan, west of Dijon (Operation Houndsworth), and in the Vienne, between Poitiers and Limoges (Operation Bulbasket). These now became the key locations for SAS operational bases and supply dumps from which sabotage and ambush parties could sortie, and upon which they could be withdrawn in the face of effective enemy reaction. 4 French Para's operations in Brittany had always been planned separately, and were not affected by the revamp; the operation planned for the Le Mans area (Haft), which was too close to the main battlefield, was downgraded to a reconnaissance mission, and much of it was reallocated, under different code-names, to 5 SAS, in order to get the Belgian contingent into action.

The SAS Brigade's operational philosophy was very much to follow the gospel according to Stirling, too; there is an annex to the SAS Troops War Diary for June which describes how the combat parties in the field were controlled:

Only the broadest directives were ever sent to the parties in the field. In one or two cases they were directed on to particular targets, but in general their modus operandi was left at the discretion of party commanders, who had been trained before leaving in the Brigade's doctrine on what types of operation and organisation was feasible. This doctrine was justified by events and every departure from it in the direction of building up cumbrous guerrilla armies met with swift disaster. [This was actually untrue; the operations in Brittany did just this and were successful, eventually.] It was always accepted that the local commanders understood local conditions and was doing his best, and should be left to fight his own battle as briefed with as little redirection as possible.

This was the only possible approach, of course, but it presupposed operational commanders having the necessary strategic, tactical and man-management skills. Some did; some did not, and the results their operations produced reflected their abilities.

The actual operational areas were nominated by SHAEF or 21st Army Group, and not by the SAS Brigade, and the decision as to the exact location was made from information derived from reports from SOE or the Office of Stategic Services (OSS), its American counterpart and passed on by SFHQ; SOE personnel – or Frenchmen they had trained – on the ground in France were to receive the SAS reconnaissance parties, and SFHQ personnel in the shape of Jedburgh teams were to accompany them. These were entirely appropriate arrangements and worked well enough to begin with, but soon SAS HQ became suspicious that SFHQ had a somewhat different agenda and that there was an obstructive political element at work which seemed to be intent on reducing its effectiveness if it could not bend it to its own will. SFHQ, in turn, had no doubt that SAS would inevitably muddy the waters for its Jedburgh teams and the partisans they were to work alongside, and perhaps even endanger them, if it were not held severely in check and preferably restricted to working under SFHQ's direct orders. SFHQ's voiced objections took the form of concern that the insertion of uniformed commando-style troops would provoke harsh reprisals from occupying forces as well as disrupting its pre-existing (i.e. SOE- and OSS-sponsored) Resistance support operations. Actually, it was probably more worried that uniformed SAS troops would ride roughshod over its precious plan to favour rightist *maquisard* groups at the expense of those who owed their allegiance, however nominally, to the *Parti Communiste Français* or had agendas of their own, and thus upset its attempts to play power games in order to interfere with internal (French) politics.

At the outset, the relationship between SAS and SFHQ was a close one, with the former passing its intentions to the latter, and the latter very much in control of arrangements, as is indicated by the order for the first major operation 1 SAS mounted in France, Bulbasket, which emanated from Special Forces HQ. All emphasis, underlining, etc is in the original, and spelling and punctuation are left unchanged. 'F.Sec' is SOE's F Section; 'DR/JD' is the Director, Jedburgh operations. Notable points are that the impetus to mount the operation came from SAS Brigade; that de Gaulle's intelligence service, the *Bureau Central de Renseignements et d'Action* (BCRA) was not to be informed of the operation in advance (because that would have given it, and the General, key information about the proposed date of the invasion, a secret to which he and they were not privy), although SOE's RF Section was on the distribution list, and that the Jedburgh team leader was to make it clear to those on the ground that the SAS base was not to become the focal point for a popular rising. We may note also that at this time the SAS operation was still known as Jockworth.

	BIGOT
SF. HQ	TOP SECRET
D/R OP. ORDER. NO. 4.	Copy No....
	26th May '44

Ref. Map FRANCE — GSGS 2738 1/250,000
Sheet 21

INF.

1. SAS intend to send a recce party of 2 SAS officers of 1 SAS Regt. to CHATELLERAULT-CHATEAUROUX — L. 5101. on night D-1/D with the intention of establishing a base which can be reinforced by further SAS troops, and from which raids can be carried out on enemy L. of C.

INTENTION.

2. One JEDBURGH will accompany the recce party in order to act as liaison between the SAS tps. and such resistance as may be available in the area.

METHOD

3. <u>Responsibility for Operation.</u>

SFHQ is responsible for despatch of both SAS recce party and JEDBURGH, and for the provision of A/C.

4. <u>Section responsible for mounting operation.</u>

F. Sec.

5. <u>Method of dropping.</u>

To reception committee arranged by F. Sec.

6. <u>Preparation of brief.</u>

(a) Brief will be prepared by F. Sec. assisted by DR/JED briefing officer.
(b) To be completed and submitted by F to D/R by 021800 B.
(c) BCRAL will NOT be consulted during preparation.

<u>Briefing of JEDBURGH and SAS recce party.</u>

Arrival: JEDBURGH and SAS recce party will arrive SF HQ 031100 B. They will report to 46, Devonshire Close.

Briefing: 031100 B to 041300 B for SAS recce party and JEDBURGH simultaneously. SAS IO is to attend in order to pass on relevant information to future re-inforcements.

8. <u>Move to STA. 61</u>

(a) Departure from SF HQ 041300 B.
(b) Tpt. for both parties will be arranged by DR/JED.

(c) DR/JED briefing officer will accompany both parties to STA. 61.

9. Action on arrival in the field.

(a) JEDBURGH will provide the link between SAS recce party and the local F. Sec. organiser: contact may also be made with DMR if deemed necessary, or in his absence with the local FFI chief.

(b) JEDBURGH will explain that it is proposed to develop a base (which will be further reinforced by SAS) for the purpose of raiding enemy L. of C. and NOT with a view to creating and holding indefinitely a base for resistance. JEDBURGH will accept such offers of assistance from Resistance as SAS may require for their task, but will NOT engage in any general recruiting or encourage any mass rising unless so ordered by SF HQ.

(c) The base must be located so as to enable parties despatched from it to harass important enemy L.of C.

(d) JEDBURGH will also report to SF HQ state of resistance in terms of personnel, arms and potentialities, and any specific requests made.

(e) It is NOT intended to alter the existing command arrangements, but if command is clearly defective the JEDBURGH will report this fact to SF HQ.

ADM.

10. Containers and Packages.

(a) SAS will NOT require packages to be made up as all equipment is carried on the man. SF HQ will provide parachutes for SAS recce party. AL/Q will arrange.

(b) JEDBURGH equipment will be brought on reporting for briefing and will be packed under
arrangements made by AL/Q for delivery to
Tempsford by 041800 B.

(c) Balance of A/C load will be decided by F. Sec.
in consultation with DR/JED.

11. Messing and Accommodation.

SF HQ will provide messing and accommodation for
SAS Recce party w.e.f. 031100 B. DR/JED will
arrange.

12. Supplies.

(a) SF HQ will be responsible for re-supply, if
required, of SAS base until arrival of SAS
reinforcements.

(b) After arrival of SAS reinforcements, respon-
sibilty for supply of the SAS base will pass
to SAS.

(c) SF HQ will continue to supply resistance in
accordance with the military situation.

INTERCOMN.

13. Code Names.

(a) JOCKWORTH: SAS base area.

(b) Code name for JEDBURGH will be notified later.

14. W/T Comn.

(a) JEDBURGH will take two sets and will establish comn. with Home Stn. as soon as possible.

(b) JEDBURGH will also be responsible for passing
traffic from SAS recce party to SAS HQ via SF

```
HQ until the arrival of SAS reinforcements
with independent comns.
```

```
15. Ack.
```

```
RH Barry
```

```
Colonel, G.S.
SF HQ
```

It is clear from this order that SFHQ was determined to keep the SAS party on a short leash initially, and ensured that its Jedburgh team would act as the sole conduit between the SAS party and the personnel on the ground. As we shall see when we come to look at the operation in question, the arrangement worked perfectly.

SHAEF was no more ready to give the SAS its head, but for rather different reasons. A later (28 May) SHAEF directive to SAS forces seemingly reveals an astonishingly optimistic view of the outcome of the invasion, and perhaps explains why it wished to put a brake on its activities; it tied the Brigade's hands once more, though not as tightly as before, saying:

> No railway demolition likely to take more than eight days to repair is to be carried out. No permanent destruction is to be done to industrial or electrical installations – powerplants, water works, gas works, locks, etc. Temporary damage to output [sic] is allowed – e.g. the cutting of power line pylons.

This is rather difficult to understand in any meaningful context, since it is inconceivable that any element within SHAEF actually believed that the invasion could possibly be so successful as to require that railway lines and the socio-industrial infrastructure in France be put back into operational order in such a short time. Nonetheless the instruction was issued, though it was short-lived, rescinded on 5 June with the caveat that operational commanders should 'use their own judgement' in regard to the extent of sabotage operations.

Later the obstructive elements in SFHQ seemed to get more of their own way. Within ten days of the invasion having taken place, and with just a handful of SAS operations under way – Titanic, which was a complete waste of resources and energy; Bulbasket and Houndsworth, which were still in the process of establishing themselves, and 4 French

Para's operations in Brittany which, up to that time, had accomplished little and looked as if they might well be heading for disaster – McLeod was already writing to Browning at 1st Airborne Corps HQ to say that he was 'not satisfied that the strategic employment of SAS troops is being properly considered'.

> SAS troops are trained on special lines and their organisation, equipment and communications are based on four essential factors [the emphasis is in the original]:
>
> (a) They are military forces carrying out military as opposed to political tasks. This has been continually stressed especially to the Allied troops under my command [presumably this is a reference to the French and the way they were operating in Brittany]. It is therefore a misuse of these troops to employ them more than necessary on organisational duties.
>
> (b) They must work from a safe base. This has always been unquestioned and it is for this reason that SAS troops should not be employed on operational tasks unless they have a safe base to which to withdraw for supplies.
>
> (c) They must keep dispersed and work in small parties. They should not, by nature of their equipment or organisation, engage in pitched battles.
>
> (d) Adequate information. Each SAS operation requires to be separately mounted and the more such planning is 'skimped' the less effective will be the operation.

McLeod was especially concerned that more and more of the operational requirements he was receiving were:

> undoubtedly the result of SOE [more accurately, SFHQ] suggestions and I have the impression that SAS troops are regarded as a military adjunct of SOE to undertake those tasks that SOE cannot undertake. It seems that the policy for the employment of SAS troops is becoming a short term one and is largely governed by the advice of SOE. There is therefore a grave danger of SAS troops being employed on the advice of SF HQ rather than on the advice of the Commanding Officer, Airborne Troops, and I am not satisfied that there is really any clear policy in existence for the employment of SAS troops.

This was a rather different conclusion to the one reached elsewhere, and betrayed a somewhat different attitude to the one Bill Stirling had adopted earlier, when he had suggested a very close relationship between SAS and SOE elements on the ground.

McLeod finished:

> I am certain that the employment of small numbers of SAS troops on tactical projects at short notice [the sort of 'fire brigade' operations to which they had been committed in Italy] will result in a complete loss of control over SAS operations as a whole and a wastage of many high class troops without a proper dividend.

These were strong words for a brigadier to write to a lieutenant-general (and hardly those of a man who had less than the interests of his brigade at heart), but perhaps McLeod was hoping to foment the very sort of turf war he was ostensibly trying to suppress. In any event, it is clear that his experience of (or perhaps talent for) this sort of in-fighting was limited but the correspondence goes a long way towards invalidating any suggestion that Rory McLeod was anything but a whole-hearted supporter of the SAS concept.

McLeod, however, was so far making little headway in his battle with the 'fourth armed service', as some within SOE liked to regard it, for on 2 August he was writing to Browning again, urging him to use what influence he could summon to counteract what he saw as a deliberate policy on the part of SFHQ to do everything possible to keep his men out of the war. He wrote:

> It is clear that the next few weeks may prove to be the decisive weeks of the war in the West. At present under half the available SAS troops are deployed. One and a half British Regts still remain unemployed, and the basic reason for this is the obstruction and difficulties caused by SFHQ. The following proposals have all been made for the employment of British troops:-
>
> (a) Haggard SFHQ are flatly opposed to this.
>
> (b) Rupert SFHQ are not in favour of this plan and there have been continual difficulties in attempting to arrange DZs. It appears that the SAS are not wanted and nothing is being done to help them in spite of the SHAEF directive.

(c) <u>Loyton</u> SHAEF ordered the establishment of this base over a month ago but SFHQ are still sending cables to the field asking whether SAS troops are acceptable.

I am convinced that now is the moment to deploy all possible SAS resources in order to exploit the crack which is beginning to appear in the West. This is no time for nice considerations as to the effect of uniformed troops on resistance groups. The SAS Regts were raised, formed and trained for operations behind the enemy lines at just such a time as the present and if they are not to be used at this moment of all others, the whole of the effort put into the organisation of this formation has been wasted and the troops themselves would have been better employed in infantry units, who are short of first class material.

There are now only two reasonable alternatives:-

(a) The fullest possible employment of the first class troops which are available on the tasks for which they have been prepared, accepting the use of uniformed troops in areas where SFHQ thinks it undesirable.

(b) The frank acknowledgement that there is no task for SAS troops which cannot be done equally well by the Maquis and the immediate disbandment of the SAS Bde.

This was a high-risk strategy, and McLeod did go some way towards softening the ultimatum contained in the final paragraph, requesting 'that this matter be given the most immediate and serious consideration, and that if necessary I may be permitted to state my views to higher authority'. The risk may have paid off, however, for within three weeks the regular report on the Operational State of SAS Troops for 22 August reflects a different position, with a total of 234 officers and 1,422 ORs in the field (and a further thirty-six officers and 268 men reported as killed or missing), and only eighty officers and 677 ORs remaining in the UK, of whom the vast majority were either HQ Squadron personnel or were scheduled to become operational within days.

We may note in passing that the notion of disbanding the SAS Brigade entirely was not to go away, and over the next month McLeod himself was discussing it, as one of four options available, in correspondence with Mayne and Franks, his two British regimental commanders. In the end the SAS Brigade, reduced to two regiments, and with Mike

Calvert in McLeod's post, *was* to be disbanded, on 8 October 1945, as part of the wholesale downsizing of the British Army.

It was not only in the rather rarified atmosphere of policy-making that the interface between SAS and SFHQ broke down; it happened at the operational planning level, too. A letter from Franks to McLeod on 4 August reporting on the operational situation protested bitterly at SFHQ's obstructive attitude towards assisting in the insertion of SAS parties, its refusal to share information about suitable drop zones and, even worse, its occasional recommendation of DZs which were in fact quite *un*suitable. It also failed to inform the SAS of all the *parachutages* it organised and carried out (which is perhaps understandable), and almost as a matter of policy misrepresented the situation on the ground vis-à-vis the *maquis* groups. Clearly, the situation had changed beyond recognition over the two months since the invasion had been launched. Franks continued:

> There is a prevalent view amongst some members of the staff at SOE, and this view has unfortunately been successfully inculcated into some of the SAS Liaison Staff Officers at Baker Street, that uniformed troops are NOT welcomed by the Maquis and further that in known Maquis areas it is better to supply them with arms and explosives and let them do the tasks rather than send SAS to the area.
>
> This is in direct contradiction to the views of both French and British Maquis leaders who have returned recently to this country and with whom I have had the opportunity of discussing this question. I quote two in particular, 'Marksman' [Lt-Col R H Heslop, also known as 'Xavier'] and M. Gausse, both of whom stated categorically that uniformed troops, even in small numbers, in any area would be welcome and of the greatest possible value. Commandant Lejeune has endorsed this view. Their views are more likely to represent those of the Maquis than the views of staff officers in London.
>
> Another view held by certain members of SOE staff is that uniformed troops in the area prejudice the chances of SOE representatives who are operating in plain clothes. This is clearly arrant nonsense. There is plenty of room in France for both SAS and SOE.

The latter was an extremely naive comment; there may indeed have been plenty of room in France, but since SAS and SFHQ personnel needed to be in the forefront of the action, that inevitably meant they were trying to occupy the same limited space. Franks' letter concluded:

> You will, I think, agree with me that the present arrangements for mounting SAS operations are highly unsatisfactory. None of these operations can be said to be simple, either for those going on the operation or those mounting them, but I am determined that all detachments of 2 SAS Regiment shall leave this country fully briefed and with every possible assistance from staff officers, which I consider they fully deserve. They are not getting it at present.

This storm had been brewing for some time, of course, and relations between the two organisations had deteriorated as soon as it became obvious that the SAS would assist any group, no matter what its political persuasion, to obtain arms if it showed any sign of wanting to use them to kill Germans. It seems entirely reasonable to put much of the blame for the situation on SFHQ. As we shall see, on the ground the SAS and SFHQ parties (the Jedburghs and the Inter-Allied Missions) worked well enough together in most circumstances, mutual criticism notwithstanding, but there is reason to suggest that they would (both) have been more effective still had they operated within a unified command structure from the outset. Bill Stirling himself had suggested something very similar in his critical letter rebutting Operational Instruction No. 2, stating his belief that SAS should be used 'as a stiffener to SOE and the Maquis'.

Any attempt to impose a solution on the two parties to this dispute was out of the question at this juncture, however, for that would have required a full-scale overhaul of the entire structure of unconventional forces in mid-battle, but one can still wonder why heads could not have been banged together at the highest level in an attempt to unstiffen a few necks. Instead, both sides settled down to investing time and energy in a fairly low-intensity power struggle; no clear victor emerged, but the SAS certainly lost out. Time after time its operations were less effective than they might have been as a result of recalcitrance on the part of SFHQ. It was thus unequal to the task of demonstrating that it was indeed a valid and important addition to the British Army's Order of Battle, and this led directly to it being disbanded in October 1945. The failure cannot be laid directly and exclusively at the door of SFHQ, but the latter played its part in it before it, too, was broken up. Brigadier-General Mike Calvert, writing to interested parties, among them his regimental commanders, their deputies and some staff and operational officers, in an effort to build a dossier of reasons why the regiment should not be disbanded, said:

> My experience is that SOE and SAS are complementary to each other. SAS cannot successfully operate without good intelligence, guides, etc. SOE can only do a certain amount before requiring, when their operations become overt, highly trained, armed bodies in uniform to operate and set an example to the local resistance. SOE are the 'white hunters' and produce the ground organisation on which SAS operates. All senior officers of SOE with whom I have discussed this point agree to this principle.

But this was too little, and he was too late.

That is not to say that there was any real appetite at HQ level for combined operations with the Resistance; the SAS Brigade's 'official' preference, as expressed by McLeod in a memorandum to 1st Airborne Corps on 26 June, when the early operational reports had been analysed, was for the SAS parties to operate in isolation, on the principle that a well-organised partisan group always drew the attention of German security forces. In fact, that was an over-simplification; in some areas, notably the Morvan, the Resistance proved to be entirely trustworthy, while in others, such as the Vosges (where, ironically, the SAS party was to be actually instructed to operate alongside the partisans), it was in large part the reverse. There was certainly no hard and fast rule.

In analysing the way in which the SAS Brigade prepared itself to go to war in mid-1944, one thing becomes clear: the defining characteristic was still the sort of supercharged 'where there's a will there's a way' enthusiasm which had fired Stirling and the others in 1941. This was entirely understandable in the circumstances, for these were brave, dedicated (and typically young; Lt-Col Mayne, for example, with a DSO and bar already to his credit, was still just twenty-eight) men who were about to commit themselves to operating for prolonged periods behind enemy lines, in areas with which they were entirely unfamiliar, relying on the RAF to deliver supplies and the shadowy and amorphous 'French Resistance' to lend support, to fight – and help to expel – a powerful enemy whose presence had been established for four years and who had a well-deserved reputation for cruelty in the way he treated those caught engaging in the sort of commando-style activities which would be their mainstay. This would be no ordinary campaign, for as well as the courage required to go into battle, meet the enemy face-to-face and beat him by superior determination and skill-at-arms, the men who engaged in it could expect to be deprived of anything resembling comfort and security from the moment they pulled on their parachute overalls, overloaded themselves with equipment and struggled to board the aircraft which would roar away through the darkness to deposit them they knew not where, save that it was likely to be within rifle-shot of a very hostile enemy.

And what of that enemy? So far, we have identified the broad strategic requirements set before the men of the SAS Brigade: the disruption of lines of communication, and the prevention of reinforcements from streaming into the battle area. But reinforcements of what nature, and from where were they to come?

By mid-1944, the war in the east was going badly for Germany. The high tide-mark had been reached in late 1942, and from then on the *Wehrmacht* and the *Waffen-SS* had been pushed back almost inexorably westward. In the process, whole units were decimated and their equipment either destroyed, lost or worn out; even those that suffered 'acceptable' levels of loss could only survive in the front line for so long without refitting, not to mention resting and recuperating, and many of those divisions withdrawn after the winter of 1943 and the Spring Offensive which followed were sent to France. In the run-up to D-Day, the occupation of France was divided between Army Group G, south of a line which followed the Loire inland as far as Orléans and then continued eastward to Geneva, and Army Group B, which controlled the area north of that line save for Alsace and Lorraine. Five German armoured divisions were within striking distance of the Channel coast: 1. SS-Panzer Division *Liebstandarte SS Adolf Hitler*, with forty-five Pz.Kpfw. IV medium tanks, fifty-four Pz.Kpfw. V 'Panther' battle tanks and forty-two tank destroyers, at Turnhout, near the Dutch border; 2. Panzer Division, with ninety-eight Pz.Kpfw. IVs and seventy-nine Panthers, near Amiens; 116. Panzer Division, with thirteen Pz.Kpfw. IIIs, eighty-six Pz.Kpfw. IVs and six *Jagdpanzer* tank destroyers, near Mantes; 12. SS-Panzer Division *Hitlerjugend*, with ninety-eight Pz Kpfw. IVs and sixty-six Panthers, at Lisieux and 21. Panzer Division, with 112 Pz.Kpfw. IVs, south of Bayeux. Of these, three were at almost full strength and battle-ready. The *Panzer-Lehr* Division was some distance further back, between Orléans and Le Mans, with ninety-eight Pz.Kpfw. IVs and eighty-eight Pz.Kpfw. V Panthers.

A further three armoured divisions, withdrawn from Russia, were rebuilding themselves in southern France: 11. Panzer Division, with seventy-eight Pz.Kpfw. IVs and forty Panthers, at Bordeaux; 2. SS-Panzer Division *Das Reich*, with fifty-four Pz.Kpfw. IVs, seventy-eight Panthers and forty-two tank destroyers, at Montauban, and 9. Panzer Division, with seventy-eight Pz.Kpfw. IVs, forty Panthers and five tank destroyers, at Aix-en-Provence (strengths and locations, some by then already out of date, are derived from a report Heinz Guderian, the Inspector of Armed Forces, sent to Hitler on 10 June). There were also a total of ten Panzer regiments equipped with a total of 250 Panthers and five Heavy Panzer battalions with a total of 102 Pz.Kpfw. VI 'Tiger' and 'King Tiger' tanks in France by 10 June, though by no means all of them were battle-ready either, and it was a fair bet that 9. SS-Panzer Division *Hohenstaufen* and 10. SS-Panzer Division *Frundsberg* would soon be on their way, probably by rail via Saarbrücken, as soon as they could be withdrawn from the Eastern Front and refitted (in fact, a battalion of each was assembled behind the front and ready to go into action by 29 June). A division of mechanised infantry (17. SS-Panzer Grenadier Division *Götz von Berlichingen*, with forty-two tank destroyers) was situated in and around Châtellerault, and as well as the eight assault infantry and two airborne divisions (and the seventeen divisions of inferior occupation troops, many of them conscripted Russian and other ex-PoWs) in the northern coastal zone and Brittany, other elite infantry units, in the process of re-equipping and retraining, and thus available for immediate relocation, were to be found at Bayonne, Perpignan, Carcassonne and Nîmes.

All the units situated outside Normandy could be expected to receive urgent movement orders as soon as the invasion was launched. Indeed, as the battle wore on, additional units from the Eastern Front and from Italy would also be detached; as late as the end of August, two reinforced Panzer Grenadier Divisions were moved from Italy to France and soon after, seven of the fourteen independent Panzer Brigades created to plug gaps in the Eastern Front battle line were also re-deployed to eastern France. Thus, a very significant portion of available German forces was potentially vulnerable to being delayed en route for the Normandy battle area, and the routes they would follow were designated as prime targets for sabotage attacks carried out by special forces combat parties as well as (Jedburgh-assisted) partisans.

*

The SAS Brigade was to carry out a total of thirty-six separate operations in France during the period between 6 June and October 1944 (thirty-eight if one counts Lost, a sub-operation mounted to check on the progress the Digson/Samwest party was making in Brittany, and Wolsey, which was actually carried out by a Phantom team attached to the SAS Brigade). In his book *Airborne Forces*, Otway divided the operations in France into six phases. The use of the word 'phases' is itself misleading, for it implies a chronological hierarchy; that Phase One gave way to Phase Two and so on, and that is not the case. Adopting a quasi-chronological format forced Otway into basic errors of classification, especially since some operations were planned to have been mounted long before they actually were, and others fell outside the framework completely, and neither are the groupings he chose entirely logical. It would perhaps have made more sense if he had stuck to what were to be three basic groups:

1 Those which called for the establishment of a semi-permanent base, from which small ambush and sabotage parties could operate, that base to be run on fairly orthodox lines, with proper administration and as many of the standard facilities as possible (allbeit in fairly skeletal form), and resupplied regularly by air. We can take the Houndsworth base, which was in use for almost four months, as an exemplar of this type.
2 Peripatetic affairs – the so-called 'flying columns' of armed jeeps, of which the only real examples were Spenser and Wallace.
3 Operations mounted in support of organised Resistance, such as Harrod/Barker and Jockworth.

Seven further operations were carried out in Belgium and Holland: Noah, Brutus, Bergbang, Fabian, Gobbo, Keystone and finally Amherst, the most complex to date; two – Gallia and Tombola – were mounted in Italy under the command of 15 Army Group, and three more in Germany: Archway, Howard and Larkswood. At the war's end a further operation, ostensibly non-combative in nature, was mounted in Norway.

The operational code-names by which the operations were known were allocated *en bloc* to the Brigade by the Inter-Services Security Board. Those which commenced on or around D-Day (and some later), were made-up words such as Bulbasket (which seems originally to have been 'Bullbasket'), Cooney, Digson, Houndsworth and

Samwest. The biggest group were names of classic British authors (Defoe, Dickens, Haggard, Hardy, Kipling, Shakespeare and Spenser, for example). Others were the names of London department stores of the period, including Barker, Derry, Harrod, Marshall and Snelgrove; those of biblical figures, such as Abel, Moses and Samson, and finally recognisable but meaningless names and everyday words (Benson, Rupert and Wallace, Gaff, Gain and Haft etc). There were other code-names allocated for operations which never took place, and they fell into the same pattern. While it is obviously convenient to refer to the operations by their code-names, they were not necessarily so known by all the participants themselves at the time; the only code-names many men would have recognised were those allocated to officers and senior NCOs, the men who were earmarked to lead small combat teams in the field. These were designated by the letter-group 'SABU' followed by a number.

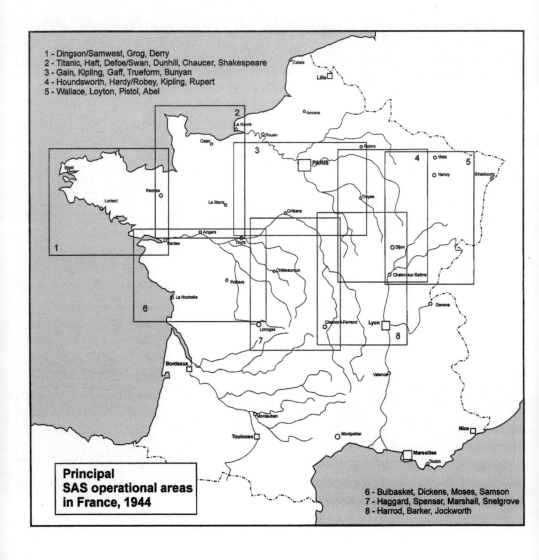

1 - Dingson/Samwest, Grog, Derry
2 - Titanic, Haft, Defoe/Swan, Dunhill, Chaucer, Shakespeare
3 - Gain, Kipling, Gaff, Trueform, Bunyan
4 - Houndsworth, Hardy/Robey, Kipling, Rupert
5 - Wallace, Loyton, Pistol, Abel

**Principal
SAS operational areas
in France, 1944**

6 - Bulbasket, Dickens, Moses, Samson
7 - Haggard, Spenser, Marshall, Snelgrove
8 - Harrod, Barker, Jockworth

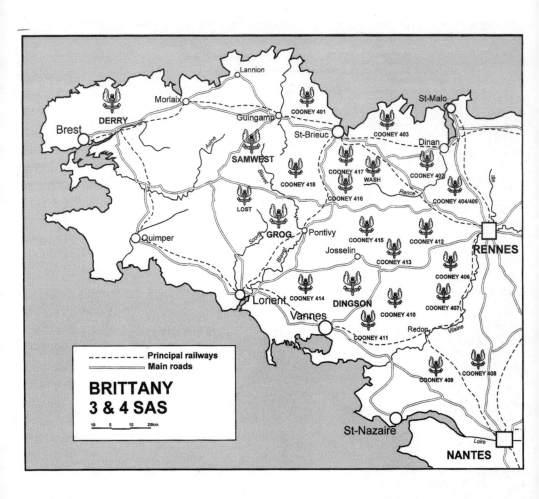

Principal railways
Main roads

**BRITTANY
3 & 4 SAS**

10 0 10 20km

Lannion
Morlaix
DERRY
Brest
Guingamp
St-Brieuc
COONEY 401
St-Malo
COONEY 403
Dinan
SAMWEST
COONEY 417
COONEY 402
WASH
COONEY 418
COONEY 416
COONEY 404/405
Aulne
Blavet
LOST
GROG
Pontivy
Scorff
Quimper
COONEY 415
COONEY 412
RENNES
Josselin
Blavet
COONEY 413
COONEY 406
Lorient
COONEY 414
DINGSON
COONEY 407
Vannes
COONEY 410
Redon
Vilaine
COONEY 411
COONEY 409
COONEY 408
St-Nazaire
Loire
NANTES

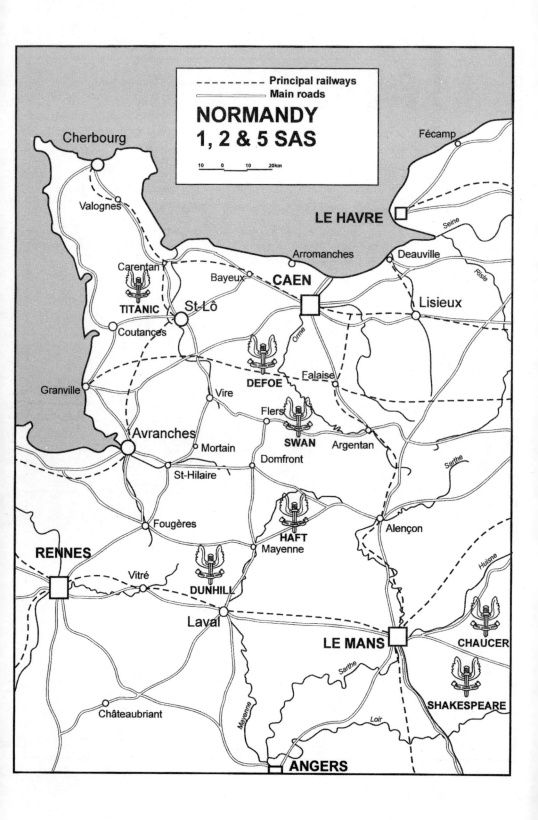

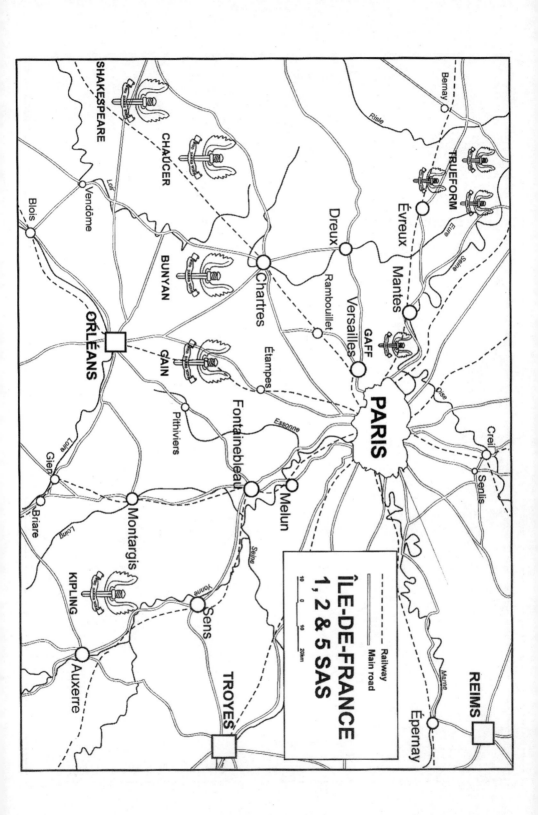

ÎLE-DE-FRANCE
1, 2 & 5 SAS

Railway
Main road

10   0   10   20km

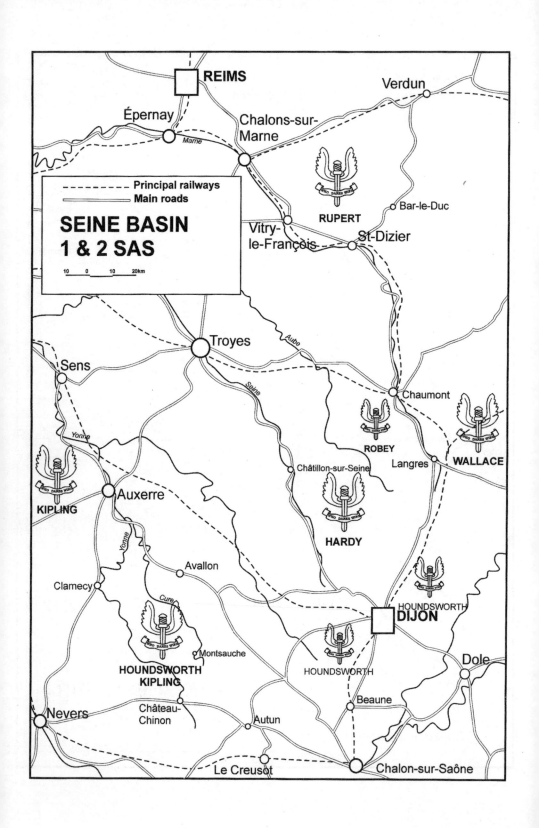

SEINE BASIN
1 & 2 SAS

Principal railways
Main roads

10   0   10   20km

REIMS

Épernay

Chalons-sur-Marne

Verdun

Marne

RUPERT

Bar-le-Duc

Vitry-le-François

St-Dizier

Troyes

Aube

Sens

Seine

Chaumont

Yonne

ROBEY

WALLACE

KIPLING

Auxerre

Châtillon-sur-Seine

Langres

HARDY

Yonne

Avallon

Clamecy

Cure

HOUNDSWORTH
DIJON

Montsauche

HOUNDSWORTH
KIPLING

HOUNDSWORTH

Dole

Château-Chinon

Autun

Beaune

Nevers

Le Creusot

Chalon-sur-Saône

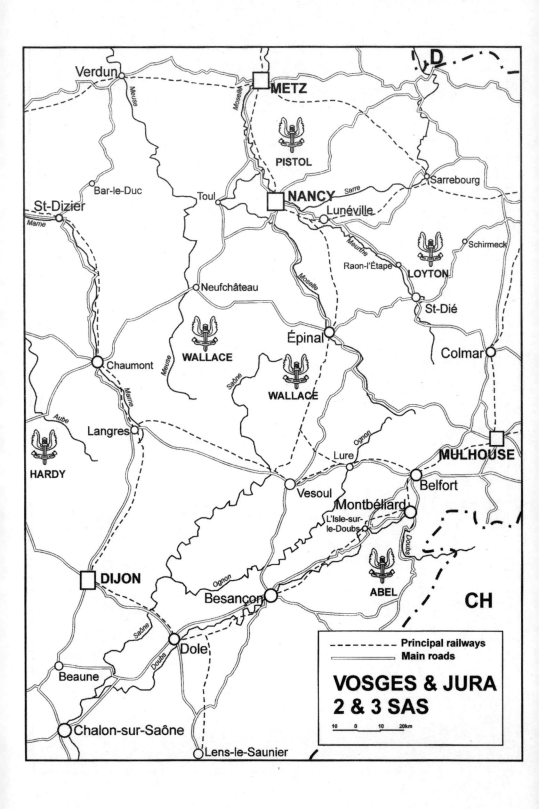

VOSGES & JURA
2 & 3 SAS

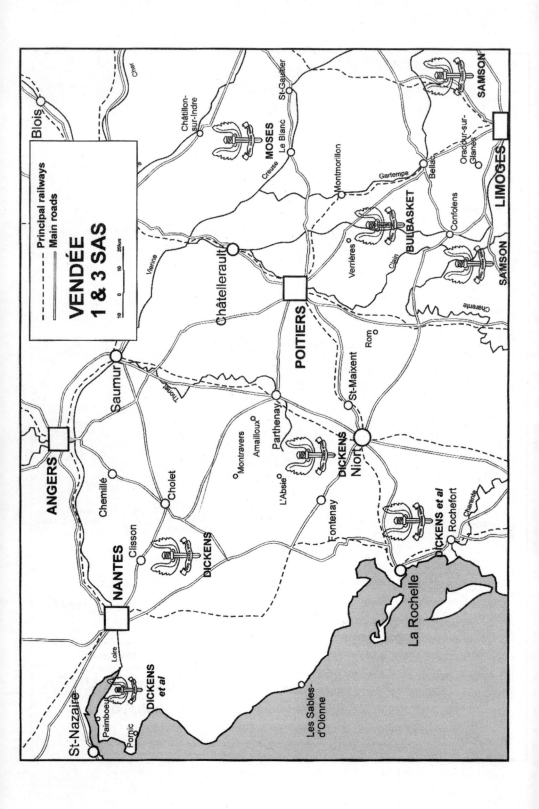

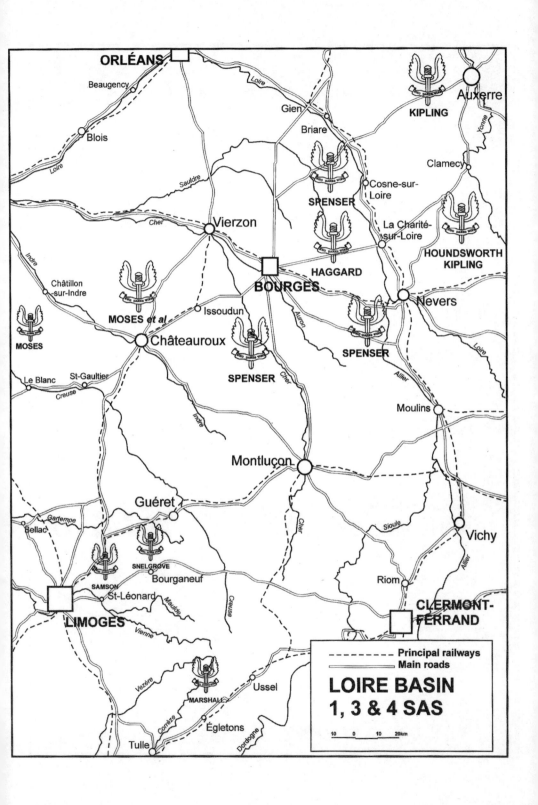

ORLÉANS
Beaugency
Loire
Gien
Blois
Loire
Briare
Sauldre
Cher
Vierzon
BOURGES
HAGGARD
Issoudun
Châtillon-sur-Indre
MOSES et al
Châteauroux
MOSES
Le Blanc
St-Gaultier
Creuse
SPENSER
Indre
Montluçon
Guéret
Gartempe
Sellac
SNELGROVE
Bourganeuf
SAMSON
St-Léonard
Maulde
Creuse
LIMOGES
Vienne
Vézère
MARSHALL
Corrèze
Ussel
Égletons
Tulle
Dordogne

Auxerre
KIPLING
Clamecy
Cosne-sur-Loire
SPENSER
La Charité-sur-Loire
HOUNDSWORTH
KIPLING
Nevers
SPENSER
Auron
Allier
Moulins
Loire
Sioule
Vichy
Riom
Allier
CLERMONT-FERRAND

Principal railways
Main roads

**LOIRE BASIN
1, 3 & 4 SAS**

10 0 10 20km

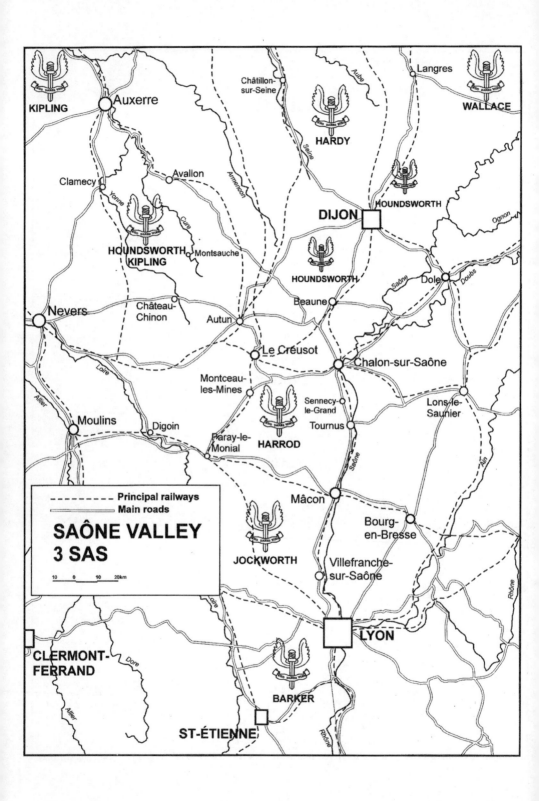

KIPLING

Auxerre

Châtillon-sur-Seine

Langres

WALLACE

HARDY

Clamecy

Avallon

HOUNDSWORTH

DIJON

DIJON

HOUNDSWORTH
KIPLING

Montsauche

HOUNDSWORTH

Dole

Nevers

Château-Chinon

Autun

Beaune

Le Creusot

Chalon-sur-Saône

Montceau-les-Mines

Sennecy-le-Grand

Lons-le-Saunier

Moulins

Digoin

Paray-le-Monial

HARROD

Tournus

Mâcon

Bourg-en-Bresse

JOCKWORTH

Villefranche-sur-Saône

- - - - - Principal railways
———— Main roads

SAÔNE VALLEY
3 SAS

10 0 10 20km

CLERMONT-FERRAND

LYON

BARKER

ST-ÉTIENNE

Part Two

1 SAS

TITANIC

Those elements of the SAS Brigade assigned to first-phase operations from 6 June 1944 moved from Scotland to RAF Fairford in Gloucestershire by train and lorry under strict security late in May, and were then locked into what became known as 'the cage'. There they stayed, with little more than briefings, PT, many games of cricket and oft-repeated equipment checks to break the monotony, until they were transported to waiting aircraft to be dropped over occupied France. The only men allowed out of camp at Fairford were those few who were to be dropped ahead of the advanced parties, and they were under very close guard, although later 1 SAS's padre, Fraser McLuskey, was later issued with a motorcycle and permitted to leave the cage to shop for the men in Oxford; toothbrushes were much in demand, and in short supply, he noted in his autobiography, *Parachute Padre*.

Among those who moved to Fairford in May were the two officers and four men from A and B Squadrons who made up the two parties briefed to carry out Operation Titanic-4. Of the other elements of Operation Titanic, Titanic-1 was to have been carried out by three three-man parties from 2 SAS, inserted between Dieppe and Rouen, but was cancelled on 24 May. Titanic-2 and -3 were drops of dummy parachutists and noise-makers, and did not involve SAS Brigade. The Titanic-4 parties, which landed at approximately 0400 on 6 June, had a singular aim – to deceive the German defenders into thinking that Allied airborne forces were landing in strength in an area south of the town of Carentan, at the base of the Cotentin Peninsula, which occupied a key position between the American landing beaches, Omaha and Utah, in the hope of drawing them back from the real drop zones, which were north and east of the town. To this end, the two groups, led by Lts Poole and Fowles, were equipped with Lewes bombs, non-lethal noise-makers and Very pistols, to fire flares.

*

Dummy parachutists were dropped alongside them, as were containers, most of them filled with sandbags. There was considerable confusion over the dropping zone (DZ), and the party landed some kilometres out of place. When the troopers met up, neither officer was present. Poole had 'rung the bell', and knocked himself out leaving the aircraft – an Albemarle, with its too-small floor hatch. He lay unconscious on the ground for some time, and was subsequently disoriented; he was found by a *résistant* named Edouard Le Duc, who was to be the party's saviour, and reunited with the others on the morning of 7 June. Fowles landed away from the others and then set off in the wrong direction, and it was 10 June before Le Duc located him. There was no sign of the containers with their stores, which left them unable to carry out their instructions to attract attention to themselves in any spectacular way.

That the men survived at liberty for over a month is a tribute to their tenacity and the reliability of their Resistance contact. On 28 June they were forced to break cover when a German *Fallschirmjäger* (paratroop) unit moved into the locality where they were laying up, near Remilly-sur-Lozon; reinforced by three US parachutists – a medical officer and two privates, one of whom was wounded – who had been captured on D+1 and then escaped when the trucks in which they were travelling were strafed from the air, they moved very cautiously round the area, their priority being to avoid German security patrols which were much in evidence. They were discovered by a pair of German paratroopers on the afternoon of 10 July; the Germans were the quicker-thinking, and lobbed two grenades, which injured Lt Fowles and two of the troopers, Hurst and Merryweather, as well as two of the Americans. The party made the cover of an adjacent farm, but the farmer refused to help them, and indeed denounced them. Within thirty minutes they found themselves surrounded, and had no option but to surrender; unlike other captured SAS troopers they were relatively well treated, probably thanks to the fact that they were in, or at least adjacent to, a battlefield proper, where Hitler's order to kill commando-style troops, rather than take them prisoner, the *Kommandobefehl*, did not apply, although the fact that they were the prisoners of other parachutists may have had some bearing on that. The wounded were liberated at the beginning of August in Rennes, where they had been hospitalised, but the others were transferred to PoW camps, where they stayed until near the war's end. The *résistant* Le Duc was betrayed and subsequently shot. There is no disguising the fact that as a military operation, Titanic-4 was a complete waste of time and effort. There have been suggestions that it occupied the attention of an entire German infantry regiment for much of 6 June and therefore played an important role in the first phase of the invasion, but they are not substantiated.

BULBASKET

The first major operation to be mounted by 1 SAS in France, Operation Bulbasket, was focused on the routes the *Waffen-SS's Das Reich* Armoured Division and the *Wehrmacht's* 11. Armoured Division (as well as two infantry divisions) could be presumed to take to reach the Overlord battlefield from their base areas in south-western France. The location was selected because of the supposed viability of the organised Resistance in the area where SOE F Section agents were first inserted, in 1941, and which had regularly received other missions in the intervening period.

Captain John Tonkin, a veteran of SAS operations in Italy, was given command of the party, his orders based on a directive issued by SHAEF to SAS Brigade on 19 May 1944. He was to take 1 Troop, B Squadron, 1 SAS Regiment, enlarged to include four officers in addition to himself plus forty-three other ranks, and reinforced by 3 Patrol, F Squadron, GHQ Reconnaissance Regiment and a Royal Army Medical Corps corporal, to a location west of Châteauroux, in the Indre, 'with a view to mounting strategic operations against the enemy lines of communication from south of France to the Neptune area [Overlord, actually; Neptune was the naval phase of the invasion, and gave way to Overlord as soon as the troops got ashore] as occasion may occur, or as developments in the main battle may dictate'. Subject to Tonkin locating a suitable base for operations and meeting certain other criteria, Bulbasket was later to be expanded to include the whole of B Squadron, under the command of Major Eric Lepine, the total force to have a nominal strength of twelve officers and 109 ORs.

Tonkin and Lieutenant Richard Crisp were inserted, together with the three men from Jedburgh team Hugh, led by Captain (later Colonel Sir) William Crawshay, whose initial responsibility was to assist in establishing Bulbasket. They were dropped blind (that is, without a reception party to mark the location of the ground) by a Halifax of 161 Squadron, RAF, based at Tempsford, on to a not-entirely-satisfactory

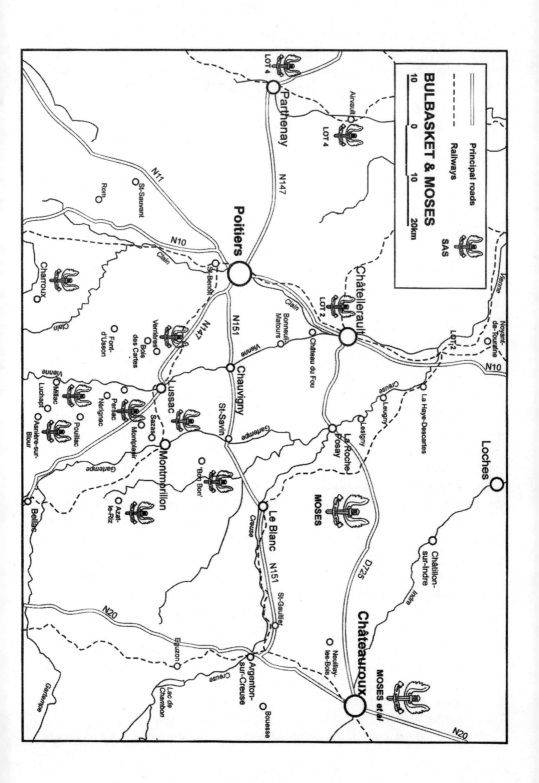

DZ code-named 'Sanglier' ('Wild Pig'), near St-Gaultier, in the Brenne marshes, some thirty kilometres south-west of Châteauroux. They landed without mishap just after 0130, and were thus probably the first Allied troops to land on French soil as a part, no matter how small, of Operation Overlord.

They were soon joined by locals who collected containers, hid parachutes and took the men to a nearby farm. Just after daybreak there arrived a young man from F Section, SOE, whom Tonkin recognised, from photographs he had studied in London, as 'Samuel' (Capt Amédée Maingard). Samuel, taken aback to learn that the invasion had been launched, since 'his' coded message to that effect was for some reason not broadcast by the BBC, took the five newcomers the short distance to Neuillay-les-Bois, where they met the then departmental commander of the FFI in the Indre, 'Colonel Surcouf' (*Commandant* Paul Mirguet). He advised that their basic plan – to divide the party into two teams, to operate against the Montauban–Limoges–Vierzon railway line, which ran through Châteauroux ('Lot 1') and that between Bordeaux (or Limoges and points south, via a connecting line) and Tours, which ran through Poitiers ('Lot 2') – would be unworkable, since the distance between the two lines was too great, and that in any event the *maquisards* could be relied upon to keep the former out of commission permanently. (A third target known as 'Lot 3', the line between Tours and Orléans, a considerable distance to the north, had already been dropped from the list.) He 'suggested' that Tonkin should establish his base of operations some sixty kilometres to the south-west, towards Poitiers, and the latter agreed, but in the meantime it was necessary to move some twenty-five kilometres in the other direction, toward Neuvy-St-Sépulchre, where a resupply drop was expected that night.

On the morning of 7 June, Tonkin learned, via Hugh's radio, that more of the Bulbasket advance party, with Lt Tomos Stephens in command and including a signaller, would arrive that night at a DZ ten kilometres to the west of Neuvy, near the village of Bouesse. Surcouf arranged transport for the nine-strong party, which was dropped successfully by a Stirling from Fairford, together with nine containers and around five tons of 'soft' stores (uniforms, tents, sleeping bags and the like, destined for the *maquisards*), the only casualty being the Eureka radar beacon, a most useful accessory to airborne resupply operations, which was never found.

That same night the enlarged party, which numbered close to a score including FFI minders, moved sixty-five kilometres west to Le Blanc, where Surcouf had his headquarters. On 9 June they split up, the Hugh team remaining at Le Blanc to liaise with the *maquis* bands in the area south of Châteauroux.

The Bulbasket party, accompanied by Samuel, headed south, beyond Montmorillon in the Vienne, to meet up with the FFI departmental commander there, 'Bernard' (Col Félix Chêne). Bernard allocated a young lieutenant, Albert Dupont, to act as liaison officer between the SAS party and the *maquisards*, particularly the local 'Amilcar' group, fifty strong and originally Communist-leaning FTP but now very cosmopolitan. Amilcar himself (Capt Robert Artaud) established the Bulbasket party in a pine wood, a few kilometres from his own headquarters at a farm named Sazas, south of Montmorillon, and together he and Tonkin set out to reconnoitre suitable DZ sites, finally selecting one a little way to the south-west, not far from the main N147 Limoges–Poitiers road, which they called Montplaisir after a nearby house.

The next morning, Tonkin received a report of eleven tanker-trains carrying petrol assembled in sidings at Châtellerault, heavily camouflaged and well guarded. (Published reports in English usually place them south-west of the city, but sources in Châtellerault make it clear that the sidings were located next to the main railway station, in the centre of the city, where they are still in use today.) He was frankly sceptical, and the only way to confirm the report of what was, it had been stressed at his briefing, a priority target was to send someone to look. 'Someone' was the diminutive Twm Stephens, dressed in borrowed civilian clothes, and mounted upon a bicycle, who set off around midday to pedal the sixty kilometres to Châtellerault, accompanied by a *maquisard* and the railway worker who had brought the report. They were to return the following afternoon, with confirmation that there was, indeed, a considerable quantity of fuel in the marshalling yard. There is some confusion as to the extent; 'eleven trains' and 'a train of eleven tanker trucks' have both been mentioned, and local reports talk of the fuel being in '*bidons*', which translates as drums but could mean jerrycans. The best indication is perhaps the size of the site: the sidings in question cover six sets of tracks and are perhaps 300 metres long.

Tonkin signalled to Moor Park, asking for an air strike, and somewhat unusually one was laid on almost immediately. The mission was planned overnight, and the following evening, 11 June, twelve de

Havilland Mosquito FB VI fighter-bombers from Allied Second Tactical Air Force bases in southern England dropped ten tons of bombs on the target, and then strafed it with 20mm cannon, reportedly destroying it completely. Eleven people died on the ground, and around a score were injured. All aircraft returned safely. The crews were never told the source of the target information, but rather that it came from 'a reconnaissance flight'.

The petrol they destroyed had seemingly been intended to refuel the vehicles of the SS-Panzer Division *Das Reich*, which had been forced to move by road, the railway lines between its bases around Montauban and the Normandy beachhead having been damaged sufficiently by repeated sabotage that it was unusable by heavy wagons carrying tanks. Many of these wagons – eighty-two specially adapted low-loader flat-cars – had been put out of action anyway, 'lubricated' with grease containing a significant quantity of abrasive carborundum powder, which caused their axles to seize up when they were collected from the rural railway sidings where they had been dispersed and left unguarded. This sabotage campaign was carried out by urban *résistants*, particularly railway workers in and around Montauban, recruited by 'Alphonse' (Tony Brooks), the organiser of SOE F Section's Pimento circuit; it is said that the most effective saboteurs Brooks had in the Montauban area were two sisters, fourteen and sixteen years old. Later, Jedburghs, notably team Quinine, led by the bekilted Tommy Macpherson, also became involved, but the essential damage was done before they arrived on the scene. Not only did the sabotage campaign contribute to delaying the German armoured division's arrival in the battle area – by perhaps ten days – but it put a considerable extra strain on both the vehicles and their crews by forcing them to make the journey on their own wheels and tracks.

The delay in *Das Reich* being committed to the battle for Normandy is often presented as being Bulbasket's most significant achievement. In fact, most of the credit for delaying its movement should go to the men and women who carried out the sabotage further south and forced the division to take to the roads in the first place. (There are persistent suggestions that the division had intended to go by road all along, to mount anti-partisan operations on the way, but that is hardly appropriate duty for an armoured division, and they can probably be discounted.) There is also a further factor to be considered: even when the division *did* arrive in Normandy, it was not committed to combat straight away, but was held in reserve until early July.

More important than delaying the commitment of one armoured division to the Normandy battle at an early stage, perhaps, was the broader economic and thus strategic effect caused by the weakening of the French railway system. Even a very approximate calculation shows why: the Mk IV and Mk V tanks (fifty-four and seventy-eight of them, respectively, plus forty-two Mk IV-based tank destroyers) which the *Das Reich* Division fielded at the time measured their fuel consumption in litres per kilometre: a Mk V Panther had a capacity of 730 litres, which was sufficient to take it little more than 200 kilometres. Moving this division alone by road from Montauban to Normandy thus probably cost Germany well over half a million litres (over 100,000 gallons) of petrol, and that was fuel she could ill afford, since the nation no longer had natural oil reserves available, the Romanian fields on which she had relied having been lost in the Russian advance, so that all her supplies had to be synthesised.

The next night, of 12 June, RAF Bomber Command bombed what is described in its War Diaries as 'communications, mostly railways' in half a dozen locations including Poitiers, but this was clearly part of an organised campaign and there is no evidence that this raid was developed from intelligence supplied by the Bulbasket party. There was a second air raid on 'a fuel dump at Châtellerault' on the night of 15 June, destroying '8 fuel sites out of 35 in the target area. No aircraft [out of 110 Lancasters involved] lost'; it is known that there was an 'Army Fuel Depôt, Châtellerault', but not what form it took; it could have been a distributed dump of fuel in drums, a more permanent dump with buried tanks or, indeed, a very temporary measure involving tanker trucks in railway sidings. A further raid on the same target – now described as being in 'the Forêt de Châtellerault', which lies to the south-west of the city – in somewhat greater strength (this time a total of 190 aircraft were involved), was made on the night of 9 August; the record states simply that the attack was 'successful'. Since the depot still existed almost two months after the first raids, it seems likely that this was a permanent structure of some sort, however, and it is doubtful that the second and third raids were simply follow-up missions built on the success of the initial 11 June sortie to attack the railway sidings.

While Stephens was away on his reconnaissance mission, during the night of 10 June, Tonkin and the rest of the advance party were waiting in vain at Montplaisir for the arrival of the main party. With no Eureka signal to guide it, the solitary Stirling was a long way wide of the mark; Tonkin heard no sign of it and therefore no signal fires were lit, and after fruitlessly searching the area, it returned to Fairford with the SAS troopers still aboard, to try again the following night. In fact, when the rerun came it was to involve two aircraft, a five-man Phantom team under the leadership of Capt Sadoine, which had not been ready the previous night, having been added to the twenty-strong SAS party. Once again, the reception party was in place well in advance, but this time, to Tonkin's horror, the main N147 road just a few kilometres to the south-west of the DZ proved to be alive with German vehicles – the advance party of the *Das Reich* Armoured Division, with its 15,000 men, more than 200 armoured vehicles and many more half-tracks and trucks carrying its *Deutschland* and *Der Führer* motorised infantry regiments, perhaps heading for Châtellerault to refuel from the dump which was even then lighting up the sky to the north-west.

The drop zone itself was in dead ground, not overlooked from the road, and Tonkin decided that the signal fires necessary to mark it for the Stirlings would not be seen. On hearing them, he ordered the markers lit; both aircraft made a pass over the DZ and then disappeared, but only one made a second pass, dropping twelve men and a similar number of containers from a height of 125 metres (400 feet). To the dismay of the men on the ground, the falling containers showed coloured lights. Intended as an aid to locating the containers when they landed, they should have been actuated on impact, but were initiated instead by the jerk of the parachute opening. The effect on the Germans was immediate – the vehicles stopped, dowsed their own lights and switched off their engines; clearly they believed themselves about to come under air attack, and took such precautions as they could. The SAS party made great haste to smash every tell-tale lamp in sight, load the containers on to waiting ox carts and clear the area; almost amazingly they were able to do so without being fired upon.

It transpired that the pilot of the second aircraft, seeing the lights of the convoy, had opted for a more prudent course. A hurried consultation with Sadoine, the senior army officer present, led him to search out an alternative drop zone, and he identified a clear hilltop area some twenty-five kilometres east of Montplaisir, where he safely deposited his thirteen parachutists – the five Phantoms and eight SAS troopers led by Sgt Eccles – and their containers. In the light of his later actions, there may be some speculation that Sadoine – not his true name, which may have been Octave Dupont; he was a Belgian who had escaped to England at the time of Dunkirk, and had joined the British Army – actively encouraged the pilot to drop them away from the main party. It was to be some time before the missing men were to make contact with the rest of the Bulbasket party; the reduction in its size was especially significant since it had been decided, at SHAEF's request and without Tonkin's knowledge, to insert fifteen men, including two lieutenants and a sergeant, away from the main operational area, and they had in fact been dropped the previous night, in four groups, directly on to railway targets at some considerable distance from his location.

As originally written, the orders for these parties, contained in Operation Instruction No. 20 of 8 June, were for the 'Lot 2' line north of Poitiers to be cut for four days starting from the night of 10 June; in fact, the plan was to be expanded to include the Bordeaux–Saumur line, known as 'Lot 4', well to the west, though it seems that no attempt was made to comply with the instruction to keep the line(s) cut until 14 June. Two teams were to cut 'Lot 2', north (Sgt Holmes plus two men, who were inserted near the village of Noyant-de-Touraine) and south (Lt Morris plus three) of Châtellerault, while the other two, Lt Weaver plus three and Cpl Kinnivane plus three, were to focus on 'Lot 4'. The four parties were to link up with Tonkin after they had carried out their initial assignments, and the first the CO knew of the change of plan was when Sgt Jessiman reported to him on his arrival at Montplaisir.

The only mishap suffered by the two parties which targeted 'Lot 2' was the temporary loss of Tpr Brown, who became separated from Lt Morris and the others when they were dropped about five kilometres off target. Brown was an experienced and resourceful man, with a Military Medal, earned in Italy, to his credit; he set off for the rendezvous, some fifty kilometres away, alone, with only a map and a compass to guide him. He was lucky enough to be intercepted by a *maquisard*, and was passed from band to band until he reached Bernard's headquarters. Sgt Holmes, one of the veterans of North Africa and Italy (where he had been Tonkin's driver), safely led his small party the ninety kilometres to the RV without outside assistance, and Lt Morris did likewise. Tonkin had moved on by that time, but they were met by *maquisards* and taken on to join the main group, arriving on 17 June.

The aircraft ferrying Lt Peter Weaver's and Cpl Kinnivane's parties dropped the former out of position by twenty-five kilometres, but it located its target railway line successfully, south of Parthenay, and placed charges which derailed a train on the morning of 14 June. Weaver and his men – and two of the troopers in Kinnivane's party – had all been members of the Scout Section of the Auxiliary Units in Dorset, and the fact that they had worked together for four years clearly stood them in good stead; the demolition successfully carried out, they set off to make their way the best part of a hundred kilometres through enemy-occupied territory to the RV.

Cpl Kinnivane's party – himself and Tprs Biffin, Ogg and Pascoe – was dropped closer to its objective, but directly on to the small town of Airvault, which had a German garrison. They were involved in a firefight almost immediately, and were forced to flee, abandoning all the equipment they were not actually carrying. George Biffin failed to link up with the other two and was captured in the town after an effort to evade. He survived interrogation accompanied by a degree of brutality, and a fairly lame plot to encourage him to escape, which was clearly intended to give his captors justification for shooting him. Managing, with the help of a *Luftwaffe* officer, who seemingly abhorred the policy of executing saboteurs out of hand, to conceal his true regimental identity, he passed eventually into the relative security of the Stalag 9C PoW camp at Mulhausen, and was eventually liberated by American forces in Bavaria.

Weaver and his men were to have an arduous ten-night journey cross-country, moving cautiously and living very poorly off the land, reaching the RV south of Montmorillon on 24 June only to find it deserted. Later that day they fell into company with a partisan band which had a stock of arms and explosives but no idea how to use them, and were then delayed longer, 'detained' for three days by never-quite-fulfilled promises, to act as weapons instructors. Weaver eventually saw through the subterfuge, and insisted on being taken to meet up with the main party, which was by then installed in the Verrières forest. He arrived, accompanied by Tprs Ashley, Cogger and Ryland, on 28 June, the same day as Cpl Kinnivane and Ogg and Pascoe, and the solitary Tpr Brown. Tonkin had been far from idle in the meantime, despite the fact that the area was 'lousy with Germans', many of them in transit towards the battlefield further north, but some of them looking for him and his men. Sabotage parties had temporarily halted rail traffic half a dozen times, and in the early hours of 13 June Richard Crisp had also successfully mined the N147, while Sgt Jessiman had mined the N10, south of Poitiers.

After the successful *parachutage* in the early hours of 12 June, Bernard had told off a dozen men from the Amilcar *Maquis* under a young lieutenant named Jean Dieudonné ('Maurice') to act as Bulbasket's minders. They had helped with security and the procurement of extra rations and had found some vehicles – three cars and a small truck – to transport the party to a new campsite near the village of Nérignac, about twenty kilometres away across the N147 to the south-west. This move was necessitated by increased German patrol activity around Montmorillon and took place during the night of 13 June. Tonkin was increasingly frustrated by lack of mobility. On the night of 12 June, while reporting the safe arrival of one stick of parachutists and the non-arrival of the other and the Phantoms, he had asked for a delivery of jeeps, and was promised that they would be sent three nights later; as soon as the party was settled into the new campsite, he despatched Twm Stephens on his bicycle once more, this time to reconnoitre the DZs suggested by the *maquisards*, with a senior (Communist) *résistant* named Camille Olivet ('La Chouette'; The Owl) to keep him out of trouble. The resupply operation was delayed until the night of 17 June, but when it was finally carried out all went well; two Halifaxes from 298 Sqdn each dropped a jeep, five containers and two men, two more from 644 Sqdn dropped jeeps and six containers, while a Stirling from 196 Sqdn dropped seventeen containers, all on to the drop zone at Font-d'Usson. The aircrafts' flight plans were uncoordinated, and each arrived at the DZ individually, but there was no mishap. The four huge parachutes attached to each vehicle deployed perfectly; holes in which to bury the protective carrying-cradles had been dug in advance – a very necessary precaution; the cradles were unavoidably big and cumbersome, and disposing of them quickly was to be a recurring problem – and the containers full of fuel, spares and tools were all located successfully. One jeep's chassis was found to have been twisted by the impact, but it was declared driveable by the master mechanic, Sgt Bob Heavens, and tanks were filled, the Vickers Type K machine-guns were mounted, and just after daybreak the little convoy set off.

It came under fire almost immediately from a German patrol, and the lead jeep swerved off the road and into a ditch, where it overturned; the other vehicles returned fire and drove off their assailants. The jeep was recovered with little trouble – one of the undoubted advantages of such a light vehicle – and after a hurried check, it was discovered that no one had been hit in the exchange, although Tpr O'Neill had suffered a crushed hand. That was not the last excitement of the short trip back to Bulbasket's base, for there was still the D11 to be negotiated; although a relatively minor road, it was in use by a steady succession of German vehicles, mostly stragglers from *Das Reich*. Tonkin waited for a significant gap in the spare stream of traffic and then hurried the jeeps across in a group, at high speed. Not a shot was fired, and the party made good its escape.

On 19 June, Tonkin received news from London that the Bulbasket party would not be made up to squadron strength. His original orders had required him to report on the number of SAS personnel the region could support, and in the light of his comments about the area being 'lousy with Germans' it is likely that it was agreed that bringing the number up to over a hundred would simply be too dangerous. Certainly, there is evidence that Tonkin was feeling anything but secure, for that same day he changed locations yet again, this time in daylight, the jeeps supplemented by a commandeered bus, moving about six kilometres south to the area around a hamlet named Pouillac.

Tonkin had another cause for concern, too: the continued failure of Sadoine and his Phantoms (not to mention the eight SAS men with him) to link up with him. Sadoine had established himself near the village of Azat-le-Ris, some thirty-five kilometres to the east. Tonkin located him on 19 June and seemingly ordered him to join up with the main party, but he declined to do so. Tonkin then returned to Pouillac with Sgt Eccles and four men – all that he could carry in the jeeps – leaving Cpl Bateman in charge of the rump of the SAS party.

At this point, as author Paul McCue has suggested in his book on Bulbasket, a rift started to develop between Tonkin and Sadoine, who had never met before. Citing an account Tonkin wrote many years after the fact, McCue implies that, on 23 June, and following a further order from London for him to do so, Tonkin tried to insist that Sadoine co-locate with him, but that he again refused, and Lt Morris, who had carried the order, returned with Cpl Bateman and the remaining two troopers. Sadoine, in his own after-action report, portrayed Tonkin as a fellow-worker in a common cause, and certainly not as his commanding officer, saying, 'Capt. Tonkin visited me here (this was his second visit) and told me where he was located and where he was operating.' They were, of course, of equal rank. It is interesting to note that Capt Tom Moore, Sadoine's counterpoint in Operation Houndsworth, who had and maintained a good relationship with the SAS party, clearly also felt that his operation was not an integral part of it: Moore said in his report 'Being a Phantom patrol *attached* to A Sqn 1 SAS did not cause embarrassment to either party. Major Fraser, his officers and men, cooperated, assisted and helped us from the moment we joined them ...' [author's italics]. McCue made much of the breakdown of the relationship between Sadoine and Tonkin who, he maintained, 'privately ... remained convinced' that the Belgian had betrayed him and the SAS party. There is certainly some confusion; Sadoine made it clear that he was operating independently, both organising and arming local partisan bands and sending back details of potential bombing targets to London. He had already received a resupply drop (on 16 June) and was to receive two more, with a total of over seventy containers and four panniers of 'soft' items, the last of them on the night of 3 July, despite seemingly having been ordered by Moor Park on 22 June, and again on 24, 27 and 29 June, to link up with the main party forthwith. It is interesting to note that on 22 June, Boy Browning, the commander, Airborne Forces, was writing to HQ 21st Army Group that 'two small bases ... some twenty miles apart' had been established by the Bulbasket party, as if this was desirable.

Sadoine, in any event, never did co-locate voluntarily with Tonkin; in the early hours of 6 July, by which time events had taken a dreadful turn, Tonkin sent Lt Weaver and a party of men to fetch him, and thereafter he was held under close arrest, his guards having orders to shoot him if he made any attempt to abscond. There were deeper reasons for this, and we shall examine them later, in the proper context.

Tonkin received a resupply drop on the night of 21 June, while Lts Stephens and Crisp were out with parties cutting the 'Lot 2' line both north and south of Poitiers, and the following night he ordered another move, this time to Persac, some fifteen kilometres to the north. Three nights later, on 25 June, the Bulbasket party moved yet again, across the River Vienne to a site near the edge of the Verrières forest, less than two kilometres from the village of that name and within twenty-five of the regional capital, Poitiers, and it was here that it was brought up to full strength by the arrival of the last seven men from the four small parties dropped blind on 11 June. There must be some criticism of the choice of this campsite – it was located on the edge of the forest, and not deep inside it, in a rough rectangle of woodland on a gentle slope running down to a stream, about a kilometre wide and two long, near to a farm and with tracks on all sides. Tonkin apparently regarded this latter as an advantage, because it allowed the party's vehicles to approach the site from any direction.

By now, sabotage or reconnaissance parties were out most nights, and were able to drive around the back roads unmolested; German security units rarely left their barracks except in considerable strength, and the pattern of their patrol activity was well known. As a result of missed resupply drops, however, Tonkin's men were in danger of running out of certain vital commodities such as ordnance and fuel. In fact, the situation by 30 June was such that Lt Morris, with Tpr Brown as his driver, on a mission to reconnoitre an airfield near Châteauroux and to cut a railway line, was forced to travel by way of Sadoine's Phantom base to obtain additional supplies of explosives; their jeep turned over between the base and the supply dump, damaging the steering and injuring both men slightly, but with fortuitous results, as we shall see.

The first blow fell on the night of 28 June, when Sgt Eccles and Cpl Bateman failed to return from a mission to destroy points in the marshalling yards at St-Benoît, in the southern suburbs of Poitiers. Prudence dictated that on the return, alone, of the sabotage party's driver, Tonkin should have cleared the area immediately. Had the two men been captured – which was the most likely explanation, for the driver had not heard gunfire – they would certainly be subjected to hard interrogation and could not be expected to remain mute for longer than forty-eight hours. Tonkin failed to shift camp until the night of 1 July, largely, it is reported, because of the presence of the stream close to the Forêt de Verrières site – the summer of 1944 was very dry in this region, and the provision of fresh water was a serious problem – and then only moved a few kilometres south, to the Bois des Cartes, the other side of the hamlet of St-Laurent-de-Jourdes, so as to be within reach of the DZ at Font-d'Usson for a supply drop scheduled for every night since that of 28 June and repeatedly cancelled because of weather conditions. Unfortunately, a well in the Bois des Cartes – the reason this new location was chosen – ran dry almost immediately, and Tonkin made a fateful decision to return to the old campsite in the Verrières forest, at least overnight, while scouting parties went in search of a new location, on the rash assumption that since it was now four days since Eccles and Bateman had disappeared, and there had been no untoward activity, either the two men had been killed, or that they had somehow not succumbed to interrogation and the location of the campsite had not been disclosed. In fact, it seems that the two SAS NCOs had been questioned in a somewhat desultory fashion by *Wehrmacht* officers from 80th Corps HQ at the Poitiers *Feldkommandantur* on 29 and 30 June, and were only handed over to the *Sicherheitspolizei-Sicherheitsdienst* (*Sipo-SD*, commonly but erroneously known as the 'Gestapo') for more serious interrogation late on 30 June. From German sources it is clear that the men were forced to reveal everything they knew, probably by early on 1 July.

As well as the presumed capture of Eccles and Bateman, there were other factors which should have convinced Tonkin to leave the Verrières site, the most compelling being reports that girls from the village, perhaps informed of the SAS party's presence by partisans, had visited the campsite, and that in consequence, some of the men had quite casually made their way to the village and had been seen drinking in the bar there. Samuel, who kept in close touch with the operation throughout, reported this to Tonkin on 1 July, and told him that if the Germans had not received reports of their presence already, they soon would. Early that same afternoon, two men dressed as civilians appeared on the road at the forest margin, pushing a motorcycle combination. They were challenged by an SAS sentry (John Fielding), and claimed to be *maquisards* (one report has them armed with Sten sub-machineguns), explaining that they had a puncture; Fielding, alone and relatively inexperienced, made the decision to take them to the campsite, where they remained for some time while their tyre was repaired. Eventually, after being interrogated at some length by Maurice, but without any other confirmation of their identities having been sought, they were allowed to leave. Post facto, there was considerable speculation that the men were in fact *Miliciens* or agents of *Sipo-SD* and that seems to be confirmed from German sources. There were further disquieting incidents that day too: reports of an unknown vehicle touring the forest roads, slowly and seemingly aimlessly, and the arrival of a small *Maquis* group bringing a stranger who introduced himself as Lt Lincoln Bundy of the 486th Squadron, 352 Fighter Group, USAAF, and claimed that his North American P-51 Mustang had been shot down by anti-aircraft fire. Tonkin radioed London asking for some sort of confirmation, but received no reply; for all Tonkin knew, the uninvited newcomer could have been a German 'plant'.

All these factors combined finally convinced Tonkin to move the campsite to the Bois des Cartes, but as we have seen he reversed himself within twenty-four hours; on the surface, at least, they seem to add up to a set of very compelling reasons to have quit Verrières completely, and Tonkin's motives for not doing so are difficult to comprehend, unless he thought he could execute a dangerous double-bluff by withdrawing quite obviously and then slipping back quietly. If so, the stratagem did not work.

When the extended Bulbasket party bedded down for the night on 2 July there were in all forty-eight men in the Verrières forest: thirty-eight SAS men, nine *maquisards* (two others had been given leave to spend the night in Verrières) and one American flyer. Tonkin and his driver, who had been scouting for a new campsite location, returned in the early hours of the morning and settled down to sleep. It seems likely

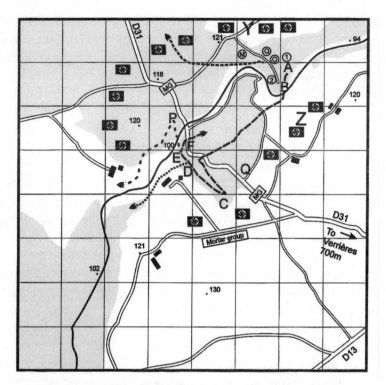

The raid on the Bulbasket party campsite, 3 July

Key

Third-class road	Ⓜ	Maquisards
Communal road	Ⓠ	Headquarters
Track	◎	Officers
Route of main party	①	Number 1 Party
Route of Sgt Holmes' party	②	Number 2 Party
Route of Lt Weaver	MG	Machine guns
Route of Cpl Rideout's party	✶	German infantry
Course of stream	130	Spot height in metres
Extent of woodland		

250   0   250   500m

that the German forces had been in position when Tonkin returned, and that he was allowed to pass through their cordon. The men were in the open, in sleeping bags, in five groups within a roughly triangular area a hundred metres or so to a side, with the three jeeps and some other vehicles parked adjacent to a track close at hand. There were no sentries posted, nor were there any other security precautions in force.

By late on 1 July, plans were being laid at the *Feldkommandantur* at Poitiers for a security operation to arrest the men camping in the Verrières forest. It would employ elements of the *Sicherheitsdienst* under the local (acting) second-in-command, *SS-Obersturmführer* Hoffmann, who was in overall charge of the operation; of the Reconnaissance Squadron of the 158th Security Division under an *Oberleutnant* named Vogt, which was attached to the 80th Corps for anti-partisan operations, and elements of 17. SS-Panzer Grenadier Division *Götz von Berlichingen*'s holding battalion. These troops probably began moving into the area soon after darkness fell on 2 July; they clearly knew exactly where their objective was situated and there can be no reasonable doubt that a fruitful reconnaissance operation had been mounted beforehand. Had it not been for the fact that two young *maquisards* had been given permission to visit girlfriends in Verrières and were returning, by a roundabout route, just before 0700, the Germans' surprise would have been complete. As it was, the two 'bumped' a sentry on the minor road to the north of the campsite and ran when he challenged them. He opened fire, and that, perhaps a little prematurely, became the signal for the assault to begin. Even as the men woke, mortar bombs were falling and bursts of machine-gun fire were cutting through the trees (though the survivor of the pair referred to above, Marcel Weber, was to say that the *maquisards* at least, if not the SAS party, had stood-to, alerted by the initial bursts of gunfire from the road leading into the forest); disoriented no doubt, and completely unprepared, the troopers struggled to react. In addition to John Tonkin's after-action report, which is hardly comprehensive on the subject of the assault on the campsite, two individual accounts of it, both set down some considerable time after the event, have survived. Lt Peter Weaver described the events thus:

On the 4th July 1944 'A' Troop, 'B' Squadron, were betrayed, surrounded by 450 SS troops armed with field-guns, mortars and heavy machine guns. At 0700hrs shells were fired into the immediate area, with automatic fire sweeping the camp from point 'Y'. [This and the other indicators refer to the sketch map Peter Weaver later drew, which forms the basis for the map on page 66. Weaver used some indicators twice, and 'Y' and 'Z' substituted for the duplications in the interests of clarity, while two, the Holmes/Cummings laying-up position and the point at which the maquisards were murdered, have been added as 'P' and 'Q'.]

Headquarters section had no time to dress before they were heavily fired on from point 'Y'.

No 1 Party and No 2 Party concentrated at point 'A' with Lt Stephens, Lt Weaver and Lt Crisp. This was then approximately 27 strong.

Lt Stephens contacted Capt Tonkin and came back with orders for every man to scatter and try to break through the ring individually.

We went as a body to point 'B' and were fired upon by automatics from point 'Z'. We were able to cross the third class road [i.e. the D 31] owing to the bend and went to point 'C', where we were fired on again by automatics.

The men were repeatedly told to scatter and hide up. They were fired on again at point 'E'. Then one party cut back with Lt Crisp and crossed the road [at point 'F'] and were fired upon, and Lt Crisp was wounded in the thigh. Lt Stephens went back to point 'C' for a recce and was also wounded in the leg. I crossed the corn field at point 'D' and was fired on halfway across. Another small party followed and were stopped by shells, where Tpr Pascoe was badly wounded.

Weaver himself then hid in a thorn thicket, where he passed the rest of the day and the following night before re-joining the remnants of the party the next day.

The other report was made by Thomas Cummings. He said:

Just after day-break on the 4th July, a heavy burst of automatic fire cut through the branches of the trees we were sleeping under. (J. Holmes, R. Guard, E. Richardson, T. Cummings) Our position was just off the path that ran through the woods, marked 'A' on the map. Immediately J. Holmes ordered us to get dressed and take up a fire position. In the two or three minutes after the first burst of fire one of the Maquis lads attached to us crawled up the slope to our position [this was seemingly Marcel Weber]. He had a very bad wound in his thigh. He was calling out "Les Allemands" were coming. Lt Stephens spoke to him, they went to see Capt Tonkin, two of the lads helping him, all the time fire was directed on the wood but the Germans never ventured into the wood. They must have thought they had the place properly closed up.

After Lt Weaver and Lt Crisp got us all together Lt Stephens came back with orders for us to disperse. As J. Holmes was strict on our group always to have our escape pack ready we were ready to go. At no time was there any panic, as a matter of fact the last I saw and heard of the group that went from point 'A' to point 'B' was Jock Govan cursing the Jerries for waking him up.

We discussed our position and went in two's, R. Guard, E. Richardson went with a large group from point 'A' to point 'B'; we never saw them again, as at this time the firing increased. J. Holmes suggested we go down the slope across the stream and cross about thirty or forty yards of open ground. (This open ground is now covered with trees) On our way across firing came from our rear, so we assumed there was no Jerries in the wood facing us. By the small bridge Victor White was firing at an enemy position and Johnnie [i.e. Sgt. Holmes] asked him to come along but he said he would be along in a minute, he never did. Further on Cpl Kinnivane was asked but he said he was getting his breath back. Another twenty yards or so he would have been safe.

We lay in this wood [at point 'P'] for about three hours listening to German traffic on the third class road and orders being given. I think this was the most trying part as we were only about ten yards from the road. When things went quiet we made our way through the woods and eventually joined the rest of the lads who got out. It was a small farm where we met, just off the third class road around the forest. Capt Tonkin, Lt Weaver, Sgt Holmes, Cpl Rideout, Tpr Keeble, Tpr McNair, Tpr Cummings all met up at the farm.' [Thomas Cummings clearly had a lapse of memory, for Trooper William Smith also escaped.]

These two reports are somewhat at odds with each other, but agree in most respects. Crucially, they contradict the personal account prepared later by Tonkin and reproduced by Paul McCue in *Operation Bulbasket*, which talks of men panicking and setting off in headlong flight which Tonkin said he tried to arrest by sending Lts Crisp, Stephens and

Weaver after them. Not all the men of the party were capable of evasion, for some, probably including Joseph Ogg and John Williams, were disabled in the initial mortar and machine gun barrage. The RAMC corporal, William Allan, could have accompanied those who did try to escape but instead remained at the campsite, tending wounded men, a task he continued to perform in captivity (William Allan's self-sacrifice was recognised by the award of the Military Medal, which was not gazetted until 14 February 1946. A posthumous award of the Military Medal was irregular at that time, and it can only be surmised that Tonkin put his name forward on his return to the UK in the belief that he was still alive). Tonkin, who had made his way due westwards from the campsite in company with Cpl Rideout and Tprs Keeble and McNair, realised that no effort had been made to secure the party's code pads, and went back to try to find them; he failed, though he was apparently able to place time pencils in some blocks of PE, which later exploded, and by that time German infantrymen were in the camp and he had no recourse but to hide himself as best he could. He was later to tell how he lay so close to a group of Germans who helped themselves to the SAS rations that the wrappings they discarded actually fell on him.

Of the SAS party in camp that night, just the seven men named by Thomas Cummings, together with William Smith, survived. Almost incredibly, none of the others was actually killed during the assault, but were taken into captivity.

Lt Tomos Stephens was the first of the prisoners to die. Wounded, he is said to have tried to surrender, but was beaten to the ground with a rifle butt (other reports state that he was shot once in the head); whether he actually succumbed to his wounds then or later is unclear, but his body was later put on show in Verrières. The six captured *maquisards* were next, shot at the side of the road in the forest (at the spot marked 'Q'; a monument was later erected near the site) and their bodies thrown in a heap in the village square. The captured SAS men and the American airman Lt Bundy were taken to the *Feldkommandantur* in Poitiers. Three of them were badly wounded – Tprs Ogg, Pascoe and Williams – and were soon removed to the Hôtel de Dieu Hospital, where they stayed for five days before being returned to the custody of the *Wehrmacht*. Their return to close confinement was ordered following the rescue from the hospital of two members of a *Maquis* band; ironically, the three wounded SAS troopers were actually in the same hospital ward, and had the rescue party been aware of that fact, could perhaps have been saved as well. The remaining twenty-eight men, some with non-life-threatening wounds, together with Lt Bundy, were held in makeshift accommodation at the *Feldkommandantur* in groups of six to eight, in rooms which were bugged; they were interrogated but not, by German accounts, mistreated. They were at some point reunited with Sgt Eccles and Cpl Bateman, already in captivity.

The fate of the prisoners was sealed by the Special Handling Order Adolf Hitler himself had issued some thirty-two months previously, but there seems to have been reluctance all round actually to take responsibility for seeing it carried out. The senior figures in the *Sipo-SD* in Poitiers simply refused to take the prisoners, and their counterparts at 80th Corps juggled with the situation until they were eventually backed into a bureaucratic corner and dared prevaricate no longer. The task itself was given, by Colonel Herbert Koestlin, 80th Corps' Chief of Staff, to *Oberleutnant* Vogt who, pre-war, had been a minister of the church. He seems to have made no objection.

During the night of 6 July, three pits were dug beside a track deep within the St-Sauvant forest, some thirty kilometres south of Poitiers, just west of the N10, at a spot previously reconnoitred by Vogt and in an area where his unit had ambushed the FTP *Maquis* Noël on 27 June. The prisoners and their extensive escort arrived at the execution site before dawn on 7 July. The thirty-one men were lined up along the track and Vogt gave the order to fire, while *Hauptmann* Dr Erich Schönig, the 80th Corps Intelligence Officer, looked on as the official observer. Schönig later reported that 'The parachutists died in an exemplary, brave and calm manner ... They linked arms ...'. In fact, when the bodies were disinterred the following December they were found to have their hands bound behind their backs. Field autopsies carried out after the bodies were recovered revealed that all had died from gunshot wounds. (Frenchmen in the vicinity at the time of the executions later testified that they had heard two rounds of cannon fire, bursts of machine-gun fire and several individual pistol shots.) There is no physical evidence, but it seems clear from (German) documentary sources that six days later the three wounded men, too ill to stand before a firing squad and with no real hope of recovery following a week of neglect, were killed by lethal injection, almost certainly an overdose of morphine. The thirty-one men executed in the forest, seventeen of whom were identified beyond doubt (despite the identity disks having been removed from all but two of them), were subsequently reburied on 23 December, 1944 in the communal cemetery at nearby Rom, all but four of them in a common grave;

Tomos Stephens was interred at Verrières and of Ogg, Williams and Pascoe, no remains have ever been found.

After belatedly escaping the campsite, Tonkin, by his own account, spent the rest of 3 July wandering around in a daze, eventually stumbling into Verrières. Most of the other troopers seem to have been rather better organised, and by evening all but Peter Weaver and one trooper had reached the fall-back RV at a farm called La Roche (or La Rocherie), east of Verrières, where they met up with Maurice and were joined by Samuel. Maurice had news of Tonkin's presence in Verrières, and Tpr McNair set out to find him. The two were given shelter on the outskirts of the village that night, and returned to rejoin the others the following morning. During that day, Lt Weaver and the remaining missing trooper also rejoined, as did a sabotage team made up of the two Smiths and John Fielding, who had been away from the campsite on the fateful morning, warned that something had befallen the rest of the party, and then fortuitously happened upon a *Maquis* patrol, which brought them to the RV. On the night of 5 July the party moved, with *maquisard* assistance, some fifteen kilometres to the south, in the direction of Millac, to a campsite in the Forêt de Plessac. There the group grew to thirteen with the return of Lts Morris and Brown from Azat-le-Ris with the one remaining jeep. As soon as they rejoined, Tonkin despatched Weaver, with a corporal and six *maquisards*, to bring in the Phantom patrol. He was motivated chiefly, it seems, by the need to replace his signallers (Cpl Chick, with Tprs Adamson and Hill to assist), who had been captured at Verrières, but also, perhaps, had finally lost patience with Sadoine whom he now placed under close arrest.

To trace the reasons for that, we have to return to the meeting Tonkin had with Maurice, Samuel and others on 1 July, where he was told that Sadoine was operating on his own, arming *maquisard* bands and setting up some kind of support network; that he had been heard to say that he considered Bulbasket's operations were likely to put both the *maquisards* and him and his men in mortal danger, and that he had suggested that the best way to combat that danger would be pre-emptively, by 'eliminating' Bulbasket. Now Samuel renewed his advice to bring Sadoine before a field court-martial and if necessary execute him, but Tonkin demurred again, and simply held him under armed guard, seemingly all the time until the Bulbasket party was evacuated, more than a month later. No formal charges were ever brought against Sadoine – and indeed, he was Mentioned in Despatches at the conclusion of the operation – but he was subsequently returned to his unit (the Irish Guards) and later dismissed the British Army. He was subsequently conscripted into the Belgian Army, was invalided out, and reportedly spent the rest of his life in a psychiatric hospital.

Also on the night of 5 July, and perhaps with revenge for Twm Stephens and the seven Frenchmen in mind – though he had no way of knowing the fate of the other men of his party, and in fact did not learn of the murders in the St-Sauvant forest until he read a newspaper report of the discovery of the mens' remains in January 1945 – Tonkin sent a message to Moor Park, asking for an air strike on barracks at Bonneuil-Matours, home of the holding battalion of 17. SS-Panzer Grenadier Division *Götz von Berlichingen*, which had provided most of the force that had attacked the Verrières camp.

The establishment was a permanent affair, originally built to house Belgian refugees in 1940. Jedburgh team Hugh was said to have provided the co-ordinates of the target, but its signals log shows that it actually asked for a strike upon the same target itself, in a communication of 12 July, saying:

'Request special bombing of HQ Boche Colonel commanding repression columns Indre Vienne Creuse et Loire. Situated Bonneuil-Matours. 15 kilometres south Châtellerault. Château 450 metres south east of crossroads east of village. 100 metres south of road from Archigny. Defense company in wood 30 metres east of trenches along River Vienne from crossroads TTT 200 yards to south. Also probably tanks.'

and it may well be that it was this second signal which actually prompted the mounting of the raid. The Mosquito strike which resulted, which may have seen the first operational use of napalm in the European Theatre of Operations, together with both instantaneous and delay-fuzed high explosive munitions, was made at dinner time on 14 July, and French accounts speak of seven barracks blocks being destroyed with eighty to a hundred dead and wounded, while Tonkin's report states that about 150 were killed and team Hugh put the toll at around 200. While the attack on the SS barracks was in progress, Tonkin and his depleted party, having moved yet again on 9 July, and by now installed temporarily near Charroux, to the west, were guests of the *Maquis* at a Bastille Day parade and dinner at Luchapt.

At this point, French records (compiled from *maquisards)* and those derived from Tonkin's after-action report indicate different locations for the Bulbasket party. Tonkin states that they moved during the night of 14 July, some thirty kilometres east again, to Asnières-sur-Blour, to co-locate with a large *Maquis* band which provided a much-needed extra element of security, and straightaway established a new DZ adjacent to it, using it for all subsequent resupply operations. French sources suggest they moved to the the Forêt du Défant and first employed a DZ code-named 'Kent', to the north-east of there, and later another called 'Milton', to the south-west, near to Luchapt, and that only the last resupply drop, which saw Lt David Surrey Dane join the party, was made on the site adjacent to the Asnières camp. During this period the party was to be reinforced, too, from an unexpected source, when two out of seven downed American flyers brought to the *maquisard* campsite asked to be allowed to join in offensive operations; Lt Flamm D Harper, USAAF, subsequently accompanied Tonkin, Fielding and the *maquisard* Maurice to cut the 'Lot 2' line and was extremely disappointed that the raid had to be aborted when the party ran into a sentry who gave the alarm.

In fact, Bulbasket's task was nearly over, and the following night, 24 July, Tonkin was informed that the next resupply drop would include a specialist in airstrip selection and preparation, who would set up their exfiltration. Lt David Dane arrived as promised on the night of 28 July, and soon identified a site north of Montmorillon, which was code-named 'Bon Bon', to the environs of which the party immediately decamped. From then on, they busied themselves preparing the strip – hedges and a tree (for which the landowner extracted payment) had to be removed and the surface evened-out, the jeep employed to pull a harrow – but there were still operations in prospect: air strikes on a barracks in Poitiers, the Caserne des Dunes, which was home to both German troops and the *Francs Gardes* of the local *Milice* detachment, who were seemingly preparing for a large-scale action against the *Maquis* groups in the Vienne, and another on the Château du Fou, south of Châtellerault, to which the survivors of 17. SS-Panzer Grenadier Division *Götz von Berlichingen*'s holding battalion had moved after the attack on Bonneuil-Matours. Both operations, carried out by 2 Group Mosquitoes on 1 and 2 August respectively, were successful, though one aircraft was lost over France from the former; both crewmen survived and evaded capture and were subsequently picked up by an RAF Hudson.

All the survivors from the Bulbasket party save for Cpl Stephenson, effectively the Phantom leader since 5 July, and one of his signallers – sixteen in all, together with Samuel, who returned to France some days later, and three American airmen – were extracted by two RAF Hudsons which landed, not without some difficulty, at Bon Bon on the night of 6 August. The remaining two Phantoms, Lt Dane and four more American flyers were taken out three days later by a USAAF C-47 Skytrain (Dakota), the C-47, though bigger, being much better adapted to the dimensions of the field than the faster Hudson. Trooper O'Neill, still in hospital in Poitiers, was liberated by American forces on 8 September.

The Hudsons brought eleven French troopers from 3 SAS (three officers, one of them British from 2 SAS, together with a party of signallers, had been dropped earlier by parachute to act as the advance party), and the C-47 brought in eight more, to establish Operation Moses (q.v.), and thus the transition from Operation Bulbasket to its replacement was seamless. The Moses party, whose numbers grew to a total of forty-two (some reports quote forty-six), was to be effective in harassing German attempts to withdraw from the Vienne and the Indre, latterly in conjunction with the Samson party also from 3 SAS which had been inserted into the Haute Vienne to the south. Operation Moses concluded only on 5 October, by which time its members were involved in the operations to contain German troops in a pocket across the Loire estuary from St Nazaire.

So what of Operation Bulbasket? On balance, it is difficult to rate it as more than a partial success, not only because so many lives were lost in its course and it had to be brought to a premature conclusion as a result but also because it actually achieved very little in purely military terms. From the outset, the leader of the Jedburgh team which was inserted with Tonkin was dismissive of the SAS operation and its chances of success. In his after-action report, William Crawshay (who, according to the Hugh's radio log, referred to the SAS party as 'Sad Athletic Sacks' during a communication of 21 June; that, of course, could have been an attempt at creating a jocular mnemonic, but could equally well betray Crawshay's true opinion of the party and its operation) was to write:

> As regards the SAS, we never considered that uniformed troops, foreign to the country and its language, could carry out sabotage in better conditions than the resistance. On the contrary, they attract far more remark, and consequently draw danger not only on themselves, but on all the Maquis in the region.

The future was to show that these very factors were to bring catastrophe upon them while their positive achievements were
considerably less than were effected by the Maquis in the same period
with less facilities at their disposal.

The employment of jeeps by the SAS at that early stage, showed
how little they appreciated the true position.

And what of Tonkin's leadership? Without a shadow of a doubt, he must
bear the responsibility for the party having been in the poorly sited
camp in the Verrières forest on the morning of 3 July when clearly it
should have been elsewhere. Equally clearly, security precautions, both
then and there, and generally, were lax. More than half a century after
the events took place, John Fielding was to agree that the Bulbasket
party had become somewhat complacent by the time of the attack on
the campsite. 'When you are successful and have a low casualty rate,' he
said, 'you are liable to drop your security precautions. We thought it
was too easy, and our security was not as it should have been.'

There is also a question as to how usefully the majority of the Bulbasket party was employed. The make-up of the sabotage teams suggests
that Tonkin consistently failed to involve the majority of his party in
operations although he himself personally participated in five sabotage
raids; as the mission's commander, he should have avoided that tempta-
tion and concentrated his energies on leading the operation as a whole.
By early July, after weeks of inactivity, many of his troopers had become
bored and restless; while it is true that mobility was restricted by having
only four vehicles and limited fuel supplies, certainly more could have
been done to have kept the men better employed, with all that would
have meant for operational effectiveness. That said, surviving members
of the Bulbasket party were to praise Tonkin for the way in which he
kept the men's spirits up in the latter phase of the operation.

As for the true source of the intelligence which led to the attack on
the morning of 3 July, a memorandum written at the time of his trial by
Hauptmann Dr Erich Schönig makes it quite clear that it was the interrogation of Eccles and Bateman by the *SD* which provided information
that was confirmed by the two *'maquisards'* Fielding intercepted and
took to the SAS campsite, thereby pinpointing it. Sadoine may have
considered betraying the main party, and may even have attempted to,
but almost certainly did not, or not, at least, to any effect.

There is a further disturbing element here, however, for it is suggested that Tonkin himself was one of the few serving SAS personnel to

have personal knowledge of the existence of the *Kommandobefehl*, if only anecdotally. He had previously been captured by German forces in the course of a commando-style operation at Termoli in Italy, on 3 October 1943. He escaped while in transit and returned to the UK via North Africa (where he first met Twm Stephens), but while in captivity, he later reported, he was warned by an officer of the *Wehrmacht* that he was being transferred into the custody of 'another unit' and that the German Army could not guarantee his survival. He was in no doubt as to the meaning of what he had been told, for he said later, paraphrasing Dr Johnson: 'When a man knows he is going to be shot, it sharpens his mind wonderfully …' One may wonder why, then, if he had particularly good cause to know the true nature of the risks they were running, he had not briefed his men on the likely outcome, should they be captured, as well as why he did not take more precautions than normal rather, it seems, than less, not to expose them to surprise attack.

We know now that the infamous *Kommandobefehl*, which unequivocally ordered the killing of all commando-style forces – either in combat, whether they tried to surrender or not, or immediately afterwards – was issued on 18 October, 1942. It is by no means clear, however, just what the Allies knew of it at this point. The official position seems to be that they had no knowledge of the existence of the order, but there is evidence to the contrary, though not from an entirely reliable source. An American Jedburgh, William Dreux, states in his book *No Bridges Blown* that at his mission briefing in the first days of July (he went into the field with team Gavin on 11 July), he and his colleagues were warned – he says 'reminded' – by their briefing officer, a Frenchman he calls 'Colonel Girard', that

> Hitler had recently issued a strict order that all captured commando-type personnel were to be summarily shot, whether in uniform or not. … It was his opinion that most German commanders would obey this order, and as to the SS it didn't matter for they would have shot you even before Hitler's order. It was clear that Colonel Girard believed all of this was inconsequential and as far as he was concerned it was all very simple: don't get captured, and if you're cornered go down fighting. I thought he was right … for it was a known risk we assumed.

Unfortunately, it is clear from reading Dreux's published account against the official records that he was fairly liberal in his interpretation of the truth, and the one surviving (in 2002) participant in that briefing, a British Jed, 'Troff' Trofimov, who was a member of a team which operated alongside Dreux's, was unable to recall what one might imagine to have been a rather memorable aspect of it, though he certainly did recall a general opinion amongst the Jedburghs that capture probably meant death. Dreux's assertion is contradicted by Jedburgh teams' orders issued long after this date, which stated that since teams would be wearing uniform, if captured they would 'be taken [prisoner] as soldiers … performing their ordinary military duties. Every established law of warfare would apply to them'. Many Jedburgh teams were actually to operate (and even to be inserted) wearing civilian clothes, and so, of course, were some SAS soldiers; no such protection, whether illusory or not, was expected to apply to them.

One further contentious point remains. It has been suggested by Max Hastings, in his book *Das Reich*, that the personnel of the Bulbasket team had only pistols when they were captured at Verrières. Hastings says: 'By one of the most extraordinary, indeed almost fantastic misjudgements of the operation, the entire SAS party had been sent from England with only .45 pistols as their own personal weapons. Beyond the Vickers guns on their jeeps they had no means whatsoever of resisting the German attack.' There was no such misjudgement. Whereas it may have been true that the men carried no weapon other than an M1911 pistol *on their person* when they were dropped, they were issued with folding-stock M1A1 carbines which were usually packed in the leg bag or strapped across the chest. Moreover, weapons, in nine containers, were certainly dropped with the advance party which arrived during the night of 7 June, and survivors confirmed that throughout the operation the men were conventionally armed, with carbines and Bren LMGs.

Captain John Tonkin was awarded the Military Cross for his part in Operation Bulbasket, standard procedure for a surviving commanding officer. Somewhat surprisingly, given its outcome, and in view of the poor judgement he had displayed, he was subsequently promoted major, and led D Squadron, 1 SAS, throughout the later stages of the North-West Europe campaign.

Little (some would say, nowhere near enough) was done in retribution for the murder of the thirty-three SAS soldiers, despite a very long and painstaking investigation carried out by Major Eric Barkworth's SAS War Crimes Investigation Team. Vogt, who commanded the actual perpetrators, was killed in action before the war ended; some minor figures were exculpated and only General Curt Gallenkamp, the commander of 80th Corps, together with Koestlin and Schönig, were found guilty of their part in the mass murder at St-Sauvant, while Doctor Georg Hesterberg, an 80th Corps medical officer, was implicated in the killings of Ogg, Pascoe and Williams. Hesterberg's guilty verdict was quashed on appeal. He maintained that the men had died of their wounds, and there was no substantial evidence to gainsay that, the men's bodies having been irretrievably lost. Koestlin and Schönig served short prison sentences, while Gallenkamp, originally sentenced to hang as the officer ultimately responsible (about which opinion there was considerable legal argument), had his sentence first commuted and then reduced, and was released from prison in February 1952.

HOUNDSWORTH

The outline plan for Operation Houndsworth was very similar to that for Bulbasket and the other long-term operations targeting German lines of communication and planned for the period immediately after the Normandy landings. A Squadron, 1 SAS, was to base itself in an area known as the Massif du Morvan, which covers much of the *département* of the Nièvre and a bit more besides, to the west of the city of Dijon. Now a National Park, it is a very different landscape from that of the Vienne, where Bulbasket was mounted – hills and valleys thickly covered with woodland, mostly unmanaged although logging was the major economic activity, interspersed with small farms. The SAS party's primary objectives were the railway lines linking Paris with Lyon, which passed through Dijon and Chalons-sur-Saône to the east (code-named 'Toby 1'), and the less important Le Creusot–Nevers line to the south ('Toby 2'). It originally had a subsidiary target – lines of communication between Orléans and Paris ('Toby 3') – but this was hopelessly optimistic, and the latter became one of the objectives of Operation Gain (q.v.). The Operation Instruction which defined the mission made it clear that 'these targets will [probably] be of greatest importance between D+8 and D+25', which gave the Houndsworth party very little time in which to establish itself and become effective.

The reconnaissance party, Lts Ian Stewart and Ian Wellsted, was inserted together with Jedburgh team Harry on the night of 6 June. It was to have a harder time of it initially than Bulbasket's reconnaissance party, for the pilot of the RAF Hudson which delivered them failed to find the designated DZ near Vieux-Dun. Capt Duncan Guthrie, the leader of Harry and the senior member of the party, told him to drop them in the approximate area anyway, and they landed some fifteen kilometres off target and dangerously near the main N6 road, outside the village of Rouvray. The Hudson, like all aircraft of that type, was fitted with an exit slide, which tore off the SAS officers' leg bags;

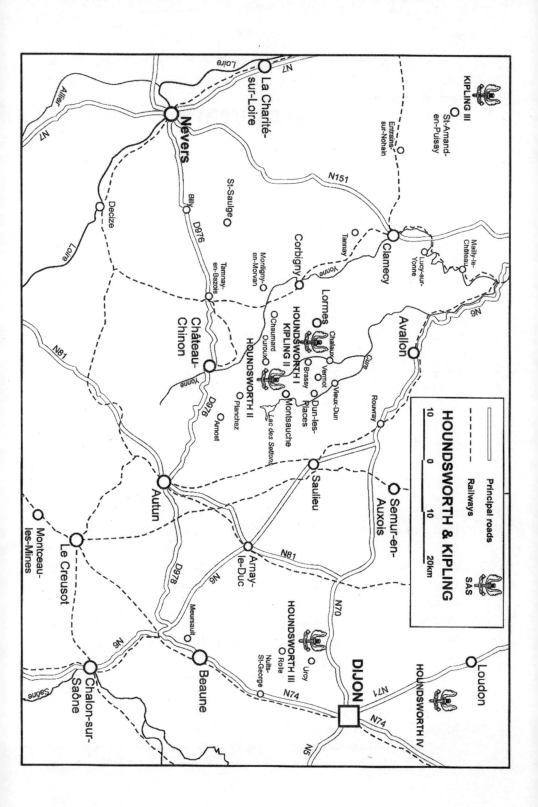

fortunately for him, Wellsted managed to hold on to his, and it was only superficially damaged, but Stewart's rucksack plummeted to the ground and disintegrated, destroying most of his kit. To make matters worse, the only radio the party managed to find at the DZ was also smashed beyond repair, and they were thus completely isolated. Worse still, an SOE agent who was supposed to have made rendezvous with the party on any one of the next five nights never turned up. All in all, the auspices for the success of Houndsworth did not look good. After a series of small misadventures and an arduous cross-country night march the party met up with a *Maquis* band, led by an engineer who was known as 'Grandjean' (Jean Longhi), near to the intended DZ at Vieux-Dun, on the evening of 8 June, and the next day Guthrie managed to contact Moor Park on a borrowed radio set.

The Houndsworth advance party, with Major Bill Fraser, the squadron commander, at its head and including a Phantom party under Capt Tom Moore, dropped into the Morvan on the night of 10 June. Like the recce party, it missed the DZ completely, and was further hampered by being separated into three groups, but at least two of its elements had functioning Jedsets. News of the whereabouts of one of the sticks reached Wellsted the following day via the FFI *Maquis* Bernard (the *nom de guerre* of Louis Aubin, a gendarme-turned-farmer from Montsauche, who formed the band early in 1943) and he later accompanied a *maquisard* party aboard a commandeered bus to pick up the sixteen men; of the other nine SAS men (and Lt-Col Jim Hutchinson, 'Colonel Hastings' and his signaller, Sgt John Sharp, who had accompanied them; these two formed two-thirds of Jedburgh team Isaac, which was later to be transformed and enlarged into an Inter-Allied Mission, Verveine) there was no sign. The party set up camp south of the village of Montsauche-les-Settons, adjacent to the *Maquis* Bernard and near the FTP group known after its leader, Serge, the leader of a dance band in 'civilian' life, which was installed a few kilometres further south in the Bois du Château. Within four days the missing elements were located, and squadron headquarters was established near Vieux-Dun.

On the night of 17 June, three Stirlings took off from Fairford; they failed to find the DZ and returned to base, but tragically, one of the aircraft was not to arrive. No sign of the plane, its crew or the sixteen-strong SAS party under Lt Leslie Cairns was ever found. The other two sticks under Capts John Wiseman, 1 Troop's commander, and Alex Muirhead (2 Troop) were dropped successfully on two separate DZs four nights later, on the night of 21 June, together with elements of Capt Roy Bradford's 3 Troop and of Squadron HQ, including the regiment's chaplain, Rev Fraser McLuskey, and a second non-combatant, Dr Mike McReady, the Regiment's medical officer, who went to work alongside the many doctors who had either joined the *maquisards* or who were prepared to help in times of need. Among the former, his closest collaboration was to be with a Parisian surgeon, Dr Alec Prochiantz, known as Martell, who based himself with the *Maquis* Bernard. Ably assisted by his wife, also a medical practitioner, he established a hospital in the Château de Vermont, and later in the forest, but also maintained a mobile surgical unit; in his Citroën *traction avant* he covered over 5,000 kilometres around the Haut Morvan during the month of August alone, looking after seven *maquisard* bands. From 1 June to the liberation of the Morvan on 11 September he performed ninety-eight surgical operations, saving all but twelve of his patients – a high success rate remarkable in the circumstances.

For the majority of the SAS party, there was very little that was truly productive to do from one day to the next, and life soon became monotonous; as the weeks went by and it became apparent that the occupying forces had no taste for offensive operations in the wooded hills and valleys, the men relaxed into a simple routine, sharing basic security duties with *maquisards* and trying to make campsites more comfortable. (Muirhead's 2 Troop occupied the same site in the Bois de l'Essart, about a kilometre away from the much larger camp occupied by the *Maquis* Bernard and adjacent to that of an offshoot band of more militant partisans known as the *Maquis* André, until 28 August, though others were more mobile: Fraser moved his squadron headquarters three times in the same period, and eventually separated from 3 Troop, with which he had originally co-located, but continued to stick fairly close to the *Maquis* Camille in the forest above the hamlet of Chalaux.) The men bartered for additions to their very basic rations and even, in some cases, ventured out to local *estaminets* for rather more palatable meals in the company of local people. By the end of their stay, officers and men, particularly from 2 Troop, were regularly to be found in the Hôtels de la Plage, Morvandelle and Beau Rivage on the nearby Lac des Settons, drinking in the bars and eating in the restaurants, much to the disgust of bourgeois patrons who had put up there for the duration, and who had no wish to mix with scruffy, dirty guerrilla fighters who dined with their weapons very obviously to hand.

A similar situation has been identified as at least a potential cause of the catastrophe which befell Bulbasket; the reason Houndsworth did not suffer a similar reverse is probably due to the strong hold the *maquisards* had on the Morvan, the solidarity of the population and the fact that Germans were only very occasionally to be found outside Château-Chinon, where they were garrisoned. In general, the majority of the men seldom moved far afield and were only occasionally selected to take part in sabotage operations; not unnaturally, the more experienced were always chosen first. It could be argued that the insertion of an entire squadron to be held under centralised command put too many men into a relatively small area (certainly Fraser thought so); to a degree, the law of diminishing returns applied: the men were needed to handle the containers after a *parachutage*, but their presence required more containers to be dropped, which needed more men to handle them … This problem could have been overcome by associating the SAS party more closely with just one partisan band, but this alternative was dismissed both for security reasons and because, as Capt Moore was to say in his report, 'The Maquis in Sqn HQ area [i.e. the *Maquis* Camille] could not be trusted, their chief effort [sic] being to get 'chutes and pilfer containers. We built up a series of small dumps hidden in the woods, which were never found by the enemy but the Maquis pilfered them if they got the opportunity'.

Padre McLuskey helped to maintain morale, visiting each camp-site in turn, carrying his collapsible altar, to conduct church parades and to distribute books he had managed to get included in one of the resupply drops, as well as simply making himself both available and generally useful. The award of the Military Cross to the chaplain at the operation's end was greeted with universal approval. His presence in the party raised one interesting question: should a priest carry a weapon in a combat situation? In his official report McLuskey himself said:

> Whether chaplains should bear arms or to what extent they should be combatant was a question which presented itself more than once in warfare of this nature. However the question be decided in theory it is certain that a chaplain's usefulness increases as he shares the lot of his fellows. Whether this involves the use of arms is perhaps an academic question as there are many combatant jobs which do not involve shooting people … Some jobs can usually be found for the chaplain which will take him where the others go and that is where he ought to be.

Is it perhaps selfish not to carry arms? If he goes unarmed where the others go does the chaplain not make a nuisance of himself to all concerned. Should he carry arms as does the M[edical] O[fficer]? The Department [presumably the Army Chaplains' Department, to whom this report was addressed] will no doubt continue to explore these questions. In this case, the chaplain did not carry arms, but whether rightly or wrongly, he was not always sure.

Rory McLeod had no such uncertainty, and in a letter to HQ Airborne Forces commenting on McLuskey's report, wrote:

I consider that in the circumstances described the Chaplain should be armed in order that he may protect himself. If captured by the Germans experience has shown conclusively that his cloth would be most unlikely to protect the Chaplain. An unarmed man who must be protected specially is a tie to the remainder of the party.

McLeod was being rather disingenuous; as far as can be ascertained there is no instance of a chaplain having been illegally killed, or singled out for ill-treatment after having been captured, during the entire history of World War Two in Europe. And much as he had regard for McLuskey's report, he did not want it widely published. 'I do not consider there is any necessity for this report to receive the wide circulation afforded to the majority of SAS reports,' he concluded.

Padre McLuskey had other, sadder duties to perform, too; in addition to the loss of the RAF Halifax and the USAAF B-24 Liberator which collided over Mazignien on the night of 18 July, another Halifax, this time a bomber variant from 640 Squadron, RAF Bomber Command, also crashed, near Ouroux, about four kilometres west of Muirhead's campsite in the Bois de l'Essart. The aircraft – Y-Yoke, with Pilot Officer Paul Hellegers at the controls – was one of 124, most of them 4 Group Halifax Mk. IIIs, which attacked the railway junction and marshalling yards at Dijon, the second time the RAF had targeted those objectives. Hellegers and his crew died in the crash, but their bodies were immediately recovered, and were taken next day to the Bois de l'Essart, where the curé from Ouroux, Père Benoît Legrain, and Fraser McLuskey performed burial rites, while villagers and an honour guard of *maquisards* looked on. The bodies of the Allied airmen were removed to Nantes after the war, and reburied in the war cemetery there, while the bodies of eighteen *maquisards* temporarily buried in the forest graveyard were also reinterred in approved cemeteries.

Much of the SAS troopers' time, naturally, was taken up with 'house-keeping'. Apart from basic rations, an individual knife-fork-spoon set, a mug and a jack-knife (though many found the Fairbairn-Sykes fighting knife handier), the SAS men were supplied with very little. Cooking pots and utensils had to be fabricated from whatever was at hand – container cells were a prime source of the former – as did living accommodation. In contrast to the *Maquis* bands, who, in the Morvan, at any rate, usually built semi-sunken huts which offered an additional measure of protection against small-arms fire and were very difficult to identify, even in daylight, the SAS troopers lived under canvas – or rather, under silk, their tents being made from parachutes. A pair, one inside the other, were suspended from a pole lashed to a handy pair of trees and then pegged out around their circumference and stretched taught so as to keep them from touching. The inner, which came down to the ground, was provided with a surround of packed earth, while the outer finished a couple of feet up in the air, and the whole was ringed by a drainage ditch. Such tents accommodated two or three men, who slept in sleeping bags on a bed of straw or bracken. Later, when the jeeps arrived, the very much larger parachutes employed to drop them were also adapted as living quarters, particularly by the *maquisards*, arranged in a similar fashion to the smaller canopies; a pair of jeep parachutes accommodated a typical *maquisard* section of a dozen men and a sergeant. The tents were essentials, not luxuries; unlike the Vienne, where Bulbasket had to contend with a drought, the Morvan had an uncharacteristically wet summer in 1944, with periods of a week or more during which it rained almost constantly. Campsite security here and elsewhere was achieved by combining sentry posts, which usually consisted of two men with a Bren gun, with a system of trip-wires attached either to No. 36 grenades or to Gammon bombs loaded with loose metal objects. The level of security at the Houndsworth campsites was generally fairly lax, in that sentries were not always posted (though the access routes were always booby-trapped); but given the overall situation in the area, that was entirely reasonable. There was never an occasion when any element of the party was taken by surprise by hostile forces.

On the evening of Saturday 24 June, elements of 2 Troop went into action for the first time, in support of the *Maquis* Bernard alongside which it had set up camp, ambushing a small German convoy on the road running south from Montsauche to Planchez. A total of seven parachutists with two Brens and fifteen partisans with a Bren and a captured German machine-gun were to attack two trucks full of infantrymen, with attendant small cars and a motorcycle. As with Tonkin's sabotage teams, there was a preponderance of officers (three, including the troop commander) and senior NCOs (three) in the SAS party. The ambush site was on a slight slope, three-quarters the way up a 500-metre straight stretch of road, where it was crossed by a track which emerged from the wooded hills to the west, where the SAS campsite lay, and descended, through open fields, towards the Lac des Settons. Large piles of cut timber left at the crossing provided cover for the main body of the ambush party, while the supporting machine-guns were sited in pairs, on higher ground some distance away from the road, at the limits of the killing ground and controlling it. The ambush was a great success; three French hostages, whose presence was unsuspected (some reports say that the release of these three was the reason for the ambush having been laid, but there is no evidence to support that), were released, and thirty-three enemy, the majority of them actually conscripted Russians, were killed and one Russian officer taken prisoner, for the loss of one *maquisard*.

Reprisals for the attack were swift, and followed a familiar pattern: next day, German forces burned La Verrerie, a farm adjacent to the ambush site. Then they turned to the town of Montsauche, which was razed to the ground, save for the *Gendarmerie* and the Post Office; one man who resisted was shot, and 302 were left homeless. Much of the village of Planchez, south of the ambush site, followed, although night fell before the work could be concluded there; once again, one man was killed, and this time 182 were left homeless.

Although the *maquisards'* camps did not come under attack that day, as they had feared, there was considerable panic, but there was more and worse to come. The next afternoon the makeshift *Maquis* hospital in the Château de Vermot, near the village of the same name and just a few kilometres down the hill from Vieux-Dun, came under attack from a strong German force (once again, most were actually conscripted Russian PoWs); the small nursing staff managed to evacuate the wounded under covering fire from the *maquisard* guards and escape into the surrounding woodland. The partisans asked Lt-Col Hutchinson to call in reinforcements from the SAS, and two hastily assembled detachments, under Fraser and Wiseman, set out from the camp near Vieux-Dun at 1900, in torrential rain. Wiseman's party bumped a German squad; SSM Seeking was wounded but L/Cpl Gibb used his

Bren to considerable effect while the party retired. Fraser spotted elements of the German party before they saw him. He waited, and eventually a contingent which he estimated to be fifty strong assembled and began to march off in column of threes. He gave the order to fire, and the two Brens, particularly that of SQMS McClennan, 'had a field day' (in Fraser's words), not more than ten men escaping uninjured. Fraser and his men then followed Wiseman's example, and the two parties were reunited at their campsite, which they hastily cleared, while 'the Germans and the Maquis expended considerable ammunition but caused no casualties throughout a most disturbed night'.

The action was renewed the next morning, and this time the Germans were more successful, locating the (deserted) *Maquis* camp and nearby vehicle park above Vermot and destroying them (they passed close to the SAS supply dump, too, but missed it). Then they turned their attention to the local population. After returning to the château and burning it, they moved on to the hamlet of Vermot, looting and burning every house and shooting, beating and raping its inhabitants. Then it was the turn of the much larger village of Dun-les-Places, a few kilometres to the east. Here they hung the village priest from the tower of the church before the assembled population and separated out every able-bodied man who had remained in the village. They shot eighteen beside the church and a further nine elsewhere, and then piled the bodies in the square and mutilated them with hand-grenades, leaving sentries posted to prevent their loved ones from approaching for two days. Needless to say, they looted and burned much of this village as well.

This was not an isolated incident, and one is left reflecting if *actions* like that near La Verrerie, which at best killed small numbers of low-grade troops but provoked such vicious retaliation, were ever really worthwhile. Certainly, post-war there was much criticism of the *Maquis* Bernard, and particularly of its leader and his counsellors, for having mounted the ambush on the Montsauche–Planchez road and calling down wholesale slaughter and destruction on the local population. The *maquisards*' position is a simple one: they were at war, and their act was thus justified; they point out that this incident actually led to the deaths of up to a hundred German troops, including those killed in the original ambush and many more who died near Vermot, to say nothing of the degree of demoralisation it caused.

Save for a raid on a *Maquis* camp at nearby Chaumard on 31 July, which, due to lax security, resulted in the death of twenty-seven parti-

sans, that was to be the last major German incursion into the heart of
the Morvan until mid-August, when troops retreating from the Normandy battlefield began streaming through there on their way towards
the Belfort Gap. With the benefit of hindsight, it was clearly a serious
mistake on the part of the occupying forces not to have cleared the partisans out of the area before they could be properly armed. At that time,
for example, Bernard's hundred or so men had perhaps fifty weapons
between them (and had had far fewer before the ambush of 24 June),
and that was fairly representative of the general situation. The *Maquis*
Camille was the best equipped of the bands in the area; by mid-August
it even had an armoured car, stolen from a factory south of Paris, as well
as a 6pdr anti-tank gun and a crew to man it, provided by the SAS.

As it was, after the *actions* of 25/26 June the partisan bands were left
in good order, and though somewhat disturbed and disorganised, they
were to regroup most effectively, thanks in some degree to the presence
in their midst of a hard-working Jedburgh team, an Inter-Allied
Mission and an SAS party which was eventually to number around 150.
The presence of that party, incidentally, seems not to have been suspected; in the two days of fighting it suffered only minor casualties, the
worst wound being that inflicted on SSM Seekings, who took a 9mm
round in the back of the neck. A *Maquis* doctor tried unsuccessfully to
extricate the bullet, which was lodged at the base of the skull; Seekings,
an SAS man since the first days, and made of stern stuff, simply sol-
diered on. The projectile was eventually removed on his return to the
UK. Fraser reported the situation to Moor Park, and was told, though
not in quite so many words, to stop messing about fighting the partisans' battles and get on with the real job of blowing up railways and
disrupting communications, though it was hardly Fraser's fault that he
had not yet been able to start that campaign – he had no reliable transport save for a few folding bicycles, and the nearest point either of the
target railway lines came to the base area was, in realistic terms, two
nights' hard march away.

It was the night of 5 July before A Squadron got the mobility it badly
needed and, as the after-action report says, 'things began to get serious',
with the arrival of three jeeps. According to Padre McLuskey, 'The
first fell conveniently in a field. The second fell not so conveniently
among trees. The third fell most inconveniently on a wooden bank by
the roadside, and hung upside down, suspended from the trees which it
brought down with it.' German patrols were known to use the road,
and so the job of recovering it had to be finished before daybreak; it

was, but it was touch-and-go. Bill Fraser was more laconic, saying simply that some forty trees had to be felled before all the vehicles could be recovered. This *parachutage* also marked the end of a period during which food and comfort items had been in very short supply, thanks to aircraft being unable to locate the DZ in an area covered with thick low cloud; Fraser had instigated strict rationing and there was no real hardship, but morale had suffered as a result.

Without reliable transport, not only was it very difficult to mount sabotage operations, but communications between the individual campsites the squadron occupied, which were widely distributed, were both poor and complicated. Muirhead's 2 Troop base was some twenty kilometres from Fraser's Squadron HQ, and the journey from one to the other necessitated an hour's walk into the forest at each end. The *Maquis* camps were equipped with clandestine telephone connections to the public exchange and so too, eventually, were the SAS camps. The few elderly *gazogène*-powered vehicles the *maquisards* were able to provide from time to time, prior to the arrival of the first jeeps, were usually capable of making the journey between the two campsites, but were far too unreliable to be trusted to carry sabotage parties the considerable distances to their target areas. (*Gazogène* is akin to coal gas, but manufactured from charcoal rather than coke; as a fuel it produced about half the power of petrol.) Once jeeps were available, of course, it was possible for parties to visit larger towns, such as Saulieu, where more serviceable vehicles were to be found, and requisition them; the jeeps thus solved the Houndsworth party's transportation problems both directly and indirectly.

The jeeps were not universally successful, however, particularly deep in the forest, where tracks were rudimentary. The day after they arrived one of the vehicles overturned; Cpl Adamson sustained a pelvic fracture, and spent the next nine weeks, prior to evacuation, in primitive conditions and very severe pain. Damage to the front axle and suspension took days to repair with the assistance of a blacksmith, a charcoal brazier and a very large hammer.

That evening a party of six men, with Capt Wiseman in command and with the newly arrived Lt Tony Trower, left in another of the vehicles to establish a base from which to attack railway targets south of Dijon, the jeep returning for reinforcements and additional supplies the next day. Johnny Wiseman's party was to work detached from the main body for the rest of the Houndsworth operational period, receiving its own resupply drops. 'Toby 1' was cut for the first time the following night, and the next morning more SAS men and a party of signallers from Tom Moore's Phantom patrol arrived. The entire group still numbered only sixteen men, and Wiseman judged that to be insufficient both to maintain security and carry out his sabotage programme; in consequence he decided to co-locate with a partisan band, selecting one at Urcy, twelve kilometres south-west of Dijon, and arming it from a resupply drop he requested. The arrangement proved to be an unhappy one, and eight days later the campsite was attacked by a force of *Milice*; the assault was driven off, but the same night Wiseman moved his men back to the original site near Rolle, some eight kilometres away. Wiseman heard later that the campsite near Urcy, now deserted, had been attacked again the following night by a combined force of *Milice* and Germans, who had approached their objective from opposite sides and ended up by firing on each other, leaving twenty-two dead. The party stayed at Rolle until mid-August, and then moved to the north of Dijon to co-locate with another, and more reliable, *maquisard* band, arming and training it and two more, and since it lacked the transportation necessary to mount ambushes on the busy through-route between Dijon and Langres, it mined it frequently instead. It was recalled to the main Houndsworth base at the end of August. In all, the 1 Troop party cut railway lines seven times, derailing three trains, and destroyed a *gazogène* production plant, as well as spotting numerous targets for the RAF; it suffered no casualties.

On 8 July, with repairs to the damaged jeep completed, Lt Dickie Grayson used it to mount a reconnaissance mission which ventured west as far as La Charité, on the Loire, returning the next morning without mishap. Later Lt Wellsted and a small party were transported in it some eighty kilometres south, out of the Morvan proper, to reconnoitre and if possible attack two airfields near the town of Digoin in the Saône-et-Loire, which were said to be in use by the *Luftwaffe*. In the event, neither was in service, and the party had to content itself with blowing a railway line and some high-tension pylons, surviving a skirmish with a German patrol (thanks largely to the work of Tpr Jemson, who later received the DCM in recognition of it), which temporarily caused its members to scatter before finally being picked up and returned to base on 18 July. The 2 Troop jeep, despite occasionally revealing potentially fatal steering defects, was by now in daily use. In the most audacious operation yet, on 10 July Alex Muirhead used it to transport a party armed with a 3in mortar to attack a synthetic oil plant on the outskirts of Autun, to the south-east; the forty rounds of high explosive and incendiary fired caused some superficial damage to the factory, and set a loaded train on fire. Otherwise, it kept up a shuttle service, transporting sabotage parties out to operational areas and then retrieving them when their tasks were accomplished. In all, Houndsworth's troops were to cut main railway lines twenty-two times, derailing six trains and destroying three locomotives and between forty and fifty wagons in the process. By means of ambushes, strafing and mining, it was to destroy many German vehicles and occasionally close roads completely for days at a time.

Even in the relative safety of the Morvan, the use of jeeps was risky. Chief among the dangers was the clear possibility of running into a concentration of German troops by pure accident; this was exactly what was to befall one of the Houndsworth parties in the operation's first and only really major setback on the ground, on 20 July.

The base in the Morvan hills had originally been conceived as an administrative and logistical centre; it was in an isolated, reasonably well-protected area, but too distant from the main lines of communications to serve as an effective operational base. Following the first successful deployment, of John Wiseman's 1 Troop into the area south of Dijon, the next was to have seen the rump of Roy Bradford's 3 Troop, which numbered eighteen – the rest having been lost in the aircraft which went missing on the night of 17 June – move off in the opposite direction, to the west and north, to set up a satellite base in the Nivernais. Its centre of operations was to have been the Forêt des Dames, well to the west of the German-garrisoned town of Clamecy, the point at which three railway lines converged. The forest was some sixty kilometres, as the crow flies, from the Houndsworth HQ base near Chalaux and conveniently placed for attacks on the important main roads and rail lines in the Loire valley, still further to the west. Earlier, raids had been made into the area from the Morvan, including one which saw the SAS jeep crossing the Loire by way of a bridge in the centre of the busy town of Nevers in full daylight, under the eyes of the German garrison, but the long transit involved considerable and unnecessary risk.

On the evening of 17 July, the 3 Troop advance party, seven in all, under Lt Ball and Sgt Jeff DuVivier, a decorated L Detachment 'original', who had accompanied Bill Fraser on the first desert raids, set off, on totally unsuitable folding 'airborne' bicycles, loaded down with personal kit, weapons and explosives, on a journey which was to take them four days. Each day was more frustrating than the last, and the men were later to report that they could have carried very nearly as much on their backs, and made the same journey on foot in half the time. Two days later the troop commander, Roy Bradford, set off to join up with them in a jeep manned by Sgt 'Maggie' McGinn as driver, Sgt 'Chalky' White, a decorated veteran of the desert and Italy, now recovered from an injury he sustained in the 18 June parachute drop, which had left him partially paralysed, as front gunner and Craftsman Devine, a REME fitter who had dropped with the first consignment of jeeps, as rear gunner, together with a member of the *Maquis* Camille, Jacques Morvillier, as interpreter. In his book *Parachute Padre*, Fraser McLuskey gives a garbled account of the sad climax of the operation; Ian Wellsted's is more accurate but heavily dramatised. That which follows is based on Sergeant McGinn's official report to Bill Fraser.

Roy Bradford had decided to take a roundabout route to the Forêt des Dames RV in order to liaise with the leader of a *maquis* group based closer to his new operational area. The party drove through the night, sticking to very minor roads and observing all the correct procedures at junctions (SOP was for the vehicle to halt well short of the crossing while a foot patrol made a reconnaissance), and arrived, at around 0800, at the small village of Lucy-sur-Yonne; taking a side road to the right towards Mailly-le-Château, and just after having crossed the Canal du Nivernais and the river which runs just metres away, north of Lucy, the jeep came face to face with a German officer, who waved it down, presumably having mistaken it for a similar-sized *Kübelwagen*, which the *Wehrmacht* used in large numbers. He realised his error when White opened up with his twin Vickers Ks. McGinn accelerated the overloaded and underpowered Willys as best he could (it would not top thirty miles per hour, he wrote). Almost immediately they were confronted by a truck full of infantrymen and White fired on it too, but within seconds it was clear that the situation was even worse than it might have appeared, for beyond lay a sizeable convoy and a large detachment of men, many of whom had dismounted and were standing in the road or in the fields at either side. There was no alternative but to continue, and as soon as his guns bore, Devine also began firing while Bradford, sitting between White and McGinn, kept both machine-gunners supplied with fresh magazines.

Although the Germans were undoubtedly unprepared, some managed to return fire even before the jeep had reached the last truck in line; Cmn Devine, exposed in the back of the car, was killed instantly by a short burst from a machine-gun, while Bradford was hit in the arm.

The loss of the rear guns made it impossible to maintain suppressive fire as the jeep passed the last German vehicle (where, as part of standard procedure during rest stops, a machine-gun could be expected to be sited), when White's guns would become ineffective. There was indeed a gun at the tail of the column, and as soon as the SAS jeep passed, its crew had free rein; a long burst caught Roy Bradford low in the torso and killed him outright, while Chalky White took at least three rounds in shoulder, hand and leg and Jacques Morvillier's elbow was shattered. Little more than a hundred metres past the convoy, but just out of sight around a bend in the road, the jeep's engine failed; McGinn, who alone was unscathed, leapt out, saw that his officer and Devine were obviously dead, and helped the two wounded men to dismount, pushing and dragging them away, through the hedge and into the sheltering woodland to the west, the German soldiers declining to follow when they arrived at the scene, but milling about excitedly in the road.

The three made their way cautiously through what was actually a narrow belt of the Forêt de Frétoy but were stopped at the far side by German patrol activity on the minor road there, and lay up all day, no more than fifty metres into the trees and constantly in fear that the German officers and NCOs would drive the infantrymen to overcome their reluctance to venture far from the road. Luckily for them they never did, and as night fell McGinn helped the others to move off to the south, recrossing the River Yonne (McGinn swam it to bring back a small boat, then ferried the others across) and then the adjacent canal. The next morning Morvillier was able to make contact with a lock-keeper, who hid them throughout the day in his orchard before passing them on to the local partisans that night. Sgt White and the Frenchman were treated in a local *Maquis* hospital and the former was soon reunited with A Squadron (though he did not recover sufficiently to be returned to active duty, the wound in his left hand requiring the amputation of three fingers). McGinn was quickly passed from one band to another, and turned up in 2 Troop's camp in the Bois de l'Essart towards dusk the next day, 21 July, with news of the incident. He was later awarded the Military Medal in recognition of his having saved the lives of his two companions. Capt Roy Bradford and Cmn Jim Devine were buried side by side in the communal cemetery in Crain, close to where they were killed, and subsequently a memorial plaque was erected at the site of the firefight, and the road renamed 'rue du 20 Julliet'. There was some (apparently well-founded) concern that

German forces would use identity papers taken from the dead men in an attempt to infiltrate spies into the partisan bands in the area; this was allayed when a courier carrying those papers, and both men's personal effects, was ambushed and killed some days later.

On receiving McGinn's report, Fraser sent a message to London for retransmission to Lt Ball's party, ordering its return to the Morvan. In fact, the seven men had arrived at the point at which they were to have met up with Bradford and his small party only twenty-four hours before the recall order was received, but already Jeff DuVivier had led L/Cpl Weller and Tpr Marshall on a mission to reconnoitre the railway line at nearby Entrains-sur-Nohain, from the direction of which they had heard an explosion just after they had arrived the previous evening. This proved to have been a *Maquis* sabotage party blowing a culvert on the line to delay a train carrying a consignment of anti-aircraft guns, ammunition and much else besides. Repairs to the permanent way were already in progress when the three SAS men arrived, and DuVivier decided to take a ready-made opportunity to intervene. Guided by two *maquisards*, the three soldiers made a wide detour which brought them back to the line some half a kilometre away from the scene of the first sabotage attempt, and proceeded to lay three thirty-pound charges of plastic explosive at fifty-foot intervals along the track bed, to be detonated by a pressure switch on the line above the last charge the locomotive would pass over, with additional detonating devices (small 'tyre burster' mines) as a safety back-up. They then passed the word to the repair gang to reverse their normal procedure of working as slowly as possible to put right the damage, and some six or seven hours later the train, which consisted of forty goods wagons and was pulled by two locomotives, set out from Entrains. It slowed as it passed the repaired culvert, and was just picking up speed again as it tripped the fog signal setting off the linked charges laid by DuVivier and his party. Both locomotives were wrecked, as was the flatbed wagon carrying the AA guns, and ten goods wagons were derailed. By that time the SAS party was long gone, to begin the trek back to Chalaux, and it was some time before the men learned how successful their brief foray – the one bright spot in an otherwise tragic episode – had been.

It was 25 July before Ball and his men returned to the Morvan, and by then preparations for the arrival of an advance party of nine men from 2 SAS's Operation Hardy, together with their three vehicles, plus two 6pdr guns for the Houndsworth party, were under way. The *parachutage* took place on the night of 26 July, with mixed results: one

Halifax, carrying the Hardy commander, Capt Grant Hibbert, failed to find the DZ and returned to Tarrant Rushton; the other two three-man parties landed safely, but one jeep was destroyed when its parachutes became tangled (a single vehicle dropped to the Houndsworth party, along with five mechanics, on 11 July, had gone the same way). The guns – this was the first time these weapons had been air-dropped operationally – landed undamaged. Hibbert's trio arrived safely the following night, but once again their jeep was destroyed. Two nights later, two more vehicles were dropped, along with Major Bob Melot, a Belgian who had joined up with David Stirling in the early days of L Detachment at Kabrit. This time, *both* vehicles were wrecked, and the exercise had to be repeated the following night. It was successful, at last, but the net gain to A Squadron was still zero, for the jeeps were assigned to replace the vehicles destroyed on 26 and 27 July, and went to the party from 2 SAS. On 1 August, Hibbert's small party set off for the Hardy operational area to the north, in the Forêt de Châtillon (the establishment phase seems to have been known as Operation Laurel; perhaps someone at Brigade HQ had a sense of humour) guided as far as Capt Wiseman's base at Rolle, south-west of Dijon, by SSM Seekings. The vehicles stuck to small roads, observed standard operating procedure at road junctions and arrived without mishap, having covered about seventy kilometres in four hours, a fair average speed in the prevailing conditions.

The 57mm-calibre 6pdr guns dropped to the Houndsworth party on the night of 26 July were originally designed for service in the anti-tank role, but by 1944 they were in general use as infantry close-support weapons; the model dropped to the SAS was the shorter-barrelled Mk II on the lightweight Mk III split carriage, specially developed for airborne forces. The term 'lightweight' is relative; the guns weighed over a ton, and were not easy to man-handle, particularly in rough terrain, although four oxen could pull them cross-country and on the road they could be towed behind a jeep. However, they could fire a range of ammunition including armour-piercing, high-explosive and common shot to an effective range of well over 2,000 metres; one was allocated to Squadron HQ, while the other stayed with 2 Troop. In fact, they were to be of limited use, chiefly because there were few suitable targets for them in the heart of the Morvan and it was not practical to deploy them elsewhere in the Houndsworth operational area, but they had considerable effect on morale.

On one notable occasion, however, the gun deployed by the

Squadron HQ proved invaluable. It was attached to the *Maquis* Camille, with an SAS crew under L/Cpl Burgess to man it, and had been located in a commanding position overlooking a major road junction south of Chalaux, with covering Bren guns to support and protect it. When, on 4 August, Camille came under attack, seemingly from a battalion of para-troopers in training, the gun, firing HE and AP ammunition at ranges of up to 1,000 metres, was instrumental in ensuring that the attackers not only made no progress despite launching three assaults, the second and third supported by machine-guns and mortars, but suffered considerable casualties (Burgess's report says 'the most sober estimate being seventeen killed and wounded'), at least throughout the hours of daylight. When darkness fell, the balance of power changed, of course, and Burgess cam-ouflaged the gun, removed the breech block and retired, hoping for the best. In fact, his efforts at concealment proved entirely effective, the gun was not found and he was able to recover it with a pair of oxen later that night, after the enemy had retired.

The gun was to come into action once more, two days later, this time with less happy results. Sited in an alternative but no less commanding position, Burgess observed a column of men marching in close order on the St-Martin–Chalaux road. The formation displayed none of the recognition signals agreed with the *maquis*, and when it deployed off the road and began advancing towards him, Burgess opened fire, causing three casualties. At that point a recognition signal was dis-played. Neither of the 6pdrs was ever used again (though both were deployed with patrols towards the end of the month and the Kipling party, which inherited them, used one in response to a rumour of tanks having been seen in the area, in September).

The squadron's other support weapon, the 3in mortar, was scarcely of more practical use than the 6pdr, though it was at least easy to trans-port by jeep, and Alex Muirhead, who was something of an expert with the weapon, kept them deployed around the 2 Troop campsite, zeroed in on locations such as the route to the vehicle park, where the *Maquis* Bernard might be vulnerable to attack. We have seen how it was employed in an attack on the synthetic oil plant at Autun on 10 July, with very limited success; exactly a month later, that operation was to be repeated, Bill Fraser deciding that an attempt to penetrate the plant would be likely to fail. This time three jeeps, one carrying the mortar, the others with their regular complement of Vickers Ks, were to be employed. The raid went largely according to plan, and was over in less than twenty-five minutes; it was a spectacular affair, but proved, in the light of day, once again to have achieved very little. In fact, plastic explosive was far and away the most useful weapon in the SAS's armoury in operations such as Houndsworth, and after-action reports consistently agreed that jeep-mounted weapons, including the paired machine-guns, were only useful in the offensive role against 'soft' targets such as vehicles and troop concentrations.

By the first week of August plans were well advanced for Operation Transfigure, an airborne landing to take the Falasie Pocket from the rear, for which the SAS Brigade was to have provided a reconnaissance element. The SAS force was to have been under the command of 1 SAS's CO, Paddy Mayne, who had decided to drop into the area well in advance in order to assess the situation in both Gain's and Houndsworth's operational areas. The day before he was due at the former site, one of its elements came under attack and he switched his destination to the Morvan instead, arriving, together with Mike Sadler, his Intelligence Officer, and his batman/bodyguard, on the night of 7 August.

That same day, Wellsted had taken a jeep and three men to support a *Maquis* ambush of what was said to be a convoy of trucks carrying tobacco, with the secondary objective of blowing a bridge where it crossed a railway junction at Tamnay-en-Bazois. When the jeep, with a hundred pounds of primed plastic explosive in the back, reached Montigny-en-Morvan, which stands at the top of a long hill, Wellsted was well in front of the labouring *gazogène*-powered *maquisard* lorry, and stopped before the village to wait for it to catch up. Moments later he saw what were unmistakably three Germans in the village street, and opened up with the twin Vickers. They went down, but within seconds 'all hell was let loose at close range', for the jeep had stopped just outside the killing ground of an elaborate ambush which had been laid to catch the *maquisards*, the fictional tobacco convoy having been nothing but bait to lure them. Wellsted and his men escaped unscathed and were able to cover the withdrawal of the *maquisards*, who also got away without ill-effect; on their return to the Bois de l'Essart they discovered a number of 9mm projectiles buried in the blocks of explosive. Wellsted was to make another attempt on the bridge at Tamnay, a week later; after coming close to losing the jeep and one of the two rather decrepit cars in which they were travelling, his party reached the village, only to discover that the bridge in question was not the stone arch they had been led to expect, but was constructed of iron girders. They placed the charges, which were unsuited to the task, anyway, and damaged the structure, but left it usable. Other charges placed on the railway turntable, and Lewes bombs left on goods wagons, were more effective.

All in all, Mayne's visit may have been good for morale – among other things, he announced Wellsted's promotion to captain, and his appointment to lead a soon-to-be-reinforced 3 Troop – but in material terms it had a negative effect on Houndsworth, for it cost the Morvan-based contingent of the party one of its two precious jeeps when the CO left for the Forêt d'Orléans on 9 August. The deficit was to have been made good three nights later, but that jeep 'pranged' too; it was a fortnight before Fraser received more vehicles, and then he got four within twenty-four hours.

Of more direct moment than the arrival of the CO was the protean situation in the area. An increasing German presence gave Bill Fraser a pressing problem: it was now more essential than ever that both the partisans and the SAS parties should be ready to evacuate existing positions rapidly, but he had five badly injured or wounded men on his hands, including Cpl Adamson, who could not be moved at a moment's notice, and it was decided that they should be evacuated by air to the United Kingdom. After the destruction of the *Maquis* hospital at Vermot, a replacement had been constructed adjacent to the *Maquis* Bernard's base. This was perhaps the most secure location in the area, with well-screened access via a minor road which was actually rather better than appeared at first sight, an adequate water supply and a fair though small DZ immediately to hand, and it was here that the wounded were concentrated while arrangements to repatriate them were put in hand. Like the evacuation of the Bulbasket party, this called for the insertion of a specialist, trained to select and prepare a suitable site for a landing strip big enough to take a Dakota, and in this instance the man chosen was Lt Robert McReady, brother of the party's doctor, who was parachuted in on 9 August.

The very nature of the hilly, wooded Morvan, offering so appropriate a base for combat operations, made finding a suitable site there extremely unlikely, and in fact the nearest location McReady could identify, after more than week of touring the countryside in a car provided and crewed by the *Maquis*, was a considerable distance away to the east, beyond the town of Saulieu, in the Côte-d'Or. Lengthy preparations were made, and on the morning of 18 August a small convoy of cars converted to carry stretchers, with two jeeps and a truckload of *maquisards* for security, set out to make the arduous cross-country journey. It was to no avail; soon after the party arrived at the site, a radio message from London announced that the operation had been scrubbed, and worse still, postponed indefinitely.

There was nothing for it but for the convoy to retrace its steps and return to the Morvan, but in the days which followed it became increasingly clear that the small hospital in the forest was inadequate to the task of caring for the wounded men, particularly Adamson, and that an alternative would have to be sought. The result was a mutually attractive arrangement with the (ex-collaborationist) owner of the Hôtel Beau Rivage on the Lac des Settons, who believed himself in constant danger of reprisals from the *maquisards* in respect of his earlier malfeasances, and who was more than eager to offer them accommodation. As a by-product, the visits to the hotel of the British soldiers from Muirhead's 2 Troop became more commonplace, and that, it is said, led to occasional liaisons with young ladies staying at the Beau Rivage and other hotels around the lake. Indeed, so Wellsted tells us when writing of the early days in the Morvan, such goings-on were not restricted to the lakeside: 'Later, when we knew the countryside better, the men would go down to the villages in the evenings and drink in the *estaminets*, or take their girls for walks through the sweet-smelling meadows ...' Happily for all concerned, the situation in the Morvan in late August, despite fairly heavy German through-traffic, was very different from that which had pertained in the Vienne two months earlier, and no harm was done.

The Houndsworth party never had enough serviceable jeeps. There were eventually to be five it could call its own, one having been lost in the fatal firefight at Lucy-sur-Yonne, and one relinquished to the regimental commander. Five of the jeeps dropped to it were smashed far beyond repair when their parachutes failed (Capt Moore's report talks of seven lost in this way, but the chronology does not bear him out). Save for the Kipling party's operations in the Morvan, after it took over from Houndsworth (the Kipling party had brought its own jeeps, forty of them, from the United Kingdom, and its advance party had had some dropped to it), the general shortage of jeeps was a common theme in the 'static' SAS operations in France, and certainly detracted from their effectiveness. The only alternative means the combat parties had of maintaining mobility was to commandeer such civilian vehicles as they could; after four years of war, not only were serviceable examples few and far between, but most, certainly in the Morvan – a poor area where motor vehicles were relatively rare – had long been appropriated

by the *maquisards*. Obtaining fuel and common spare parts such as batteries and tyres, which wore out very rapidly on roads which were
chiefly unsurfaced, presented enormous problems. Nonetheless, by
dint of very comprehensive scavenging and a good intelligence system,
A Squadron was able to obtain some thirty vehicles of different types
during its three-month stay, the majority of them latterly, and from
bigger towns outside the immediate area; when it came to withdraw in
early September, the motorised column in which it moved included
twenty-one cars (some reports say eighteen) in good repair, including a
V8 Ford Coupé which was 'Reg Seekings's pride and joy'; he was
reported to have been most upset when he was unable to repatriate it.

During the last week of August the situation improved considerably,
because thanks to an enormous influx, Fraser was able to borrow as
many jeeps as he needed for offensive operations. First of all, on 25
August, five jeeps from 2 SAS's Wallace party, carrying Capt Lee, four
other officers and seventeen ORs who had escaped the firefight at Villaines and then become separated from the main group (see the account
of Operation Wallace, below), arrived, and on 29 August the jeep
columns carrying the Kipling party, led by Tony Marsh and with Paddy
Mayne and Bob Melot in tow, began to reach Chalaux and set up camp
at nearby Brassy. In addition, a twenty-one-strong reinforcement party
under SSM Feeberry, and a six-man sapper party under Capt Bridge-
ford arrived by parachute on the night of 27 August; by now this corner
of the Morvan was very crowded indeed with British parachutists, and
the situation got worse when Johnny Wiseman's party returned at the
end of the month, though by then all thoughts were turned towards
departure.

The general situation had somewhat eased by then, too, (although
this was just a temporary lull) and it became feasible to send out patrols,
using the jeeps as machine-gun platforms, along the lines Stirling and
Mayne had devised in the desert, three years earlier, though the first
sortie was disappointing. Fraser organised and led a 'Jock column' (the
name was a throwback to the days in North Africa, originally used to
describe a patrolling armoured column), including a jeep towing one of
the 6pdrs, which left Chalaux on 26 August and travelled through the
Morvan as far as Arnost. The adventure was short-lived, however, and
the party returned to base. The operation, which was to have culmi-
nated in an assault on the German garrison at Château-Chinon in a
combined operation with *maquisards* from many different bands, was
'discontinued as impracticable', on 29 August.

In the days that followed, both Fraser and Wellsted led parties which had some success strafing traffic with the jeep-mounted guns with relative impunity, having perfected a technique of attacking from a minor road which paralleled a major route – a not-uncommon occurrence in France, thanks to Napoléon Bonaparte's far-sighted policy of building new, straight Roman-inspired roads, the *routes impériales*, to carry his armies, instead of relying on the traditional tracks which followed old field boundaries or the contour line – at a point where there was no direct connection between the two.

Fraser took two jeeps and a car to St-Saulge, in the direction of Nevers. He had the padre with him, and when, two days later, it became obvious that there were good prospects for ambush parties here, he sent him back to Chalaux to gather reinforcements in the shape of Lt Grayson with a sizeable party mounted on three jeeps and three cars. The next day Grayson's team, together with a local partisan band, ambushed a convoy near Billy-Chevannes, between Nevers and Château-Chinon, destroying six vehicles, killing a significant number of Germans and taking five prisoners with no loss to themselves. Over the next two days Fraser's party strafed other convoys, and killed seven German officers travelling in two cars in an ambush at Souzy, while L/Cpl Cave and Tpr Dray, who became temporarily separated, mined several roads, reportedly causing the death of a minor German general named Deinherdt. The German response was typical: twenty-four civilians were shot by way of revenge.

Wellsted's objective was the road between Autun and Dijon. His party numbered eighteen SAS men plus some *maquisards* to act as guides, interpreters and liaison officers, and was mounted on two jeeps, one of them towing a trailer, and three commandeered cars. From the outset the cars proved unreliable, and the party was forced to stop in Saulieu to make running repairs. Here Wellsted learned that the Germans had by now given up using the main N6 road through the town – though they had been doing so just days earlier, when, on 22 August, Marshal Pétain had passed through there on his way into exile at Singmaringen in Germany, via Belfort – and revised his plan, deciding to move further east the following day. On 30 August he met up with one of the *maquisard* bands Wiseman had earlier armed, and he and its leader took the surrender of a large group of conscripted Poles who had deserted from their barracks at Chalon-sur-Saône. The next day he sent road watchers to survey the main routes and search out likely ambush sites, and Sergeant DuVivier strafed the road between

Beaune and Nuits-St-Georges to the north, and blew the 'Toby 1' railway line again.

One of the road-watching parties had reported a considerable amount of traffic, including convoys, on the Nolay–Beaune road, and the next day an elaborate ambush, involving SAS troopers, *maquisards* and Polish deserters, was put in place. It remained there all day, but nothing passed. It was planned to target the Beaune–Nuits-St-George road the following day, but none of the commandeered civilian cars could be persuaded to start; eventually, SSM Feebery and Sgt DuVivier set out alone, and strafed German traffic on the road from a safe distance, destroying or disabling two heavy trucks, three 3-tonners and two cars, and reportedly killing thirty-five. That same afternoon a reconnaissance in the direction of Meursault returned with two cases of that village's renowned wine, much of which was consumed that night in the Hôtel Morvandelle on the Lac des Settons at a dinner over which Paddy Mayne presided.

There were to be no more combat operations mounted by A Squadron in the Morvan. The main emphasis now shifted toward readying it for a move north, through Avallon and Auxerre, which were already in Free French hands, to the safety of the Allied lines at Joigny, on the River Yonne. The first to leave were the five jeeps from 2 SAS; two were to make their way to the Channel coast, and their crews were repatriated from there, to be reinserted and rejoin the Wallace party; the other three, with Lee at their head, turned up in Paris, where the men took some unofficial leave.

The squadron set out from Fraser's headquarters at Chalaux on 6 September, in its rag-bag collection of civilian vehicles, guarded initially by *maquisards* in two nearly-new captured trucks and a gaggle of jeeps manned by men of C Squadron and the newly arrived A Squadron reinforcements under SSM Feebery, who were to stay behind. The wounded and injured were left at Auxerre, to be evacuated by air, and the rest crossed the Yonne into undisputed territory late that evening, three months to the day after Houndsworth's reconnaissance party had left Tempsford. From there, they made their way to Orléans and were transported back to the UK by American aircraft employed in the vast resupply operation which was under way.

Operation Houndsworth cut railway lines, most of them important trunk routes, on twenty-two separate occasions, destroying three locomotives and at least forty goods wagons. It destroyed perhaps twenty-five vehicles and damaged many more; identified some thirty targets warranting attack from the air (the most unusual of which were probably the 'sunken bridges' – causeways just below the surface of the water – which the *Wehrmacht*'s engineers had constructed across the upper Seine); armed perhaps 3,000 *maquisards*; rescued and repatriated sixteen Allied aircrew; killed or wounded at least 220 German soldiers, and accepted the surrender of half as many again, while taking twelve prisoners in action. This list is not exhaustive, and takes no account of the effect the presence of an offensive force in their midst had on the morale of German or *maquisard* forces in the area. That it was able to accomplish this for the loss of just two of its number, with seven more wounded or injured to some degree, while apparently concealing from German security forces the fact that such a large party of uniformed British soldiers was operating in the area at all, is quite extraordinary. If the Houndsworth operational plan had major flaws, they were in expecting the combat party to operate over too wide an area with too small a pool of vehicles, and too great a degree of centralisation; Fraser was to suggest in his report that an operation such as this would have been better mounted by troop-sized parties, each with its own base, widely dispersed throughout the area.

We have noted previously that the most effective of the SAS operations in France were those in which the combat teams reached a high level of synergy with the partisan bands while still operating independently (and allowing them to do the same); in that respect Houndsworth stands out as exemplary, though that is not to say that the *maquisards* were universally trustworthy. The award of a second Military Cross to Bill Fraser (who had won his first MC in December 1941, in the desert), whose 'untiring leadership and spirit kept his men alert and their morale high', was both popular and well deserved.

GAIN

Operation Gain, which established the third of 1 SAS's combat bases, was undertaken by D Squadron under the command of Major Ian Fenwick. A newcomer to the SAS, Fenwick had enlisted in the elite Kings Royal Rifle Corps in 1939, but had spent much of the war as intelligence officer of the Auxiliary Units in Somerset before volunteering for the Regiment on being released from that duty. Despite a superficially somewhat unlikely background as a book illustrator and cartoonist, he fitted in well in the mess, although he still retained the reputation as 'a mad bugger' that he had earned with the Auxiliers: one of the Somerset volunteers later recalled that he had a disturbing habit of 'chucking live explosives around to make you move', though another commented more seriously that 'Nobody argued with Fenwick. He could get anything done.' His determination was, quite literally, to be the death of him.

The objectives of Operation Gain were defined by Operation Instruction No. 22, issued on 12 June. They were straightforward: to cut the railway lines in an area bounded by Rambouillet, Provins, Gien, Orléans and Chartres, primarily the double-track main line connecting Troyes and points east with the Overlord battlefield, via Orléans, Tours, Le Mans and Argentan, but including several single-track branch lines which criss-crossed the area. The operation was to begin as soon as possible, and was to have lasted for three weeks.

The advance elements of the Gain party dropped on the nights of 13 and 14 June; the first group, under Lt Jimmy Watson, went in blind, while the second, a six-strong team from 2 Troop under Captain Jock Riding, dropped on to a DZ marked by a reception party organised by SOE F Section's 'Hermit' circuit, west of Pithiviers. Watson found one of the three railway lines towards which he had been directed was kept permanently out of commission by the RAF and the other two disused, but Riding was more usefully employed. His party began

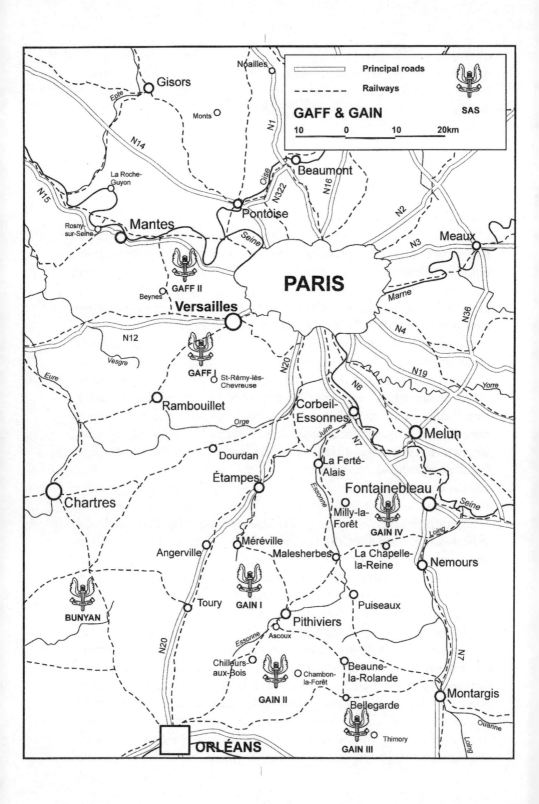

Noailles

Gisors

Monts

La Roche-
Guyon

Rosny-
sur-Seine

Mantes

N15

N14

Epte

N1

Oise

Beaumont

Pontoise

N322

N16

N2

Meaux

N3

Seine

GAFF II

Beynes

Versailles

N36

PARIS

Marne

N12

Vesgre

GAFF I

St-Rémy-lès-
Chevreuse

N20

N4

Eure

Rambouillet

Orge

Corbeil-
Essonnes

N6

N7

Melun

N19

Yorre

Dourdan

Juine

La Ferté-
Alais

Chartres

Étampes

Essonne

Fontainebleau

Seine

Milly-la-
Forêt

GAIN IV

Loing

Angerville

Méréville

Malesherbes

La Chapelle-
la-Reine

Nemours

BUNYAN

Toury

GAIN I

Puiseaux

N20

Essonne

Pithiviers

Ascoux

N7

Chilleurs-
aux-Bois

Chambon-
la-Forêt

Beaune-
la-Rolande

Montargis

GAIN II

Bellegarde

Ouanne

Loing

ORLÉANS

Thimory

GAIN III

Principal roads

Railways

GAFF & GAIN

SAS

10   0   10   20km

offensive operations on the night of 17 June, and despite being on foot, over the next twelve days repeatedly cut the Malesherbes–La Chapelle-La-Reine, Malesherbes–Puiseaux and Fontainebleau–Nemours lines, derailing an entire goods train on the first of those.

Fenwick himself, together with his six-strong Squadron HQ, which included SSM Jim Almonds – a Kabrit 'original' and one of the most experienced and resourceful men in the Brigade, who had already won the Military Medal twice – arrived at the DZ Riding had used on the night of 17 June, and the men settled into a campsite in a substantial but isolated patch of woodland which Fenwick had preselected with the aid of aerial photographs. Already, Riding and Watson had come (separately) to the conclusion that the *maquisards* in the area were a mixed bunch, disorganised, over-enthusiastic and poorly trained and equipped, despite the presence of the 'Hermit' circuit. The topography of the area was less than ideal for the SAS's purpose, too – it was largely agricultural, and thus 'managed', possessing none of the natural, wild character of the Morvan, and offered less opportunities for effective concealment of what was, eventually, to be a relatively large party of British soldiers.

For the first twelve days, while additional men were dropped to join them, the Gain parties operated on foot, and were thus limited to targets close to their base, notably the Orléans–Pithiviers–Montargis, Orléans–Bellegarde and Bellegarde–Beaune-La-Rolande railway lines which had become an important, though roundabout, supply route to the Normandy battlefield after the RAF had destroyed the Loire bridges to the south and west. Almonds led a small party to blow the Orléans–Pithiviers line the night after his arrival, and the exercise was repeated regularly from then on, despite requiring night marches of a score or more kilometres in each direction so that an element of security could be maintained by separating campsites from targets. It was not until the last days of the month that the first pair of jeeps were dropped, together with their drivers and a mechanic, and immediately the majority of the men, save for Jock Riding's 2 Troop, which remained in the original campsite, moved south to the Forêt d'Orléans; already, by contemporary accounts, Fenwick was uneasy, and feared betrayal, either deliberate or accidental, by *maquisards*. His misgivings were soon to be proved justified when Riding's party, encamped in the Forêt de Fontainebleau while they operated against the Nemours–Fontainebleau line, was 'sold' by a French contact. The next day the site was attacked by two companies of German security troops from Milly, but Riding's sentries saw their approach and the party was able to evade, killing two Germans in the course of a brief firefight. Riding then rejoined the main party, blowing the Malesherbes–Puisseaux line again on the way, for good measure.

On the night of 4 July, a further element in the shape of a twelve-man party led by Capt Pat Garstin, with Lt Johnny Weihe as his second-in-command, was due to be inserted into the very north of Gain's operational area, at La Ferté-Alais, only some fifty kilometres south of Paris. The pilot of the Stirling which carried them from Keevil found the DZ, was satisfied that the recognition letters flashed to him by the reception party were correct, and turned to begin his drop run. As the men drifted down to earth in the moonlight, it became clear that they had been betrayed and ambushed. Machine-guns began to open up on them; three were wounded and six more were also captured; Tprs Norman, Morrison and Castelow (rendered in some accounts as Costello), who exited the aircraft as numbers ten, eleven and twelve, had the good fortune to land in woods and managed to evade capture. All three evaders made it to the safety of Allied lines, Norman and Morrison together, after forty-three days behind enemy lines, Castelow after a spell in captivity, overpowering his guard and killing him with his own rifle.

The nine captured men were transferred to Paris that same night, Lt Weihe and Cpl Howard Lutton to hospital (where the latter died of his wounds the next day), the rest to the care of the *Sipo-SD*, which interrogated them forcefully over a brief period and then seemed to lose interest in them. Five weeks later, on 8 August, and somewhat to their amazement, the seven men were given civilian clothes and told that they were to be exchanged for German agents. Handcuffed, they were put aboard a truck and driven northward out of Paris, stopping in woodland near Noailles, where they were ordered out of the vehicle. One of the men, L/Cpl Serge Vaculik, a Czech with French nationality who had originally joined 4 French Para and was then cross-posted as an interpreter, also understood German, and was later to say that what he overheard of a conversation between the escorts indicated that all was certainly not well; he was helping to support Pat Garstin, who had still not recovered from wounds he suffered in the ambush, and managed to whisper a warning to him, and Garstin immediately shouted an order to scatter. Firing their sub-machineguns (reported to be Stens; there is a persistent suggestion that the episode was engineered to look like a 'blue on blue' encounter between *résistants* and parachutists) wildly, the escort gave chase. L/Cpl Ginger Jones tripped over an exposed root and fell flat; the pursuing Germans assumed he had been hit by gunfire and ignored him, and he managed to slip away deeper into the wood and hide in the confusion, while Vaculik, with a head start, outran his pursuers. Capt Patrick Garstin, Sgt Thomas Varey and Tprs Thomas Barker, Joseph Walker and William Young were shot down as they tried to flee, and their bodies buried in neighbouring woodland (they were later reburied in the National Cemetery at Marissel). Jones and Vaculik were eventually reunited by the Resistance, and later crossed into Allied-held territory. Lt Johnny Wiehe was discovered in a Paris hospital after the liberation, paralysed from the waist down from a spinal wound. He was eventually repatriated to his native Mauritius, but died within two years.

SOE's operations in the area south and west of Paris had been extensively penetrated the previous year, and there is clear documentary evidence in a variety of archive locations which demonstrate that the F-Section circuit in question had actually long been run by *Sipo-SD*. In particular, one *SD* officer, *SS-Sturmbannführer* Hans-Josef Kieffer, chief of Section IV/E in the capital and arguably the most effective counter-intelligence operative in France at the time, was known to have placed agents in Resistance groups, and had earlier ambushed SOE parties dropped by parachute in the area, including the 'Bricklayer' team captured on the night of 29 February 1944. According to a statement made by *SS-Hauptscharführer* Karl Haug on 7 March 1946, he was a member of a party organised by Kieffer and led by an *SS-Obersturmführer* named Schubert, which captured Garstin and his men. The party expected to intercept a resupply drop, and the men concerned were somewhat surprised when they realised that the parachutes supported men as well as containers. The arrest operation was thus a disorganised affair, but as we know, was largely successful; Schubert was awarded the *Kriegsverdienstkreuz II Klasse* (War Service Cross, Second Class) in recognition of a job well done.

Haug saw nothing more of the parachutists after they were delivered to *Sipo-SD* headquarters at the rue de Saussaies the following morning, but on 7 August was ordered to collect a group of seven prisoners from a hotel used as a makeshift prison by *Sipo-SD* in the place des Etats-Unis at 0330 the following morning. He recognised them as the men he had help to apprehend during the *parachutage*. The prisoners were placed in a truck which joined a convoy of fifteen to twenty cars for a two-hour journey north, separating from it just after first light. Haug goes on to describe how *SS-Hauptsturmführer* von Schnurr, command-ing the operation, ordered the men out of the truck, which was parked at the edge of a patch of woodland, had them marched some hundred metres into the wood into a small clearing and then lined up side by side facing the six German personnel present, all of whom were armed with submachine-guns. Schnurr then took a sheet of paper from his pocket, he said, and began reading from it, a short phrase at a time, pausing while *SS-Unterscharführer* von Kapri (who worked in Section IV/E's radio intelligence section, as did Schnurr) translated his words into English. Schnurr continued (in German): 'You know that saboteurs are punished with the death penalty in accordance with the rules of warfare', whereupon the two prisoners on the extreme left of the line (facing Haug) 'sprang with a cry to the left and away. At the same moment everybody began to shoot … I found it impossible to shoot at these men with whom I had formerly been on such friendly terms.' Haug continues:

> Three of the prisoners fell where they stood. The next two ran about thirty metres into the wood and then they too crumpled up. Searching and swearing now began on a grand scale. But in spite of the search the two who had broken away were nowhere to be found. When we got back to the place of the shooting after about half an hour, one of the men we had shot [presumably Jones] was missing; there were now only four corpses there. We saw a track, made by crawling or dragging along, leading up into the wood from the place where the other had been lying. We began to search again and moved out in a line in this direction. After about 500 metres, Ilgenfritz (an *SS-Obersturmführer* who was head of Section IV/E's transport section) caught sight of the prisoner running and shot him down. He and the other officers were of the opinion that he was one of the two who had got away, and that one of the dead bodies had been carried away during their absence by members of a resistance or sabotage group … [Schnurr] maintained that I was to blame for a man [sic] escaping.
>
> The three officers next discussed what to do with the dead bodies. They agreed to drive to the next village, where an air force unit was quartered, and to ask the officer commanding it to put a number of men at our disposal to search the neighbourhood once again and bury the dead. The air force put approximately one company at our dis-posal. The officer i/c was to be told that the men we had shot were saboteurs who had been surprised at a rendezvous and shot. The

whole neighbourhood was combed once again by these troops, without success. I did not see the bodies again afterwards. Schnurr then ordered us to drive into the village, where the column with which we had left that morning was carrying out its operation.

Haug, not unnaturally but nonetheless rather disingenuously, did his best to distance himself from the actual killings, but also maintained that he had no clue, right up until the time that Schnurr gave the order to march the prisoners into the woods, that he was to be part of the firing party chosen to execute them. Von Kapri told him that they were to be shot, he admitted, but he believed that he was involved in an operation to transfer them to a prison or camp where the killings would be carried out 'by a firing squad especially chosen for the purpose. Executions were, as far as I knew, always held in the yard of a fortress or a prison.'

Fenwick, of course, knew nothing of the capture of Garstin's party, and indeed, such was the unreliability of radio communications, it was some time before he learned that it was out of contact and not responding to signals. Now that he had a degree of mobility, thanks to the jeep drop, he began to carry out wider-ranging sabotage operations aimed at disrupting rail and road traffic through the entire 'Orléans Gap', between the forests of Orléans to the south and Rambouillet and Fontainebleau, to the north. In particular, this was to be the route which 9. SS-Panzer Division *Hohenstaufen* and 10. SS-Panzer Division *Frundsberg*, which we may recall had been hastily withdrawn from the Eastern Front without their equipment and were refitting in Germany, would take on their way to the battlefield, and was also very important for general resupply.

Fenwick also learned, from the 'Hermit' group with which he had retained sporadic contact, that the locomotive sheds and all-important turntable at Bellegarde were themselves vulnerable. He despatched a reconnaissance party, which returned with a favourable report, and then set about planning an operation. The plan itself was simple, of course: drive the jeeps as close to the rail yard as possible, enter on foot, place demolition charges with delayed-action fuses in all the appropriate places and clear the area before they went off. Execution proved to be another matter entirely. For a start, there was but one locomotive in the shed, where there would normally have been perhaps half a dozen, and that in itself set alarm bells ringing in Fenwick's head. He placed substantial charges of plastic explosive on both actuating cylinders anyway, and had turned his attention to the turntable when the party came under fire from German troops in concealed positions. In the darkness and confusion, the fire was not effective, and the SAS men were able to retire in good order and make a clean getaway in the jeeps. Operation Gain had been betrayed again, and on the party's return to the campsite in the forest, Fenwick lost no time in ordering an immediate move to a fresh location, still within the forest confines, under conditions of tight security.

As July wore on, the Allied Tactical Air Force's fighter-bombers, operating at low level against targets-of-opportunity, and the more systematic high-level bombing campaign carried out by the RAF's Avro Lancasters and the USAAF's Boeing B-17 Flying Fortresses and Consolidated B-24 Liberators, rendered the railway system in the area virtually unusable, so that movement was increasingly switched over to the roads. With more jeeps at its disposal, the Gain party, which had by now been increased to a strength of fifty-eight, was able to operate more widely and more frequently, and before the end of the month jeep patrols were out every night, when fuel supplies allowed, shooting up isolated vehicles in particular – a tank transporter near Ascoux; two trucks on the Orléans–Pithiviers road; a fuel tanker, fully loaded, on the same road the following night – and disrupting traffic out of all proportion to their actual presence. They regularly mixed with German vehicles in the process, relying on the similarity, particularly in the dark, between the Willys jeeps, now camouflaged according to the German pattern with fresh-cut foliage, and the *Kübelwagen* to give them an element of security; when German vehicles risked using their headlights, so did they.

Before the end of July, Fenwick, having heard rumours from Resistance sources of an impending security sweep through the forest, decided to regroup; all save Capt Riding's troop, plus the CO, the SSM and Sgt Lambert, were to disperse, Lts Bateman and Parsons and their parties to join a strong *Maquis* concentration at Thimory, sixty kilometres east of Orléans; Lt Watson and his party northward, towards the Forêt de Rambouillet. Riding provided an armed escort to Bateman and Parsons and their men, who were mounted on commandeered civilian transport, to Thimory, and on the way back almost came to grief. His jeep passed four German tank transporters, and he decided to leave the main road in favour of one with less traffic; a convenient side-turning came up rather unexpectedly (they were running without lights), his driver took the corner too fast, and the jeep overturned, coming to rest upside down in a ditch. Standard procedure was to lighten the vehicle and right it by sheer muscle power if no additional vehicle was available, and this the crew proceeded to do, assisted by three willing Frenchmen who happened along, but they had barely begun when a convoy of eighty vehicles, most of them commandeered cars, each with a load of German infantrymen, passed down the road beside them. With the benefit of hindsight, it is easy to say that in the dark, it would have been natural for the German troops to have identified the upturned jeep as a *Kübelwagen*, but nonetheless, the passing of that convoy – and pass it did, without a single one of its vehicles, not even a motorcycle outrider, turning aside – must have seemed an eternity for Jock Riding and his men.

The situation in the area was becoming more fluid by this time, as resistance in the Normandy battlefield began to crumble, and Gain's operational sorties became more audacious. They were far from being risk-free, however, as Lt Watson was to discover when one night he drove innocently into the town of Dourdan, which he had been reliably informed was free of Germans, only to find a convoy of enemy vehicles drawn up in its central square. Watson, unchallenged, drove on, but pulled up once he was out of sight, and assessed the situation. He had seen only a small group of soldiers around the trucks, and judged them to be their drivers, enjoying a break; he decided that the target was too tempting to ignore, turned and drove back into the square, opening up with both pairs of Vickers when the trucks came into sight. As he did so, hitherto concealed machine-guns in the trucks opened up on *him*, though if they had delayed a few seconds longer, they would have been more effective. As it was, Watson's driver was able to take a side-turning out of the field of fire, but not before the French guide/interpreter had been hit, causing him to release his hand-hold and fall out of the jeep as it rounded the corner (he was not badly hurt; gaining the cover of a garden, he was able to evade capture and returned to Watson's camp a few days later).

In his after-action report, Watson was to express a belief that he had been expected in Dourdan, and quite possibly lured there, and that may have been so. In any event, the incident was to have a serious consequence, for it convinced the German security forces that something had to be done to flush out the British commandos before they became too powerful. Intelligence must have pointed to the location of the Forêt d'Orléans camp, which had been occupied for far too long, and the assault came on Sunday 6 August – a day when, as luck should have it, Fenwick was absent at the Thimory camp, making arrangements to receive Paddy Mayne, who was to have parachuted in the following night. Riding and Watson were both visiting, having assumed the routine job of collecting the coming week's code pads and transmission schedules.

One can perhaps imagine the scene: it was a hot summer's afternoon in the forest glade where the SAS had set up camp almost a month earlier; there had been no sign of any untoward activity around the site, and the British soldiers were probably as relaxed as they could be, so deep in enemy-held territory, as they began the task of preparing for the forthcoming night's operations – refuelling and servicing the jeeps, cleaning weapons, filling magazines with ammunition and making up demolition charges and Lewes and Gammon bombs. At times of heightened alert, Bren-armed pairs were posted some hundreds of metres away from the campsite proper, but that afternoon the advanced sentry positions had not been manned. The first the men knew of the attack was the thump of mortars, the whine of the shells as they descended and the explosion as they hit the ground, but soon they came under machine-gun fire too, and saw grey-clad figures moving among the trees.

Thus far, the situation was a rerun of the one which had faced the Bulbasket party on the morning of 3 July, and the outcome could have been similarly catastrophic, but in the event there was some confusion but no panic; the men grabbed escape haversacks, personal weapons and extra ammunition and went to pre-established all-round defensive positions. The jeeps were parked some distance away from the campsite, and there was never any question of escape by that means, even if there had been enough space aboard the vehicles for all the men, but Capt Riding and the signaller, Sgt Bunfield, managed to negotiate the cordon unobserved and extricated their two vehicles. For the majority of the men of the party, fieldcraft and superior skill-at-arms were the key to their survival, heavily outnumbered as they were, and that was precisely what they displayed, firing sparingly at German infantrymen who showed themselves and denying them the chance to set up an assault in strength through the thick undergrowth, waiting for darkness to give them the chance to slip through the cordon.

By dawn of the following day, 7 August, there was not a single SAS man left in the forest campsite, and already they had started to regroup. With only the kit they stood up in and their emergency escape haversacks, with light weapons, limited ammunition and just three vehicles, they were hardly in fit condition to launch offensive operations, but they were unharmed and in good order and, what was perhaps more important, in relatively high spirits, having proved themselves capable of taking on a vastly superior German force and, if not beating it into submission, at least making it look very stupid indeed. That reality could not have been more different from the account Ian Fenwick received, for he was told that they had been wiped out to a man.

Fenwick's first act was to signal Mayne to abort his insertion. (In fact, Mayne decided to jump into the Morvan to join Bill Fraser's A Squadron instead, before setting off to find out for himself what was happening to the Gain party; his true purpose, however, was to take command of the SAS Brigade's component of Operation Transfigure, which is described in more detail in the account of Operation Kipling.) Fenwick then set off, with Cpl Duffy as driver, Sgt Dunkley manning the rear Vickers, L/Cpl Menginou of 4 SAS as interpreter and an FFI sergeant as guide, both to make a first-hand appraisal of the situation and look for anyone who might have survived. The jeep made good time on back roads, but was spotted from the air by a Feisler Fi.156 *Storch* observation aircraft, which radioed a report to elements on the ground. Just short of Chambon-la-Forêt and not far from the campsite it was flagged down by a lone Frenchwoman. The Germans, she said, had taken all the men and boys in the village captive and were 'waiting for them'. Whether Fenwick took her literally and simply did not care, or whether he thought she simply meant that there was some sort of German presence there, one that he could defeat, we will never know. For his part, he is reported to have said something like 'Thank you, Madame, but I intend to attack them', and ordered Duffy to drive on.

The jeep drove into the village at speed, and was met by machine-gun and 2cm cannon fire; Major Ian Fenwick and the two Frenchmen were killed instantly, Fenwick apparently taking a single 2cm round to the head. Duffy was wounded and crashed the jeep, but saw Sgt Frank Dunkley led away in handcuffs before he lapsed into unconsciousness. Dunkley was never seen again, and is presumed to have been unlawfully executed under the *Kommandobefehl*; no body was ever found, but his name is inscribed on the Bayeux Memorial. Major Fenwick is buried in the cemetery at Chambon-la-Forêt. Cpl Duffy was passed from one hospital to another and eventually escaped from one in Fontainebleau with the assistance of a French nurse, who obtained a doctor's white coat and a pair of ill-fitting shoes for him. After two painful days of stumbling around aimlessly, he had the good fortune to be picked up by a *résistant* and was sheltered until American troops arrived, whereupon he was whisked off to a US Army hospital in Milly. He later became one of the very few British servicemen to receive, rather to his surprise, a Purple Heart, the American decoration for those wounded in action, which were routinely distributed to all those in US hospital beds.

It was some time before news of the ambush which cost the lives of Fenwick and his crew reached the surviving members of the Gain party via Resistance channels, but long before that it had become clear that it was no longer an effective fighting force. Jock Riding assumed command, and was confirmed in it when Paddy Mayne arrived, having driven from the Morvan, on 12 August, and restricted its activities to observation and intelligence gathering. Lts Bateman and Parsons and their sections, still in company with the *Maquis* Agrippa at Thimory, were present when the camp came under concerted attack from infantry backed up by a squadron of armoured cars on 10 August. There was no further loss of life amongst the Gain party before the fighting front passed through the area and the operation ceased, although an American airman, Lt Edward Simpson, was killed, and Tpr Wilson had a narrow escape, in the aftermath of the attack on Agrippa's camp, when a *maquis* car in which they were travelling was machine-gunned in an ambush. Wilson, hit twice but not badly wounded, shot and killed three of his attackers with his pistol before being wounded again himself, this time more severely. Amazingly, considering what he had done, he was taken off to hospital rather than being despatched on the spot, and was still there when American forces arrived and liberated him. Two SAS soldiers, Tprs John Ion and Leslie Packman, captured on 16 August, were unlawfully executed; they are both buried in the cemetery at Chilleurs-aux-Bois. A third body found with them was too badly decomposed to be identifiable, but may have been that of Sgt Frank Dunkley. Operation Gain was officially terminated on 19 August, and its survivors were soon repatriated (though not before Almonds and Riding were 'captured' by Americans, who simply refused to believe their story, particularly that they had been driving about the countryside in jeeps for the past many weeks). SSM Almonds was later commissioned in the field and remained in the army post-war, retiring with the rank of major. In addition to his Military Medals he was also awarded the *Croix de Guerre*.

HAFT

Operation Haft was a minor 1 SAS operation which saw a seven-man party dropped between Mayenne and Le Mans to report on enemy troop movements and identify targets for air strikes; it was closer in character, perhaps, to those which a later generation of SAS troopers would recognise. The party – three SAS officers: Capt Mike Blackman and Lts John Kidner, who had earlier served with Bulbasket survivor Peter Weaver in the Dorest Auxiliary Units, and Hugh (John) Randall, who had joined 1 SAS after a long spell with Phantom and acted as the party's signals officer, with a three-man team under Cpl Brown to assist him, together with an interpreter seconded from 4 SAS – was inserted on 8 July, dropping from a Tempsford-based Halifax on to a DZ manned by *maquisards* under the leadership of an SOE operative code-named Scientist.

As we observed earlier, Haft was conceived as a much more ambitious operation than it became, and the original plan called for ten to twelve parties to be inserted in the area bounded by Flers, Dreux, Orléans and Angers, and for a base and supply dump to have been established to support them. The Operation Instruction which defined its original objectives (No. 25) was at pains to underline its nature:

The objectives of parties in this area are as follows, in order of priority:

a) Airfields and emergency landing grounds
b) Soft targets, DRs [despatch riders], staff cars etc. on main roads
c) Telecommunications
d) Bulk petrol
e) Any action which will embarrass (sic) and delay the movement of reserves and supplies up to the battlefront.

The objective of Operation Haft is primarily a military one and whilst no opportunity should be missed of profiting by the assistance of resistance groups or of directing their efforts into those channels which will most embarrass the enemy, it is not the intention that SAS troops engaged on this operation should be diverted from their main task by the necessity to arm or organise the local resistance groups. Every effort should be made to prevent large numbers of maquis collecting around the base area and so compromising it.

It may be assumed that the final instruction was inserted in the light of the experience of 4 SAS in Operation Samwest (q.v.). In the event, long before the advance party was readied it had become clear that the area in question was far too close to the Overlord battlefield to allow a sizeable SAS party to operate in anything like safety, and Operation Instruction No. 27 reduced the mission to its actual status, with reconnaissance as its task. Later, what had originally been Haft 105 became Operation Chaucer, Haft 205 became Shakespeare and Haft 305 became Bunyan; and thanks to a perceived need to get the Belgians of 5 SAS into action as soon as possible, they were carried out by men of that battalion.

It transpired that the Haft party's insertion had actually been observed by German troops garrisoned at the nearby village of Lassay, of which Blackman was very wary initially, but that information was not passed on to *Sipo-SD* until the following day, by which time the parachutists were well hidden and their surplus kit buried. On the evening of the third day, Blackman and Kidner set off on the first reconnaissance expedition, staying out one night before returning to the hiding place, where, Randall told them, there had been significant German activity. As a result Blackman ordered a move, and that established a pattern for future operations – Blackman and one or other of the lieutenants, usually Kidner, Randall being more occupied with communications, sortied to gather information, invariably in the company of a *résistant* (always, reported Blackman, of very high quality), staying out one or two nights and then returning to base to code and transmit a signal before moving to a new location. This proved to be an excellent *modus operandi*, and the party never came under any form of direct threat.

By 10 August, when the party had been in the field for over a month, meaningful intelligence was becoming very scarce, and Blackman took the decision to contact Allied forces, meeting up with an American tank destroyer unit the following day and arriving at 21st Army Group Tactical HQ the next morning. Blackman subsequently returned to the UK by air while the rest of the party travelled by motor torpedo boat from Arromanches to Newhaven, spending much of the time trying to swap bits of kit at an advantageous barter rate with the Royal Navy crewmen. In all, the Haft party passed back information on forty targets, many of which were attacked successfully from the air. Throughout, the operation was an example of good liaison between SAS and SFHQ, and relations with Resistance groups and other elements already on the ground since long before D-Day were 'particularly good and effective', to quote one later report.

HAGGARD

The penultimate operation 1 SAS mounted in France, Haggard, was a relatively brief affair – in the broadest sense, no element of the party was operational for more than a month, and by a more realistic definition, it was active for a bare fortnight – but proves rather difficult to analyse due to gaps and inconsistencies in the various accounts of its activities, which are often at odds with one another. As one member of the party was to say, many years later, 'Lepine did not encourage his officers and NCOs to write up their own reports', and he himself was very economical in his account, which runs to just five pages, one of which simply lists the kit each man carried. A copy of the radio log, missing from the file held at PRO, exists elsewhere; though it is rather terse, it usually provides a means of cross-checking the claims made in other accounts, but it is far from comprehensive.

Operation Haggard was undertaken by the elements of B Squadron not committed to Operation Bulbasket, a total of fifty-three all-ranks under Major Eric Lepine. They were to operate west of the Loire in the triangle formed by the cities of Gien, Bourges and Nevers, and close to Vierzon, an important railway junction (and thus south of the Orléans Gap and west of the Morvan), but, thanks to opposition from General Koenig's HQ, the EMFFI, were inserted too late in the campaign ever to have influenced the post-Overlord battle, for the Falaise Gap was closed before they could begin to have an impact on the lines of communication. EMFFI's hostility to the operation ostensibly centred on the likelihood of Haggard disrupting its pre-existing Resistance support operations and increasing the risk of the Germans engaging in reprisals against the civilian population, but was really more concerned with internal (French) politics and power games; SFHQ used a similar argument in other circumstances, but to less effect.

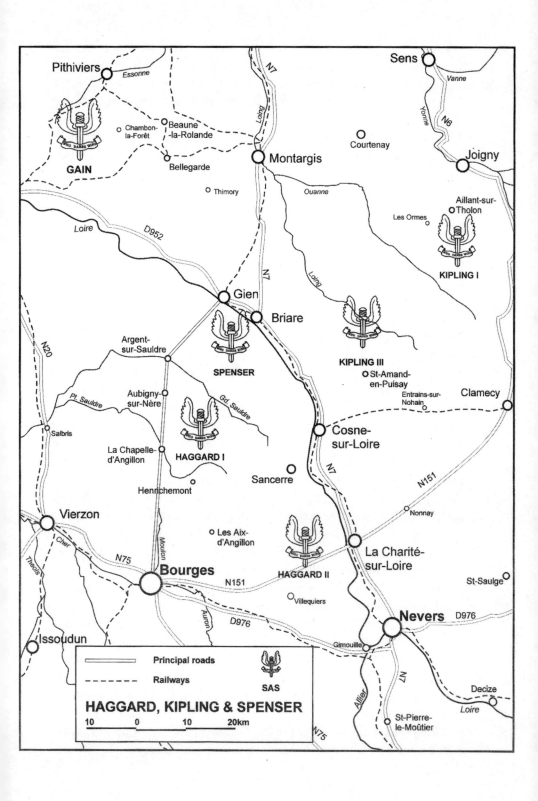

Pithiviers

Essonne

N7

Sens

Vanne

Yonne

N6

Joigny

Chambon-la-Forêt

Beaune-la-Rolande

Courtenay

GAIN

Bellegarde

Thimory

Montargis

Ouanne

Aillant-sur-Tholon

Les Ormes

KIPLING I

Loire

D952

Loing

N7

Gien

Briare

Loing

KIPLING III

SPENSER

St-Amand-en-Puisay

N20

Argent-sur-Sauldre

Pt. Sauldre

Aubigny-sur-Nère

Gd. Sauldre

Entrains-sur-Nohain

Clamecy

Salbris

La Chapelle-d'Angillon

HAGGARD I

Cosne-sur-Loire

Henrichemont

Sancerre

N7

N151

Vierzon

Cher

Les Aix-d'Angillon

Nonnay

Théols

Moulon

HAGGARD II

La Charité-sur-Loire

St-Saulge

N75

BOURGES

N151

Auron

Villequiers

Nevers

D976

Issoudun

D976

Gimouille

St-Saulge

Principal roads

SAS

Railways

SAS

HAGGARD, KIPLING & SPENSER

Allier

Decize

Loire

St-Pierre-le-Moûtier

N7

10   0   10   20km

N75

Clearly, SAS Brigade HQ was wary of offending what was in effect the French High Command, and the Operation Instruction's statement of objectives contains the telling phrase: 'Receiving operation parties at short notice *when it is decided that SAS operations can take place without prejudice to resistance*' (italics added). As a result of the delay, which extended into mid-August, Operation Haggard's contribution to the liberation of France consisted largely of harassing German forces trying to escape the advancing Allied armies, and in this it met with a measure of success at little cost to itself. It was, however, mounted far too late ever to have been truly effective in a wider sense, which must have been particularly galling since its personnel had been available for independent offensive operations ever since the mooted reinforcement of the Bulbasket party was abandoned on 19 June, and had been left idle for almost two months at a crucial time as a result.

The copy of the Operations Instruction which exists, outside the PRO archive, is unfortunately both unnumbered and undated – though the context makes it fairly clear that it was issued in the third week of July – and speaks of the advance party being inserted sometime around the end of the month. In fact, it was to be delayed still further. The advance party of seven men, four troopers from 1 SAS under the command of Lt Peter Neilson, together with two members of 5 SAS to act as signallers and interpreters, was inserted successfully, together with Jedburgh team Alec, and thus, unusually, by three B-24 Liberators operating out of Harrington, the SAS stick divided between two of them, the third carrying the Jedburghs. Jack Blandford, one of the SAS party, recalls dropping on the night of 9 August, and the SAS Brigade War Diary and the Haggard radio log bear him out. The after-action report of the Jedburgh team states it was the night of 8 August (though a hand-written note on the file header page says it was the night of 9 August) and Major Eric Lepine's after-action report, just to confuse matters still further, says it was the night of 10 August. The accounts do agree that the party landed safely, but according to Alec's report they were 'dropped sixty miles east of area intended in briefing', which makes little sense unless the team had somehow managed to become attached to the wrong SAS party. This was not unknown, and in fact, there is some circumstantial evidence to suggest that this may actually have been the case.

The Mission Directive for team Alec says: 'To accompany a reconnaissance party of SAS to Loire et Cher [sic]; to provide the link between SAS and Resistance groups, contacting Ventriloquist ('Antoine').' Now, leaving aside the error in the name of the *département* (it is 'Loir-et-Cher'; the Loire and the Loir are not one and the same river), the Loir-et-Cher is adjacent to the Cher, and north-west of it; it was there that the party from 5 SAS which was to have brought the team mounting Operation Shakespeare up to strength was dropped, in error, on the night of 8 August (see the accounts of Operations Bunyan, Chaucer and Shakespeare, below). The previous night had been the time of the cancellation of Paddy Mayne's insertion into the Orléans area and his decision to switch to the Morvan, so one may speculate that there was a great deal of activity and thus scope, at least, for misunderstanding and confusion. It may indeed have been the case that the mix-up which saw the destination of two SAS parties switched may also have extended to Jedburgh team Alec (we should note that it was travelling in an aircraft of its own; it could be that this pilot's briefing was botched, too). Early on in the Alec report there appears the note 'Met Antoine 12 August. Decided to remain in present area ...' which perhaps supports this notion. (Antoine had responsibility for an area which covered the northern part of the Cher, the Loir-et-Cher and parts of adjacent *départments*, so that in linking up with him, Alec could be said to have obeyed its Mission Directive.)

There is no reference in Lepine's report to the presence of the Jedburgh team, although the SAS Brigade War Diary mentions it in passing; Lepine's omission is surprising, to say the least, given that team Alec's stated objective was to support his party. Nor is there any mention of a Jedburgh team accompanying the SAS reconnaissance party in the latter's Operation Instruction, which says that communications would be the responsibility of the signallers from 5 SAS. It is tempting to speculate that the Jedburgh team was a wholly unexpected addition to the operation, and that Lepine simply had not included them in his plans. This might account for the distinctly cool relationship between SAS and Jedburghs, though it appears from yet another report, written by the political officer, that the Jedburghs' leader, an American, was overtly anti-British and had little affection for the SAS party, talking it down (and his nation's interests up) to the French at every opportunity, albeit to no discernible effect, and that cannot have helped the situation either.

Lepine himself, with his Squadron HQ, the political officer, one full section of ten and the remainder of Neilson's section, a total of twenty men, left Keevil on the night of 14 August in two Stirlings, to be dropped into the DZ used by the advance party. This time the 'dropping was disgraceful'; one pilot dropped his stick too high, so that its members drifted a considerable distance and finally landed, happily without incident, only a few hundred metres from the main Bourges–Gien road, along which a substantial convoy of armoured cars and mechanised infantry was travelling at the time. The other pilot dropped his stick too low, and the men had no time to release their legbags. As a result two, including the SSM, suffered broken (or badly sprained; reports vary) ankles and another, Capt Courtenay Gosling, who was attached to the party but actually reported to the Political Warfare Executive, broke a shoulder blade, an incapacitating injury which necessitates a long recovery period, and was 'unable to take part in operations'. Lepine's after-report states that Gosling spent weeks in the care of Pierre Malgras, a doctor who 'worked for the Germans by day and the *Maquis* by night', acting as a ready intelligence conduit between parachutists and partisans. He was eventually evacuated into the American-occupied zone on 26 August, and, still not fully fit, operated there.

The Haggard HQ party established its base, to the east of the Bourges–Gien road, in the Forêt d'Ivoy, adjacent to the Château de la Verrerie, the home of 'Colonel' Colomb (Comte Arnaud de Vogüe) the FFI military commander in the area, and never moved from there. Its original targets were to have been the railway lines running through Vierzon from Châteauroux in the south toward Tours in the west, and north, toward Orléans and Paris, both directly and via a roundabout route through Bourges and Montargis, so that German traffic would be forced to use the roads, where it would both consume precious petrol and be vulnerable to ambush. By the time the headquarters party arrived, the advance party had already destroyed a stretch of the double-track main line between Vierzon and Tours, in the Cher valley, although disaster had threatened when one of its number, an ex-Auxilier who should have known better, used only fifteen seconds' worth of Bickford safety fuze to set off the explosion. (Jack Blandford, the saboteur, recalled, 'As I dropped to the ground, up went the bombs! We had stones dropping all round us, plus a length of rail about eight feet in length ... I decided next time to use more than six inches of fuze!') In fact, this was to be one of very few operations Haggard mounted against a railway line, for it was clear from observations that the forces of occupation were actually making very little use of the network, presumably due to successful sabotage of the permanent way elsewhere and the shortage of rolling stock, and had decided to switch over to the roads.

Lepine's report now diverges once more from the War Diary. He says he sent for the rest of the squadron to be dropped in the area of 'Villequis', actually Villequiers, south and east of the original DZ. He says that they arrived on the night of 18 August, but the War Diary and radio log state that a party of twelve men under the command of Lt Davidson, aboard a Fairford-based Stirling, was inserted there that night, and that the remaining fourteen men were dropped to the Forêt d'Ivoy DZ on the night of 24 August; in fact, the latter party, under Lt Schlee, was inserted, from a Fairford-based Stirling, at the Villequiers DZ, after having been forced to return to Keevil the previous night.

The secondary base near Villequiers allowed the men there to concentrate on the roads and rail routes from Bourges eastward towards the important Loire crossings at La Charité-sur-Loire, Nevers and Decize, the north–south route from Bourges to Gien having already begun to lose its importance as American forces pushed eastward north of the river. Lepine was to say of this period:

> It was evident at the time that the Germans were more intent on avoiding ambushes than on looking for sabotage parties, as a result, jeeps would have proved at this stage invaluable. However, it was first difficult to lay successful ambushes owing to the density of the peasant population among which there were a certain number of collaborators who warned the enemy of the presence of British parachutists. In the south the Maquis was better organised and Major Lepine's patrols met with more success.

In fact, it was 21 August before Haggard mounted its first successful ambush (though the radio log for 19 August shows Lepine as reporting having already carried out 'extensive ambushing'), destroying two staff cars and a truck and killing perhaps twenty-five including the commandant of the *Luftwaffe* forces at Bourges airfield. Two similar operations the following night killed about fifty more. On 23 August the Vierzon–Orléans railway line was cut near Salbris, and the following day RAF Mosquitoes were called in to bomb the Bourges–La Charité line, without much success, but in five ambushes laid by both parties '6 lorries and 3 cars were knocked out [the radio log says four and three, respectively] and 47 Germans were reported killed'. On 25 August Lepine was warned of the impending arrival in the area of a column of infantry and some heavy artillery, which would be passing up the Bourges–Gien road on its way to join the resistance to the American advance north of the Loire, and his men, together with a strong force of local *maquisards*, were able to prepare a simple but very effective trap. A stretch of the road was under repair, and slabs of plastic explosive were concealed in the piles of flints and gravel by the roadside for a distance of about fifty metres; as soon as the column was abreast, the explosive was detonated. Lepine estimated that perhaps as many as 500 were killed and injured, and large quantities of stores and munitions were captured. Curiously, the radio log makes no mention of this incident.

At this point a further degree of confusion sets in. Lepine's after-action report says: 'After this operation ... it was decided to blow two canal bridges over the waterway which runs along the Bourges–Never road ...' but it only becomes clear on reading the radio log that he was referring to two separate operations. The waterway in question is the Canal Lateral à la Loire, which, as its name suggests, runs parallel with the river, which runs roughly north–south through the area. The operations would be mounted in conjunction with *maquisards*, 'owing to the fact that these bridges were guarded by SS troops ... The Maquis role was to block the road on each side of the bridges with trees and hold off any attack while the SAS patrols went in, killed the guards and blew up the bridge.'

The site of the first operation was to be the point at which the canal crosses the River Allier near Gimouille, eight kilometres from Nevers, near its confluence with the Loire, and then runs alongside the road in question for perhaps five kilometres. At some point around this time, a detachment of eight jeeps from 3 SAS, two separate four-car patrols, one led by Gabriel de Sablet, the other by an Aspirant calling himself Plowright, a *nom de guerre*, arrived in the area. The 3 SAS party was engaged in Operation Newton, the original objective of which was to reinforce the Dickens, Harrod and Moses parties; it remained co-located with Haggard for some time. Lepine implies they arrived on or about 25 August. Plowright and de Sablet report joining the Haggard party on 28 and 29 August respectively. Neither makes any mention of their involvement in blowing the canal bridge and according to them neither patrol was particularly successful; we can speculate that had either one been involved in an operation as spectacular as blowing up a bridge carrying a major canal over a major river, wrecking a major road in the process, its report would probably have made mention of the fact.

We shall return to the Plowright and de Sablet accounts, but for the moment continue with Lepine, who reported:

> At midnight [on 25 August] the patrols set out in transport. Everything went according to plan. The bridges [sic] were well and truly blown. The Maquis played their part excellently, but suffered casualties:- 2 killed, 2 taken prisoner and subsequently tortured and killed, and one man wounded. The SAS patrol had to fight a fairly stiff disengaging action as the enemy had arrived with 20mm guns mounted on trucks, which was more than was anticipated. In this action the SAS casualties were:- Cpl Wilkinson killed, L/Cpl Ewing wounded. [Corporal John Wilkinson, who was posthumously awarded the Croix de Guerre avec Palme, lies in the Communal Cemetary at Villequiers. He was the only fatal casualty of Operation Haggard.] After embussing and having gone only four miles the party ran into an oncoming German convoy of some ten trucks. Due to the coolness of L/Sgt Youngman who was driving the leading car, the party passed untouched. Unfortunately the rear jeep crew (French) lost their nerve, drove their jeep into the side, jumped out and rushed into the woods. As a result the jeep was captured intact and in perfect running order.

Neither Plowright nor de Sablet made any mention of this loss in their after-action reports either (though there is a report in the radio log from 0830 on 6 September of an intact French jeep having been captured, seemingly the previous day), but then, according to them, they had not yet even arrived in the area... In fact the radio log has Lepine reporting their arrival on 28 August ('9 [sic] jeeps 24 men arrived many thanks.'), and seemingly attacked the second canal bridge the following day. It may have been that it was to this second attack that the jeeps lent their support, and that the two incidents had become concatenated into one in Lepine's mind by the time he came to write his own report, more than a month later, but there is still no mention of any such incident in the de Sablet or Plowright reports ... The French jeeps were split between the two Haggard bases for the remainder of their stay in the

Cher, but there is no reason to think that either patrol was particularly effective.

By now opportunities for offensive action were few and far between, though on 28 August Lepine reports having blown the Bourges–Nevers railway line 'in an effort to hold up an armoured train. This train was used to evacuate wounded while the Red Cross ambulances on the road contained men and supplies' (the Jedburghs had a different story to tell; by their account the train was 'shooting up farms and killing peasants in the fields'; they also place the attack on it on 24 August). He also noted a build-up of enemy troops in Bourges, remarking that this probably included a Corps HQ, but by 30 August he was reporting that the German in the area were now 'appearing in smaller and smaller numbers'.

Lepine records that 'Major Poat MC arrived' on 31 August, but tells us no more about 1 SAS second-in-command's brief sojourn with his party, save that he left on 4 September, 'for Kipling', and the Kipling party's reports make no mention of Major Poat's absence (or, indeed, of his presence). No sooner had Poat arrived at the Forêt d'Ivoy than Lepine received a signal for him via London from Paddy Mayne, who had by now arrived back in the Houndsworth area, telling him not to 'send Haggard here unless they are mechanised'. It perhaps came as something of a surprise to all concerned, for there had never been any mention of the Haggard party moving to the Morvan (though the original Operation Instruction did talk of it linking up with the Gain party, and perhaps either reinforcing it, or providing a haven for it, should it be forced to retire from the Orléans Gap; in the event, of course, Gain had already been stood down before Haggard was up to full strength) and one wonders, with the majority of the Kipling party now installed in the Morvan, just how big a force Mayne wanted to assemble there. In reply, Poat told Mayne (on 1 September) that the Haggard area was a good one for jeeps, and that men on foot were of little use there, but said 'If 4th French come here with 60 jeeps will send B Squadron to Kipling and mechanise them. Will then send them [to] Houndsworth if you agree'. Three days later Mayne had clearly abandoned whatever plan had been forming in his head, for he asked Poat simply to return to Kipling.

Despite Lepine's failure to report bringing any of them to action after 31 August, there clearly were Germans about still, because on 3 September they 'blew the few remaining road and rail bridges in the area', while the radio log and the War Diary tell us that the Haggard party executed two successful ambushes that same day, destroying four trucks and killing forty-five in the first and destroying ten trucks and killing twenty-seven in the second, and a third, which destroyed three trucks and killed eighteen, three days later. That same day, Lepine tells us, 'the 3rd French Jeep Patrol moved off for Moses' (though Plowright reports sending two jeeps 'through the lines to Fontainebleau to be repaired' on 4 September, and leaving the Forêt d'Ivoy on 8 September, to link up with Captain Simon (the commanding officer of Operation Moses) on the following day, in which the Moses report concurs; de Sablet (whose report is extremely brief and uninformative) says he 'moved off [from Lepine's base] in the direction of Fontainebleau' (i.e. northwards) on 6 September and gives no further information, though the Moses report states that he joined that party at Châteauroux on 11 September.

By midday on 7 September Lepine was reporting to London 'Area is played out. Spent 2 days looking for Boche, but have had no luck', and the next day Mayne signalled him to 'move to Briare with all men and kit'. The Haggard party was withdrawn on 9 September, arriving in Briare the next day for a brief rest period before being re-assigned.

In the summary to his report, Major Lepine estimated that during the course of the operation, 120 enemy troops were killed, and nineteen trucks, five cars and a motorcycle destroyed, which doesn't tally with the reports recorded in the radio log. It was successfully re-supplied three times, though half the first consignment was almost lost thanks to the pilot of the aircraft carrying it ignoring clearly-displayed lights and a functioning Eureka beacon and dropping it instead into woodland ten kilometres from the DZ, where three charcoal kilns were glowing red in the darkness (the charcoal burners found the containers next day, and alerted the local *maquisards*). One of the re-supplies consisted largely of petrol which, Lepine says, 'was for the jeep patrols and later given to 4th French Bn', a solitary reference in his report to the presence of yet another SAS detachment in the area, though there are more in the radio log.

In fact, 4 SAS began to arrive in the area in strength in the last days of August, to mount Operation Spenser (q.v.). On 6 September elements of its second squadron entered Bourges, and thereafter were in action between Bourges and La Charité and Nevers, the very region Lepine was supposed to cover, for at least a further week: the Spenser report says 'During all this period, from 2 Sep – 10 Sep, all the vehicles in the Bn continuously attacked German convoys along those roads still in use. A large number of enemy were killed or wounded and a considerable amount of equipment captured', and that is definitely at odds with Lepine's version of events.

KIPLING

The last operation 1 SAS mounted in France, Operation Kipling, was focused on the area east of the Orléans Gap, and was tasked originally with establishing a base for Operation Mappin, one of three SAS operations which would have made up the advance reconnaissance element for the airborne forces' component of Operation Transfigure. The latter called for the insertion of an airborne battle group to act as a blocking force in the path of the German Army's retreat eastward out of the Normandy battlefield, that retreat to be hastened by an armoured thrust from the west; the employment of SAS troops as its forward reconnaissance element would have recognised at last that the Special Air Service had a real role to play within the formal structure of the Order of Battle. Before we examine Operation Kipling, therefore, we have to look briefly at Transfigure.

Transfigure was an ambitious operation which had as its objective nothing less than the destruction of the German Army west of the River Seine. It had two main components: a wide right hook by the armoured divisions around the Falaise Pocket, from a start line Le Mans–Tours towards Chartres, and a simultaneous landing in daylight by airborne troops, both American and British, in the Paris–Orléans Gap, to act as a blocking force. The SAS Brigade was to provide the reconnaissance element for this airborne force, and would supply three troops, two from C Squadron, 1 SAS, under the command of Major Tony Marsh, and one from C Squadron, 2 SAS, under the command of Major Roy Farran. Each would have twenty jeeps, the men and vehicles to be landed in Airspeed Horsa gliders on a landing zone south of Sonchamp, on the edge of the Forêt de Rambouillet. The units from 1 SAS were to have mounted Operation Ponting, which was to have been based with Airborne Forces Tactical HQ and concentrated on the area to the west of the French capital, from Mantes through Dreux and Nogent to Châteaudun, linking up with the Bunyan or Chaucer parties (q.v.) as necessary, and Operation Mappin, which was to have worked south-eastward on the axis Méréville–Pithiviers–Bellegarde–Châtillon, eventually making for the Kipling or the Houndsworth base; 2 SAS's Operation Fortnum was to have struck due east of the landing zone, towards Fontainebleau and Troyes, and eventually link up with the Rupert or Hardy parties. The commanding officer of 1 SAS, Paddy Mayne, was to have had overall command of the three operations, though the decision as to whether Mappin and Fortnum were to have pushed on to the bases in question was to have been taken by the Corps commander, and was thus out of SAS control. Clearly, Operation Gain would have been swamped in the process. According to the SAS Brigade's Operation Order for Transfigure, issued on 13 August, the Gain party was not to be told of Operation Transfigure ahead of time. It and the Haggard party, also ignorant of the plan before hand, were to have been alerted on Transfigure D Day and ordered to render assistance as appropriate. The plan was overtaken by events, and was subsequently abandoned.

As with Operations Houndsworth and Wallace, there exists a first-hand account of some elements of Operation Kipling, *These Men are Dangerous*, published some ten years after the event by Capt Derrick Harrison, a veteran of the Italian campaign, who led the advance party. This time, however, one must voice a caveat. Harrison worked as a journalist, post-war, and he certainly streamlined his account of his own activities in the interests of maintaining its pace. That is perhaps permissible, but any claim he has to be taken entirely seriously is eroded by an unaccountable tendency to lapse into absurd fantasy, particularly when he strays away from his own experience and retells tales that he had clearly heard at second (or more) hand. In contrast to his book, however, Harrison's official report on the part he played in Operation Kipling is extremely terse, and runs to little more than half a page. In particular, the account of the action at Les Ormes, below, uses Harrison's book as its source; no other exists.

The Kipling plan called for the insertion of three officers and twenty-four ORs, two sections from C Squadron plus signallers and fitters, with six vehicles, into the environs of the Forêt de Merry-Vaux, some way to the east of the Paris–Orléans Gap and about twenty kilometres west of Auxerre. This was a very suitable landscape for guerrilla warfare, bordered as it is by the large Forêt d'Othe to the north and with other extensive wooded areas all round; it merges with the Morvan massif in the south-east and communications between the Kipling and

Houndsworth areas, though their headquarters were perhaps 150 kilometres apart, were to be viable as a result. When the Belgian veteran of the desert campaign, Major Bob Melot, was parachuted in to join the Houndsworth party on 27 July, his first important duty was to reconnoitre and approve Harrison's DZ, and he left the Morvan in company with Paddy Mayne on 9 August to carry out his orders. By 12 August he was satisfied with the arrangements in the Forêt de Merry-Vaux, and signalled that the advance party should be despatched. Its objectives were broadly similar to those laid down for the Hardy party: to gather intelligence and locate a suitable base area for a larger party, keeping a low profile, initiating no offensive operations even if high-value targets of opportunity were identified and, if possible, restraining the local (well-organised) *Maquis*, even though the latter had effectively (and finally) been let off the leash in a broadcast General Koenig made on 1 August. That this last task might perhaps have been a tall order for a small party of foreigners did not seem to have occurred to anyone at Moor Park.

Capt Harrison and five companions were parachuted in on the night of 13 August, to be met by Major Melot and a party from the *Maquis* Chevrier. There were no mishaps during the insertion (the men carried the kitbags containing their rucksacks on their chests instead of strapped to a leg until they had exited the aircraft; this was the first time the new arrangement had been used operationally, and it was popular and successful) save that Harrison broke a finger on his left hand, and after collecting the containers, the men spent the rest of the night at the *maquisards'* campsite deep in the forest to the west of the DZ. Unlike many of the partisan bands, even this late in 1944, the *Maquis* Chevrier was well supplied with weapons, and, with a leader and a strong cadre of senior staffers who were all ex-regular army, was extremely well organised; it was also well disciplined, and its commander understood the need to keep a low profile for the moment.

Harrison had been given the option of calling for immediate reinforcement if he believed the situation warranted it, and this he did, that first night. Twenty-four hours later Lt Stewart Richardson and two men were dropped, together with a jeep, which landed heavily in the trees, away from the DZ. On the night of 16 August, ten more men and three jeeps arrived safely, and by the morning of 18 August the party had grown to a total of three officers and twenty-four ORs, with five (just about) serviceable jeeps, and had set up its own independent campsite; but it had also encountered another *Maquis* band, this one in battalion strength, which had no intention of lying low. Its leader, Roger Bardet, was an SOE F Section operative who was in fact working for *Sipo-SD* and had originally come to the area to hide out, having been implicated in the so-called Déricourt affair, which may or may not have involved a very influential SOE agent of that name having gone over to the Germans and been at least involved in 'blowing' the 'Prosper' network the year before. Bardet was in dispute with *Commandant* Chevrier for overall control of the FFI forces in the region (Chevrier was to prevail, and later became the FFI commander in the *département*). Harrison and Melot were faced with a dilemma: they had to persuade Bardet, who was very keen to re-establish himself in favour, to disobey what he deemed to be a direct order from the Commander-in-Chief of Free French forces, but were forbidden to tell him why. They were very fortunate in having the leader of Jedburgh team Bruce – Major William Colby, who was later to head the Central Intelligence Agency – to assist them; Bruce had been inserted without Harrison or Melot's knowledge on the night of 14 August, and already Colby had won Bardet over, and now he was to do so again, by demonstrating that his own orders, which also stressed the need for restraint, and which of course came from SFHQ and thus also, arguably, from Koenig, post-dated those Bardet had received in the General's radio broadcast. With the proviso that Harrison would inform him the moment the restrictions on his men were lifted, Bardet agreed to stay his hand, and Harrison tells how he breathed a heartfelt sigh of relief.

With five vehicles and adequate working relationships with the local *maquisards*, Harrison was at last able to begin making a detailed reconnaissance of the area, but the same day, 18 August, he received the news that Operation Transfigure had been cancelled, following the near-certainty of the Falaise Pocket being closed off in the very near future, whereupon the entire complexion of Operation Kipling immediately changed.

So too, of course, did the attitude of the *maquisards*, and within days the whole area seemed to have emptied of German troops, who were suddenly very reluctant to leave their strongpoints; Harrison's men took to flying Union Jacks from their jeeps and, outside the immediate area of their campsite, where they were known, to sounding a morse 'R' on their horns at every blind bend in an attempt to prevent the almost ubiquitous *résistants*, who not unnaturally took any military-looking vehicle to be German, from firing on them. (They had similar problems with Allied aircraft, too, and on a number of occasions only narrowly missed being strafed from the air, despite the jeeps carrying distinctive yellow marker panels on their engine covers.) But there were still German combat units in the area, and on 21 August the *Maquis* Chevrier camp came under attack. Harrison, at his own camp near by, was alerted by the sound of automatic fire and set out to establish a supporting position, but the SAS men's help was unnecessary; in under an hour, the *maquisards* had beaten off the attack so convincingly that the Germans had hurriedly cleared the area.

Later Melot learned via the Resistance that there was a significant amount of German traffic on the road between Courtenay, to the north-west, and the larger town of Sens, north of there, and despatched Harrison to investigate. It was rather late in the day to set out on what was a longish cross-country journey, and instead, the two jeeps selected for the mission left the SAS campsite early on the morning of 22 August. Harrison relates that they travelled by way of Aillant-sur-Tholon, finding it free of Germans, and then, after a makeshift celebratory lunch in a village north and west of there (wherever they went, the uniformed SAS patrols were taken, not unnaturally, for the spearhead of the invasion force), set off on tertiary roads which follow the track of what is today the main A6 *Autoroute du Soleil*, only to become completely lost within the hour. Relying on compass bearings rather than maps they eventually came to the Courtenay–Sens road, and crossed it at high speed near Vernoy. There, in the cover of a wooded ridge, they found a satisfactory position from which they could strafe anything using the road, but after some hours they had still seen no traffic whatsoever. It was early evening by now, and Harrison was presented with a problem: trying to run an operation such as the one he envisaged would be impossible after dark. Even as he was trying to decide whether to recross the road in daylight and return to base or find a place to lay-up until the next day, two Frenchmen came strolling up a track to their front. He and his driver, Curly Hall, covered them with their carbines and Harrison challenged them, to be asked casually if they were with the Americans! 'What Americans?' asked Harrison. 'The Americans at Courtenay, who came this morning,' he was told.

After Harrison's two FFI guides had questioned the men, and were satisfied that they were telling the truth, the two jeeps set off at speed towards Courtenay. Short of the town they ran into a platoon of M4 Sherman tanks, the advance party of a spearhead battalion of the US 4th Armored Division, which had indeed reached Courtenay that morning, and was now leaguered there. Within half an hour, Harrison was reporting to the commanding officer that in their travels that day, they had seen no sign of German activity as far east as Joigny, twenty kilometres away and the next town of any size in that direction, but the American officer preferred to believe his own reconnaissance elements, and told Harrison that he expected a counter-attack at any time. 'But,' he assured him, he would be 'alright behind our tanks', and directed him towards the unit's quartermaster. The SAS party had not received a resupply drop for five days, rations were getting low and lunch, for all its celebratory pretentions, had been a scratch affair; neither had they had a night of unbroken sleep since arriving in France. They needed no urging to set off in search of hot food and sleeping bags, but before he slept, Harrison was even able to write a brief note to his wife to add to the armoured unit's daily bag of outgoing mail.

Early next morning, laden down with American ration packs, the two jeeps set off to return to the Forêt de Merry-Vaux, arriving at the camp-site in the early afternoon garlanded with flowers from villagers they had met on the way, all of whom had heard by now of the coming of the Americans. Already the *Maquis* Bardet, Harrison was told, had left its forest base and moved in strength into Aillant.

The post-operation check of the vehicles revealed that the pintle mounting for the rear Vickers gun on the second jeep, commanded by Lt Stewart Richardson, was near breaking point and needed welding. Richardson asked permission to drive into Aillant in search of a garage which could carry out the work, and because he disliked the idea of a single jeep 'dashing around the countryside on its own', Harrison decided to go with him; they took skeleton crews – just a driver for each vehicle: Curly Hall, who had been with Harrison since Italy, and Tpr Brearton, who regularly took the wheel of Richardson's jeep – and an interpreter who went by the *nom de guerre* of Fauchois, apparently sec-onded from one of the French battalions, in the second jeep. Their route took them through the village of Les Ormes, but before they got there they saw smoke rising in the distance. It was coming from the village, and as they got nearer, the men heard gunfire, too. Just short of the first houses a middle-aged woman on a bicycle, in tears and com-pletely oblivious of them in her haste, almost ran into Harrison's jeep; there were Germans in the village, she said, and they were shooting people; she was going for the *maquisards* ...

Harrison told her that they would go to Aillant in her place, but in fact he knew that there was no time for anything but direct action. He took a quick poll of the others, and they all agreed; moments later they

were back in the vehicles and speeding towards the village square, real-
ising they would be heavily outnumbered but hoping that surprise and
speed would give them an edge.

The first German Harrison saw was an officer of the *Waffen-SS*,
walking towards them with a pistol in his hand and a look of blank surprise on his face. Harrison shot him without a word, and then took in
the scene: drawn up in the square beside the church were a large truck
and two staff cars, and near them stood a group of soldiers in battledress. Off to one side were terrifed villagers, and behind them, burning
houses. He stood and fired a long raking burst with his twin Vickers;
almost 200 rounds of mixed incendiary, tracer and ball ammunition
ripped through the vehicles and the group of men beside them, starting
fires and causing mayhem. For a moment the Germans stood trans-
fixed, but these were battle-hardened elite troops, not second-rate
occupation forces, and soon they were scattering for cover and already
returning fire. Harrison shouted to Hall to reverse, but there was no
response; looking over, he could see that Hall was badly shot up,
slumped over the wheel, and he returned his attention to the job at
hand. The firing was becoming more intense now, and Stewart
Richardson and his crew, some distance behind Harrison, had joined in
too, when, he says, 'my guns jammed'.

He jumped out of the jeep and ran round to the back, to work the
rear gun. It fired a short burst and then it, too, jammed, whereupon he
switched over to the gun mounted adjacent to the driving seat, only to
have that jam as well. As Harrison was to put it: 'A dud jeep and three
jammed guns. Hell, what a mess!' Nothing daunted, Harrison reached
for his .30-calibre M1 carbine and fired off magazine after fifteen-
round magazine from the hip, while trying to lift Hall's lifeless body
from the jeep. If he had not been sure his driver was dead earlier, he was
now. Fauchois came forward to help him, but Harrison ordered him
back. And then he was hit in the right hand.

If changing magazines had been difficult before, thanks to the
broken middle finger of his left hand, now it was next to impossible; it
seems likely that during the next attempt, he failed to seat the fresh
magazine accurately, and this caused the carbine to misfeed, for the
weapon jammed and he reached instead for his .45in Colt M1911
pistol, only to find that the holster was empty. He managed to eject the
carbine magazine and clear the stoppage, but even while he was
ramming a fresh magazine home, he heard Richardson telling him to
make a dash for the jeep; Brearton had succeeded in turning it around,

and the Frenchman was working the rear gun with Richardson beside him, handing him magazines. Harrison did as he was told, and managed to scramble into the vacant front seat as the vehicle began to move, out of the square and away from the village, to disappear into the woods.

They returned to the campsite in the forest without further incident, and later, when the *maquisards* brought word that the Germans had left, Richardson returned to Les Ormes to find out what had happened. There was no explanation as to why a detachment of *Waffen-SS* had turned up there and suddenly begun burning houses and shooting people, though there was speculation that it was done as a reprisal for the *maquisards'* activities of the previous few days. Two Les Ormais had been shot and killed before Harrison and his men arrived on the scene, but eighteen more, earmarked for execution, had managed to escape in the confusion. The body of L/Cpl James Hall had been laid out in the church, and he was later buried in the village's cemetery. The Germans had taken their dead and wounded, which reports put at around sixty, with them, leaving behind three burnt-out vehicles. Harrison was later awarded the Military Cross in recognition of his actions. The death of one British soldier was perhaps a small enough price to pay to save the lives of eighteen, but at the time that was little consolation to Derrick Harrison, who was further depressed at 'feeling something less than useless' with two injured hands (in fact, the injury to his right hand was superficial, and did no lasting damage), and he was reflecting on his misfortune that evening when a report of a large convoy close at hand reached the camp, and two jeeps were dispatched to check it out.

Much to everyone's disappointment there was no sound of gunfire, and eventually the vehicles could be heard returning, but to Harrison's amazement, not two but twenty jeeps, with a German staff car carrying Major Tony Marsh at their head, appeared down the narrow track through the trees and undergrowth. When the Transfigure airborne landing was cancelled, the orders for his two-troop contingent had been hastily rewritten, and instead of mounting Operations Ponting and Mappin he was despatched directly to the Kipling base; he had managed to procure enough Dakota aircraft to carry twenty jeeps and half his personnel, and had been deposited at Rennes on 19 August. The column had made its way through the crumbling German front with little trouble, save to a couple of ragged German convoys which it met and scattered; hence the staff car and a gaggle of disoriented prisoners.

On 27 August, Mayne and Melot returned to the Morvan, this time in company with Tony Marsh. It appears that Mayne quickly came to the realisation that Houndsworth's men were nearing the end of their usefulness through general fatigue, and just at a time when they would need to be at their most alert if they were simply to survive, let alone harass the ever more numerous retreating German forces to the best of their ability. The best course of action, he decided, would be for most of Marsh's force to replace Fraser's in the Morvan, leaving behind a small rump under Capt Davis to operate as a local security force, and for A Squadron to be evacuated.

Tony Marsh returned to the Kipling base on 29 August, waited for the rest of the squadron to arrive from Orléans and then retraced his steps towards Chalaux with the majority of the men and vehicles, leaving Capt Davis, thirty-four men and twelve vehicles behind. They travelled in groups, and by separate routes, some looping around to the west as far as the line of the Loire. The element Harrison led narrowly missed a confrontation with a German convoy near Clammecy, a known hotspot. On 1 September, a subaltern, Peter Goddard, who had volunteered for 2 SAS from a service corps, was despatched back along the route to the Kipling base to recover a jeep trailer which had become unserviceable. He got as far as the small town of Tannay, south-east of Clammecy, where he encountered a party of *maquisards* preparing an ambush; they asked for his assistance, and he agreed. His two jeeps, it was decided, would conceal themselves near a crossroads, with the partisans in an overwatch position on the hillside above. It seems, in fact, that the Germans were already at the crossroads, and that the 'small convoy' contained two truck-mounted semi-automatic 3.7cm Flak 36 light anti-aircraft/anti-tank guns, which could expend a six-round ammunition clip in just a few seconds. Goddard stopped the jeeps short of the objective, and went to reconnoitre on foot.

By Harrison's account (he heard the story from SM Lilley, who was present; Major Marsh's after-action report supports the broad details), Goddard reappeared, dismounted a single Vickers K from one of the jeeps and disappeared again, followed by the sergeant-major. The first Flak truck was taken completely by surprise, Goddard killing or wounding its occupants with machine-gun fire from the hip (no mean feat in itself with a Vickers K) and then tossing in a grenade. The second truck was a different matter, of course; as Goddard turned his attention to it, it opened fire. Goddard threw himself in the ditch and then, some moments later re-emerged and made a run for the jeep. He was hit repeatedly before he turned the corner. Of the *maquisards* who were supposed to have been in a covering position, there was no sign;

they had melted away at the first sign of trouble.

The original intention seems to have been for the operational strategy in the Morvan to have changed dramatically, from one which was essentially static in nature, with established locations acting as bases for small raiding parties, to something much more fluid, with 'flying columns' of armed jeeps pursuing and harrying retreating enemy forces, constantly threatening their security and reducing any potential they might have had for inflicting damage, death and destruction on the communities through which they were passing. In fact, by the time C Squadron had established itself in the Morvan, and A Squadron had left, in the first week of September, the German presence in the area was already becoming very patchy, and in real terms the replacements were less effective than Bill Fraser's squadron had been, despite being both considerably better equipped and fresher, although that is in no sense a criticism of them as a fighting force. On the few occasions on which patrols did find themselves in set-piece firefights, usually against larger German formations (once after being tricked into believing that the troops in question actually wished to surrender) they acquitted themselves well; the most significant single incident occurred when a patrol led by Lt Mycock played an important role in securing the surrender of the German garrison at Autun, which had been swelled by stragglers until it numbered some thousands of men.

As the equinox approached and summer gave way to autumn, weather conditions began to deteriorate and the frequency of successful resupply flights decreased dramatically, the primary result of which was an acute shortage of petrol. Meaningful patrolling was actually impossible between 9 September and 23 September, when the RAF flew a daylight resupply mission, simply because fuel was in such short supply, and only reconnaissance missions were mounted. Before the end of the month C Squadron was pulled out and sent to Cosne-sur-Loire, which was by then well within liberated territory, for a period of rest and recuperation and was then ordered to Brussels to refit before being recommitted to action in Holland, where it spent the winter operating alongside Field Security Units; it returned to the UK in March of 1945. With C Squadron's withdrawal from the Morvan, 1 SAS's operations in France came to an end.

Left to its own devices, Captain Davis' smaller contingent was in action from the outset. On 29 August Davis himself led a patrol which got off to a bad start when one of the jeeps overturned, injuring both occupants and necessitating the detachment of a second car. The remaining vehicles continued towards the objective, heavy enemy traffic on the La Charité–Clamecy road. The next morning an ambush was sprung, perhaps a little prematurely, but a map-case taken from a captured staff car revealed that the enemy column was made up of two infantry companies supported by machine-gun, anti-tank and light anti-aircraft sections. Both SAS and German forces withdrew to regroup, and in the early evening Davis re-engaged when the enemy column, composed of 5-ton lorries, three of them towing light anti-aircraft guns, civilian cars and scout cars, stopped short of Nannay, strafing with a dozen Vickers Ks and expending around 4,000 rounds of ammunition. Davis described the German resistance as 'very strong and accurate', three of the trucks dropping their sides to reveal 2cm cannon to add to effective MG and light mortar fire. When enemy infantry showed signs of outflanking them, the SAS party broke off the engagement, being forced to leave behind two jeeps which had been disabled in the firefight, regrouping first in the Forêt de Donzy and later in the village of the same name. Reports from the *Maquis* later indicated that the column, which was forced to return to La Charité, had lost between thirty and forty men killed and twice that number wounded, and that fifteen of their vehicles had been towed away from the scene, three of them burned out.

Within a week, German activity had virtually ceased in the area, and on 9 September the party moved to near St Amand-en-Puisaye, some twenty kilometres north-east of Cosne-sur-Loire, and patrolled on both sides of the river. Hearing reports of the imminent arrival of the Elster column (q.v.) Davis pushed forward into its path, and on 13 September linked up with Pierre Bourgoin, by now promoted to lieutenant-colonel, who requested that he assist the men of 4 French Para in ensuring that there were no incidents between the (still-armed) Germans and FFI elements from Bourges. From then on, Davis's detachment manned roadblocks and provided security patrols until it, too, was ordered to Brussels to refit.

By the time Kipling main force had become effective, towards the end of August, the Allied invasion of Normandy had succeeded and any danger of effective counter-attack was past; the German forces which remained at liberty in central and southern France had one main objective: to retreat towards the Reich as quickly as possible and attempt to regroup behind the last natural barriers, the rivers and the mountain ranges which form a natural frontier. Naturally enough, the best-led, best-trained units – the elite of the *Wehrmacht* and the *Waffen-SS* – were doing so in relatively good order, maintaining flank security as they went and, where necessary, fighting their way through the partisan rising with few real problems. The picture was far less clear, and far less positive, however, for second-line units like the occupation forces. These units had lost the habits of combat and on occasion got badly mauled by the *maquisards* as they made their way eastward across France; indeed, some were to surrender to regional leaders of the FFI en masse rather than risk further loss of life. Those German formations which elected to stay put generally fared little better – though there were exceptions; the Lorient, St-Nazaire and La Rochelle garrisons, for example, held out right to the end of the war – and many, such as the garrison at Gap, put up no fight at all, surrendering to the Resistance and being herded into the local cinema, where they were placed in the custody of two young men armed with rifles.

The overall picture was one of confusion bordering on chaos, with local Resistance elements exercising only very limited control. They shared the broad agenda of liberating France as rapidly as possible, certainly, but that was as far as common cause went; under such circumstances the support network which had been so important to Operation Houndsworth, for example, largely disappeared, and after a short period of initial euphoria, when parachutists in British uniforms, driving around the countryside in jeeps flying the Union Jack, were routinely fêted, the SAS parties found themselves largely ignored, overtaken by events and the tide of war.

Part Three
2 SAS

DEFOE

As we have noted, 2 SAS returned to the UK from North Africa only in March of 1944 and thus found itself a long way behind its (British) sister-regiment in the queue to make up its numbers; most of the potential recruits with combat experience had already joined 1 SAS and no less than 140 of the men who joined 2 SAS during 1944 had never previously seen action of any kind. The Regiment had also gone through the upheaval of losing its original commanding officer, Bill Stirling, and while his replacement, Brian Franks, was held in high esteem, the transition caused an additional delay. As a result, 2 SAS was not committed to the battle to liberate France until it was already some six weeks old, and that inevitably reduced the regiment's effectiveness. This reduction was not attributable to any shortcomings of its own in terms of battle-preparedness or skill-at-arms, but rather to the changing nature of the battle itself; we should remember that 1 SAS's Operation Kipling, inserted in mid-August, was also to achieve very little, and for the same reason.

The first operation 2 SAS undertook apparently fell victim to the poor organisation at Moor Park which Brian Franks was later to criticise most volubly, but fundamentally it was flawed as a result of it having been conceived outside the Brigade and foisted upon it. Operation Defoe was notionally tasked with reconnaissance in depth behind enemy lines in the Argentan area of southern Normandy, adjacent to the area into which the small Operation Haft team from 1 SAS had been inserted some ten days earlier. Like Haft, its task was to pass back targeting information to be used in planning air strikes and gather tactical intelligence which would assist in the break-out from the beachhead. On 19 July, a two-section party, twenty-two men – which seems an excessive number given the task and the circumstances, and bearing in mind that the Haft party had numbered just seven – under Capt McGibbon-Lewis and Lt Silly, was flown in to an LZ near the 2nd

Army HQ, well to the north of its designated operational area, where it was met with blank looks, the officer who had requested its presence, Col Vernon, the GSO 1 (Operations), having been transferred the previous day, leaving no warning of its arrival. (2nd Army, we may note, was still fully engaged in Operation Goodwood, the envelopment of Caen and the offensive against German armour to the south and east of the city, which had been launched just the day before; it is doubtful whether anyone at HQ had much time for, or interest in, a small party of specialist soldiers which had turned up unexpectedly.)

Almost incredibly, for the next four weeks the party was left largely to its own devices, contributing little to the battle for Normandy which was going on around them, although Lewis sent out small parties under all four of his subalterns, 'for experience', but also to try to find a place where they could cross the lines. Results were patchy. The first party, led by Lt Dick, attached itself to XII Corps. Dick mounted four reconnaissance patrols, unfortunately losing a man, Tpr James Wilkinson, to a booby trap, and concluded that it would be impossible to penetrate into German-held territory in that sector; Lewis agreed when he came to see for himself. Next, Lt Colchester took a party to operate with the Inns of Court Regiment in VIII Corps, with similar results. Lt Silly did manage to find gainful employment of a sort, acting as a local reconnaissance element for Richie's XII Corps, his party mounted on a pair of armoured cars alongside the Blues and Royals, while Lt Dennison was despatched to the American sector, attached to the 90th Infantry Division and the French 2nd Armoured Division. Dennison and two men eventually penetrated into German-held territory, and were soon surrounded. Dennison and Cpl Bovio evaded (Tpr Smithson was captured but later managed to escape and made his way back to the 90th Division) at the cost of their borrowed vehicle, and were later able to identify a well-camouflaged mobile column made up of a score of self-propelled guns, ten petrol tankers, fifty heavy trucks and many smaller vehicles. Dennison borrowed a bicycle and pedalled off to an American outpost; messages were passed and an armoured car unit arrived and called up close air support. Within forty-five minutes of the last vehicle passing Dennison's position, the column was virtually destroyed.

Eventually, on 12 August, someone at 2nd Army finally devised a mission: a short-duration reconnaissance expedition to report on enemy troop movements in the triangle formed by the towns of Flers, Falaise and Argentan, which lay directly in the path of Patton's 3rd Army as it cut through the German rear in a vast encircling movement from the west. Lewis commanded the mission, known as Swan, himself, with Colchester as his second. It finally got under way on 15 August, three days after the Americans reached Argentan and two days before Crerar's 1st Canadian Army took Falaise; thus, by the time it got into its operational sector, it was in the middle of the most important concentration of German combat troops in Europe. Meaningful reconnaissance was both out of the question and largely redundant, for the battle was fluid and continuous right across the Falaise Pocket, as it would come to be called, and 'we were shelled, mortared, bombed and almost every [sort of] lethal weapon was directed against us', Lewis said in his report. By 19 August, Canadian II Corps and US XV Corps were little more than a mile apart at its eastern extremity, and linked up the next day, cutting off many German units up to divisional size and bringing the Battle of Normandy to a close. Operation Swan terminated on 23 August, and Lewis and his men were soon back at 2nd Army HQ, by now brought up to Villers-Bocage, negotiating a ride back to the UK.

GAFF

The second operation mounted by 2 SAS, Operation Gaff, had a sin-gular aim: the capture or assassination of the commander of all German forces in an area which stretched from Denmark to the Bay of Biscay, Field-Marshal Erwin Rommel. It was quite atypical of the SAS combat missions mounted in occupied France and more reminiscent of the sort of 'stunt' one of the private armies might have undertaken two or three years earlier – a return to a modus operandi which the SAS had foregone in its search for a new and more valid strategic identity. This is not to suggest that the capture or assassination of an unique enemy asset such as Erwin Rommel was perceived to be does not have a certain merit, but the effect would have been largely pyrrhic and good only for propaganda; and we should bear in mind that it would almost certainly have been the signal for massive reprisals, probably on a par with those taken for the assassination of Reinhard Heydrich in Prague, which cost the lives of perhaps 5,000 Czechs.

The operation was got up in response to intelligence which originated many hundreds of kilometres away from the target area. One of the *maquisards* in the Morvan, Jean Lebaudy, who used the name Lemaitre and was also apparently known to some as Defors, was acting as assistant to Jim Hutchinson (q.v.), the Jedburgh-turned-Inter-Allied Missionary who was co-located with the Houndsworth party. Lebaudy had moved to the area from Paris; his family was extremely wealthy, and as well as a town house on the fashionable Avenue Foch, owned a large 16th-century château in the village of Rosny-sur-Seine, near Mantes-la-Jolie, to the west of the capital. This large country house had been requisitioned by the German occupying forces soon after the fall of France, as had several other similar properties in the area. In early July a group of workers from the Rosny estate joined Lebaudy in the Morvan, bringing with them the news that one of the neighbouring châteaux, also requisitioned, at La Roche-Guyon, was occupied by Erwin Rommel following his appointment to command the forces defending the Channel coast.

Now, Bill Fraser, the officer commanding Operation Houndsworth, had a particular personal interest in the Desert Fox. While serving with 11 Commando in North Africa, after the disbandment of Layforce and prior to joining L Detachment, he had played a (minor) part in an earlier operation aimed at killing or capturing Rommel at his head-quarters in Benghazi. His commanding officer, Lt-Col Geoffrey Keyes (son of Sir Roger Keyes VC, the first Director of Combined Opera-tions), died during this raid (in the course of which he, too, won a posthumous Victoria Cross); to him, there was something serendipi-tous about the information Lebaudy brought, and by the nature of the signal he addressed to SAS Brigade HQ in which he passed it on, he clearly felt that he had a right to another crack at the Field Marshal, even though the chances of him and the necessary small team being able to make the 400-kilometre journey from the Morvan to Mantes successfully at that juncture were extremely remote. In the event – and hardly surprisingly – the decision was that while Rommel was certainly a worthwhile target, the operation in question should be mounted from the UK. Fraser did not give in easily – with many men who had intimate knowledge of the area available to him, he argued, he was the logical choice to run such a mission – but in the face of a blank refusal from Rory McLeod, give in he eventually did, and the mission was awarded (nominally, at least; four of its six participants came from the ranks of 3 French Para) to 2 SAS. In his book *That Drug Danger*, Sir James Hutchinson was to claim the credit for developing the intelligence and says that he approached Fraser with the outline plan to kidnap Rommel; since Lebaudy was 'his' man, that may well have been the case, though equally, the signals between the Morvan SAS base and Moor Park were initiated by Fraser in unequivocal terms. An irregular larding of 'facts' inconsistent with those from other sources found in Hutchinson's book does not encourage one to believe his account unquestioningly.

Gaff's leader, it was decided, would be a twenty-four-year-old Franco-American who had enlisted in the British Army under the name of Jack William Lee (he is reported also to have used the Christian name Michael; in his book *Winged Dagger* Roy Farran calls him 'Ramon Lee', and portrays him as a hot-head and not entirely trustworthy, as we shall see when we look at Operation Wallace, the official report of which speaks of him being 'attached [to 2 SAS] from the French squadron'. In his rather bald after-action report on Operation Gaff he signs himself 'SW Lee'). Born Raymond Couraud, he is said to have joined the French *Légion Etrangère* in 1938 and fought with distinction in Norway in 1940, making his way to Britain after the fall of France and taking part in the St-Nazaire raid in the spring of 1942 before transferring to 62 Commando and thence to 2 SAS. Now with the rank of captain, and with a reputation as an effective sniper and unconventional fighter (and with a Military Cross to his credit), speaking French fluently as well as some German, Lee was selected as the operation's commander. He chose a member of 3 SAS, *Sous-Lieutenant* Robert Raillard or Roillard, as his second-in-command and three others from 3 SAS – all of them said to be ex-legionnaires: a sergeant of German origin named Mark or Marx, a Russian named Fedossof and a third Frenchman named Durban (certainly a *nom de guerre*) – together with an English lance-corporal named Moore to be the sixth member of the small group.

The Gaff party was inserted on the night of 25 July, dropping blind from an Albermarle on to an unmarked DZ near St-Rémy-les-Chevreuse, between Chartres and Rambouillet. The six men landed safely, but three leg bags were destroyed on landing, and they could find no sign of the container dropped with them, which held such useful equipment as the snipers' rifles they were supposed to have used in the attempt of Rommel's life, as well as more mundane items such as rations and sleeping bags. Nothing daunted, the six men began to make their way the forty or so kilometres northward towards the valley of the Seine, but within twenty-four hours Lee was incapacitated and the party was forced to lay up for some days. Reports attribute the cause to a bout of malaria; Lee's report makes no mention of malaria, but says he became ill after he 'ate plastic', presumably plastic explosive – though why he would do such a thing is not made clear – and cured himself by drinking six gallons of milk. On 28 July the men learned that 'Rommel had been got' (he had been seriously wounded, in fact, suffering multiple skull fractures, among other things, some eleven days previously, when RAF fighter-bombers strafed his staff car) and that changed the situation.

With much of the urgency gone, Lee made a new operational plan, electing to mount *ad hoc* ambush and sabotage operations directed at the busy rail and road routes up and down the lower Seine valley; though never well supplied with material, the party managed to mount two successful attacks on trains, halting them and later seeing them attacked by Allied aircraft, and also shot up and bombed vehicles,

On the night of 9 August, the Dakota which evacuated the last elements of the Bulbasket party brought an officer and nine ORs from 3 SAS to bring the Moses party up to full strength. (*Photographs are all from the author's collection*)

A party from 4 SAS photographed, probably in Rennes, after the conclusion of operations in Brittany. The one-armed Cmdt Pierre Burgoin, the battalion's CO, stands hatless beside the driver.

The D Squadron Sergeant-Major, 'Gentleman Jim' Almonds, one of the L Detachment originals, pictured here at the twin Vickers Ks of a jeep dropped to the Operation Gain party in the Forêt d'Orléans.

Capt Ian Fenwick, Operation Gain's CO, at the wheel of the same jeep; early-model vehicles like this offered no protection whatsoever but had impressive firepower.

John Tonkin, Twm Stephens and Richard Crisp pictured just before Stephens set off to cycle the sixty kilometres to reconnoitre the railway sidings at Châtellerault.

Some of the ill-fated Bulbasket party in the days before the raid on the Verrières forest, during which most were captured.

Sgt Johnnie Holmes, seated in shirt-sleeves, and Lt Richard Crisp with two B Squadron troopers, photographed in the Verrières forest just days before the raid on the campsite there.

Some of the survivors of the Verrières forest raid, plus two American airmen, gathered around the Bulbasket party's sole remaining jeep.

Right Lt David Dane and Capt John Tonkin. The latter carries a rare long-barrelled P'o8 Artillery-model Luger pistol, while Dane contents himself with a pair of M1911 Colts.

Below The two jeeps from the Kipling party which took part in the fire-fight at Les Ormes. Left to right: Capt Harrison, Curly Hall, Lt Richardson and Tpr Brearton.

A jeep stowed in the bomb-bay of a Handley-Page Halifax; the protective pans were designed to deform on impact to absorb some of the shock of landing.

A split-second after release, the valise containing the four parachutes has just been pulled free of its stowage in the car's back seat space.

The process was not fool-proof; roughly half the jeeps dropped to SAS parties in France finished up like this one.

Later-model jeeps featured an armoured shield before the radiator and bullet-proof glass screens for the driver and front gunner, as well as other modifications.

Capt Alex Muirhead, who led A Squadron,
1 SAS's 2 Troop in the Morvan hills during Operation Houndsworth.

destroying perhaps seven trucks and a number of light vehicles including at least one staff car. This latter seemingly contained a senior officer, and Lee tracked him to his headquarters at Monts and set up an assault on it. His party had to withdraw when the alarm was raised, but not before Sgt Mark had called out some orders in German, which set the defenders to firing at each other. Lee was told the next day that there had been a dozen fatalities.

By 12 August, the party was seriously short of ammunition and ordnance, and Lee left the others at the base they had established at a farm named St-Cyr-Rouge near Beynes, and set off to contact the American forces which were known to be approaching from the west. Dressed in the uniform of a *gendarme* and mounted on a bicycle, he passed through the American lines at Brou, near Chartres, and was eventually brought to Patton's 3rd Army Headquarters. The information he brought with him concerning enemy dispositions was of little interest, Lee himself was treated with scant respect, and was placed on a flight back to the UK. The other members of the party stayed in place until they were overrun by American forces some ten days later. Lee tells us in his report that it was his wish to be reinserted on 19 August with an additional twenty men and two jeeps, to establish five five-man ambush and sabotage parties in an arc around the west side of Paris; this was very close to the plan developed for Operation Trueform (q.v.), but it is unlikely that Lee had a hand in this. In the event he was not to return to the Seine Valley, but was to take part in Operation Wallace instead.

Some observers have held up Operation Gaff as an example of how small, dedicated parties of SAS parachutists, speaking the local language fluently, could have had an impact on affairs in Occupied France after D-Day out of all proportion to the resources required to insert them and without requiring vast technical back-up. This, they say, should have been the pattern for all SAS operations in the theatre. Frankly, that suggestion begs the question of where enough men with such language skills (not to mention the required high level of training and self-motivation) were to be found – it had proved difficult enough to recruit French-speaking Jedburghs, after all – and ignores the fact that they would indeed have required regular resupply. The Gaff party obtained its food from local people, but it was lucky to be able to do so; it could not, however, obtain ammunition and ordnance from partisan sources. Most *maquisards* were intent on keeping such arms and munitions as they had to themselves, and not sharing them with interlopers, and in this instance it is clear from Lee's account and those of the

Trueform parties which operated in the area later that the *maquisard* groups in this area actually had very little in the way of armament anyway. Gaff was essentially a *coup de main* operation which changed tack in mid-course. The only way to sustain an operation like that in the longer term would have called for the establishment of a semi-permanent base to which the raiding party – or parties – could return for resupply, and this, of course, is exactly how the conventional 'Phase One' operations were organised.

DUNHILL

Another 2 SAS reconnaissance mission into the greater Normandy battlefield area left the United Kingdom on the night of 3 August, but this time, seemingly thanks to a complete lack of co-ordination with 21 Army Group's headquarters in the field, it was to be dropped in an area where effective German resistance had already virtually ceased, and by the time it had collected itself and regrouped there was simply nothing for it to do. Dunhill was the largest operation the British component of the SAS Brigade mounted on the western edge of the Normandy battlefield; a total of fifty-nine men under Captain Greville Bell, plus a Phantom party, were dropped into the area between Rennes and Laval, but arrived only hours before the spearhead armoured forces of the US 3rd Army which had that very day liberated Rennes. Four of the five sticks dropped were actually inside Allied-held territory before they had spent twenty-four hours in France. The only useful purpose Dunhill's participants served was in assisting downed Allied airmen, following a contact made with Airey Neave of MI9 at Le Mans on 12 August. The following day the party entered the Forêt de Fréteval, where the airmen were concentrated, in a convoy made up of four buses, three jeeps and three civilian cars, dropping off small road-watching and security parties along the way. At the forest campsite it met up with Debefre's Belgians and together they escorted the evaders to safety. On 17 August Operation Dunhill was officially terminated, and the men made their way back to the UK, arriving at Newhaven on 20 August.

That the lack of success achieved by Operation Dunhill was brought about largely (or even solely) by its late insertion is, of course, impossible to demonstrate. Greville Bell had this to say: 'Everyone with me made a great effort to save this operation from being completely valueless, but as far as offensive operations go we could do little as the Germans either avoided us or moved too fast.'

TRUEFORM

Gaff was the precursor to a much bigger and more orthodox affair launched in the same general area, the lower Seine valley. This operation, Trueform, was mounted jointly by 2 SAS and the Belgians of 5 SAS (plus a small contingent from 1 SAS took part, too, though there is no clear indication why), inserted into the area between the Seine and the much smaller River Risle to the south, and was tasked with disrupting road and rail traffic and destroying fuel dumps. In all, the best part of a squadron was involved, and their endeavours met with some success largely, it is suggested, because the German forces retreating through the area were more interested in saving their skins than they were in searching out parachutists.

Operation Instruction No. 43 which defined Trueform, issued only twenty-four hours before the first parties were inserted, states that it was to be carried out by ten all-ranks from 1 SAS, forty all-ranks from 2 SAS and sixty-two all-ranks from 5 SAS, and that despite the Belgians being in the majority, it was to be commanded (from the UK) by Brian Franks, the CO of 2 SAS. The 112 men who were to mount the operation were to be inserted on the nights of 16 and 17 August at a dozen different locations and then split up into approximately twenty-five separate parties, and operate for a maximum of three weeks, by which time it was confidently expected that the area in question would have been overrun by Allied forces swarming out of Normandy. In fact, there seems to have been some to-ing and fro-ing between parties when individuals or small groups stumbled across one another in what was to prove a small operational area. It seems that the leader of each section submitted an after-action report, as did the leaders of some of the three- to six-man teams (and even some men who were separated from the others and operated individually), but not all have survived; as a result the overall picture is patchy and unclear. Those that have survived are fairly consistent, however, and we can thus make up a reasonable composite picture of the conditions under which the operation proceeded.

The area between the Seine and the Risle was stiff with Germans retreating in haste but in relatively good order despite being very short both of food and of fuel; time after time SAS personnel found themselves in close proximity to German troops, sometimes occupying the same patch of woodland, sometimes even the same house. It may well be true that in general the Germans were more interested in evacuation than they were in seeking out Allied parachutists, but that did not prevent them from patrolling offensively; thus, the environment in which the SAS parties operated was troubled and difficult, but at the same time, the degree of disruption inherent in any mass retreat worked in their favour, for they could be fairly sure that the priority for any German unit they did attack would be to clear the area, rather than to stay and search for the culprits. Each of the parties was allotted a fairly small area adjacent to the DZ on which it landed, and thus was able, theoretically at least, to go into action almost immediately. The prime targets were to have been fuel tankers and fuel dumps, but it soon became clear that these were few and far between, and that the German convoys which had been able to obtain a supply of fuel carried it with them. All parties reported heavy German reliance on horse-drawn transport, particularly for those infantrymen who were not forced to march, and that such petrol as was available was being reserved for fighting vehicles and artillery tractors. In the event, the Trueform parties had to content themselves with targets-of-opportunity, scattering diminutive tyre-burster mines on roads, bombing and shooting up vehicles travelling alone or stopped at the roadside, occasionally destroying supply dumps and sometimes even attempting conventional ambushes – Corporal Hughes and his small party captured a truck and the 8.8cm gun it was towing, and took a dozen prisoners, in this way, but that was a rare occurrence.

In the absence of a comprehensive collection of after-action reports, it is impossible to make any sort of assessment of the results obtained by Operation Trueform, but there is nothing to indicate that any of the parties met with any major success. If anything, there were suggestions that the men were undertrained, and that experienced personnel would have been more effective, and there was considerable criticism of the local *résistants*' will to fight. ('22nd August – It rained all day and night and the French ratted at the last moment. There was no cover from the rain but that was no excuse. My men were also browned off and unwilling. It was disappointing as the road was full of German traffic,' wrote

Capt Holland in his report.) The SAS Brigade's War Diary provides very little information, but suggests that 101 all-ranks were actually dropped over the two nights, on to six DZs, and goes on: 'Conditions were unsatisfactory for successful operations owing to the lack of accurate information about the enemy; the confused state of the battle and the need to operate immediately on arrival. The parties operated with moderate success for 4 or 5 days until reached by Allied forces. It is remarkable that only two men were missing from the operation.' Those two were Tpr Harold Erlis, killed apparently after having been taken prisoner on 19 August, and Sapper Thomas Bintley, attached from the Royal Engineers as a demolition expert, who died of wounds he received on 20 August, though two reports make mention of the capture of a Capt Baillie in the early hours of 23 August.

HARDY AND WALLACE

Up until the last week of July, the majority of 2 SAS's troopers were still unemployed, and remained at the training base in Scotland, but that was about to change, albeit slowly, with the commencement of Operation Hardy, the precursor to the insertion of the 'flying column' of armed jeeps which would mount Operation Wallace. We have already encountered the Operation Hardy advance party, under the command of Capt Grant Hibbert, dropping into the Houndsworth area on the night of 26 July. Three Halifax aircraft, each carrying a jeep and three men, left Tarrant Rushton that night; two of the sticks and one vehicle (the other's parachutes failed) landed safely at a DZ used by Alex Muirhead's troop, and moved off to the HQ camp the following day, where they met up with the third stick, which also lost its jeep when it was inserted that night. Two more jeeps were written off the next night but one, but replacements were eventually dropped successfully on the night of 30 July, and the Hardy party departed thirty-six hours later. During this establishment phase the operation was actually known as 'Laurel', but the name seems not to have stuck; 'Hardy' was to have been the follow-on offensive operation, but Roy Farran, the commanding officer, seems to have preferred 'Wallace', which was the name of *his* movement into the operational area.

It had originally been the intention to set up a base on the Plateau de Langres, fifty or so kilometres north-west of Dijon in the direction of Nancy, astride the N19 which runs roughly west–east from Troyes to Vesoul and on to Belfort, and which would thus be an important route between France and Germany. In the event, the base was to be located some twenty-five kilometres further west, in the Forêt de Châtillon, which was a more desirable area, being solid woodland for miles in all directions, criss-crossed with tracks passable to jeeps but with few roads and fewer villages. Capt Hibbert and his men were tasked with setting up a secure supply dump for an operation which was to follow and gathering intelligence about enemy activity in the area round about.

When it came time to leave the Morvan, Hibbert, briefed at length by Bill Fraser, and with his SSM, Reg Seekings, as a guide, proceeded cautiously – among other dangers, there were two *Routes Nationales*, including the very busy N6 with its almost-constant stream of German vehicles, to be crossed – to Johnny Wiseman's base near Rolle, where the party waited for a Frenchman who had been 'laid on' to guide them further and never materialised; it was the morning of 5 August before the party arrived, without incident, in what was to be its operational area. Reconnaissance patrols started the next day.

Hibbert's party of nine was brought up to a total of nineteen when Lt Robertson and his section were parachuted in on the night of 8 August, and on 12 August the enlarged party which had by now made contact with effective *maquisard* bands including a large one at Aignay-le-Duc, from which it obtained the use of a truck, moved a few kilometres south-west, and three nights later was brought up to thirty with the arrival of Sgt Robinson and his section. (In fact, it actually numbered thirty-five by this time, having collected evaders in the shape of one American and four British aircrew.) Five more men (one of whom, Capt Fleetwood-Hesketh, worked for the Political Warfare Executive but was attached to SAS) were dropped on the night of 17 August, together with twenty-five containers, by which time the party had moved again, to the vicinity of Gurgy-le-Château.

That same day, a large partisan force ambushed a sizeable German column moving along a road in the direction of Langres. Despite the presence of tanks and armoured cars, the *maquisards* managed to capture two half-track personnel carriers, but the Germans retaliated by taking a dozen Frenchmen from the nearest village, Recey-sur-Ource. The next day the hostages were exchanged for the vehicles, but afraid that this action would bring increased German activity, and warned that their position had likely already been compromised, the Hardy party moved again on 19 August and the following night received three more men and another large consignment of supplies. On 21 August two jeeps laid an ambush on a road known to be frequented by German vehicles, destroying two trucks and killing or wounding some thirty Germans without loss, and destroyed another truck the next day. On 23 August three jeeps carrying men who were to patrol on foot arrived in the village of Giey-sur-Aujon at the same time as a party of Russian conscripts, much to the surprise of both parties. A brief and rather one-sided firefight ensued before the Russians disengaged and ran for their lives. That night a seven-man party under Lt Pinci was parachuted in, together with yet more containers.

The next day, a month after its advance party had arrived in the Morvan, Hardy was joined by the depleted Wallace party, under the command of Major Roy Farran, after what had proved to be a rapid but arduous and costly journey halfway across France, much of it through territory still occupied by the Germans.

Roy Farran, in his book *Winged Dagger*, tells how he was hospitalised with a complication to an earlier leg wound (and then went down with a bout of malaria, contracted during 2 SAS's formative period in Algeria) at the end of July 1944, and effectively absented himself without leave, knowing that the Fortnum party as it then was, made up of the remaining elements of his squadron, was making its preparations to be transported to France, and determined to rejoin it. The original insertion plan called for a glider-borne landing in conjunction with Operation Transfigure (q.v.), and through the night of 17 August the men of the SAS struggled to load their vehicles on to Horsa gliders, one vehicle and its three-man crew per aircraft (it was a struggle; the Horsa had been designed to take no vehicle larger than a motorcycle combination, and the jeep was a very tight squeeze indeed), only to learn the following morning, just after embarkation was complete, that Transfigure had been cancelled. Fortnum, however, had not, but instead had been hastily trimmed down and transformed into Wallace, and so the vehicles had to be off-loaded as quickly as possible and reinstalled aboard a fleet of Dakota aircraft (no easy task, either), to be transported to the airport at Rennes, where one runway had been made serviceable. The airlift was undertaken by 46 Group, RAF Transport Command, from Brize Norton; eighteen of the aircraft landed safely, the other two were forced to return to base by a severe storm. The jeeps and crews they carried were delivered the following day, and caught up with the rest of the column that night.

The Dakotas landed at Rennes during the afternoon of 19 August; the jeeps leagured at Vitre that night and made contact with Paddy Mayne at Le Mans the next morning. Mayne promised to supply them with a guide to take them to the Gain base, north of Orléans, but the man never showed up, and eventually the column found its own way, missing the Gain party but leaguering that night in American positions north of the city; by the following night Farran and his men had crossed into enemy-occupied territory, with 250 kilometres behind them and a similar distance still to go. Travelling by day initially, they stuck to tracks through the Forêt d'Orléans for the most part, at least as far as Les Bordes, where, after having been fêted as liberators by the local population, they emerged upon a main road which parallels the Loire. From here on, the journey got riskier and even though the party stuck to the most minor of minor roads, there were always more major highways to be crossed, and given the weight of traffic, that often posed a problem. The textbook solution was to select a crossing point at which there was a clear view of the road for some distance on either side, deploy the two lead jeeps to cover it and then hurry the entire column across at top speed, the covering jeeps to tail on behind. Crossing the main road from Montargis south to Briare was the first test of the system, and it broke down; the covering jeeps' crews misunderstood their instructions, failed to tail onto the column, and stayed in their overwatch position for some hours. Sgt Forster and L/Cpl Bird and their drivers were to rejoin the squadron in the Forêt de Châtillon after an epic journey, during the course of which one jeep collided with a German staff car, the occupants of which were promptly despatched. They met up with Lt Carpendale, who had become separated from the main party at Villaines-les-Prévôtes (q.v.), in Auxerre, and continued together.

The night of 21 August was spent in the Forêt de Dracy (apparently unknown to Farran and his men, they were only a scant few kilometres away from the Kipling base), and much of the next day was spent resting and reconnoitring the area, Farran having decided to switch over to evening movement, a decision he was soon to regret since the majority of German movements were taking place then too, thanks to the ceaseless activity of Allied fighter-bombers during the daylight hours. The party now split into three components with Capt Lee, who had returned from Operation Gaff only days before Wallace had been initiated, in command of a section of five vehicles, then a section of eight under Farran, and with Lt David Leigh in command of another section of six bringing up the rear. In the early evening it continued its way eastward. Farran ordered a thirty-minute gap left between sections; all would set out to follow the same route, but would be at liberty to divert from it at need. Above all, Farran ordered, the sections were to put security first, moving carefully and sending out a reconnaissance party if there was any doubt at all whether the route ahead was clear. He had reckoned without what he called Capt Lee's 'Latin temperament' and what others might describe as hot-headed disregard for basic safety precautions.

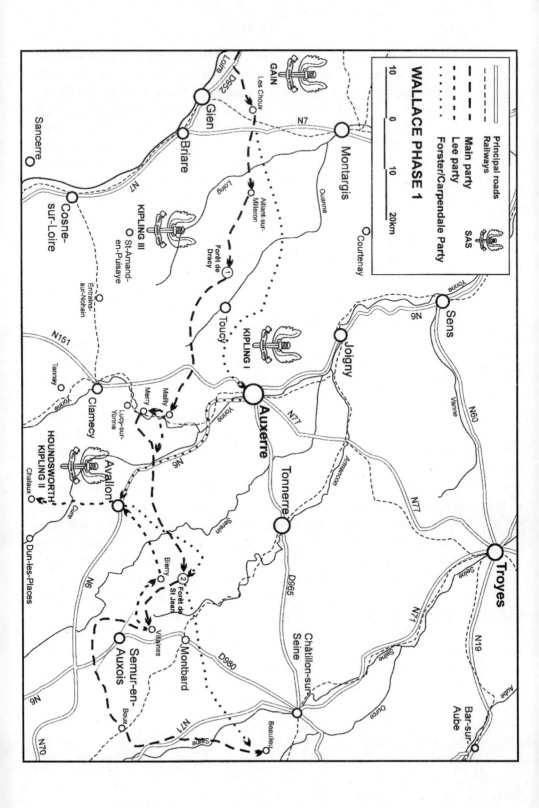

It is not clear at what time Lee's section reached the River Yonne at Mailly-le-Château (though it was certainly before dusk), but the Wallace report is clear that he was warned by villagers of the presence of a party of Germans on the far bank. Contrary to Farran's orders, which were to avoid confrontation, he elected to cross the bridge, at speed, perhaps with an eye to surprising the enemy contingent, but the fourth of his five jeeps came under fire and was knocked out. As luck would have it, its three-man crew was largely unscathed; while the other jeeps gave covering fire with their Vickers guns the men managed to clamber aboard the tail-ender and somehow rejoined the others, without additional mishap, further down the road. Farran, when he arrived at Mailly half an hour later, was more prudent, but still did not follow his own orders. Instead, he set out to reconnoitre on foot and was greeted by a burst of machine-gun fire when, rounding a corner, he came within sight of German infantry in something like company strength. Farran flung himself into the ditch beside the road, made a quick appraisal of the situation and beat a hasty retreat, pausing only to loose off a Bren magazine or two loaded with mixed ball and tracer from the top of the bluff on the far side of the river, setting one of the German's (horse-drawn) vehicles on fire.

Farran left word for Lt Leigh of his intentions with the men in Mailly, and turned south, hoping to be able to cross the river at the next bridge upstream, at Merry, only a few kilometres from the spot where Roy Bradford and Jim Devine had died, just over a month earlier. This time there was no German presence and he crossed safely under the light of the rising moon. Not long after midnight the Wallace party, now down to eighteen vehicles and fifty-seven men, was reunited at a predetermined RV near the village of Châtel-Gérard in the Forêt de St Jean, with well over half the journey across enemy-held territory behind it. The next evening, Wallace would not be so lucky.

The party resumed its odyssey the next afternoon at around five o'clock, with Lee – despite Farran's very vocal anger at his irresponsibility and largely because he was the only fluent French speaker – still in the lead, albeit with his section reduced to just two jeeps. In less than an hour he was in trouble again, having believed an erroneous report that the village of Villaines-les-Prévôtes was free of any German presence. In fact, in the centre of the village he ran into a detachment of what Farran was to describe as Afrika Korps troops (they had apparently arrived recently from Italy, and wore tropical battledress), and in moments one of his men lay dead, one was wounded, and both vehicles were destroyed. Lee himself, together with the other two members of his jeep's crew and Lt Lord John Manners from the other jeep, managed to scramble into cover, and were later able to find a way out of the village and into the safety of the surrounding hills, while the remaining man, Cpl Walsh, remained behind to assist the fatally wounded Tpr Rudd. Farran, meanwhile, was coming along behind, confident, for some unfathomable reason under the circumstances, that Lee would obey orders, act as a responsible reconnaissance element leader should, and warn him of any opposition ahead. In the event, he was not even alerted by the sound of gunfire, it would seem, for 'we turned a corner and came face to face with a 75-millimetre gun blocking the entire road' less than ten yards away. Before Farran could do more than start to react, the guncrew loosed off a round which cleared his head by inches, and his driver, Cpl Clarke, had no alternative but to run the jeep off the road, wrecking it in the process but taking them out of the immediate line of fire. Clarke grabbed the Bren gun and scrambled for a position from which he could give covering fire, while the squadron's signals officer, Lt Chips Carpendale, frantically gathered up the code-sheets and the marked-up map and joined him, while Farran doubled back down the road to attempt to organise a response from the rest of the column, which luckily had been well spaced out and had stopped short of the corner.

The firefight which followed was to last, Farran says, for upwards of an hour, and resulted in many German casualties initially, thanks largely to poor tactical leadership. Eventually, however, German performance improved, and Farran saw that he would inevitably be outflanked if he did not withdraw. He was able to do so without loss by the fairly simple expedient of abandoning the Bren gun manned by Cpl Clarke and Lt Carpendale, which gave him covering fire as he pulled out. (Both subsequently rejoined, Clarke after escaping from German custody when his guard dropped his machine-pistol into a pool of water while escorting him up a river bed and then joining up with Capt Lee, Carpendale after fortuitously meeting Sgt Foster as the latter attempted to catch up after having become separated from the main party at the first road crossing; they rejoined Farran on 28 August.) The section, now reduced to seven jeeps, retreated back the way it had come, turning south and then east, taking a wide detour around Semur. They saw no sign of Lt Leigh and his column of eight jeeps and were reassured by that, believing them to have been warned off by the gunfire. In fact, Leigh and his section entered Villaines only a short time after Farran and his men had left, and this time the Germans got the upper hand almost immediately. Leigh was killed in the first exchange of fire and there were numerous casualties in the other vehicles, three of which were destroyed. Nonetheless, seventeen men managed to make their way out of the village with five intact vehicles, and later joined up with Capt Lee, who succeeded in getting them, his own small party and Cpl Clarke back to the Houndsworth base in the Morvan, surviving another encounter with German troops in the village of Bierry-les-belles-Fontaines on the way. Lee then made the decision to return with this group to the United Kingdom, despite apparently being ordered to remain where he was, await resupply and then rejoin Farran, and sixteen officers and men chose to do so via Paris, and remained there for some time. Six men – Lt Hugh Gurney, L/Cpl Tanky Challenor and Tpr Will Fyffe in one jeep and Lt Birtwhistle, Cpl Clarke and Tpr Roche in a second – made their way back through American lines to Normandy and thence to the UK; they were subsequently parachuted back into France, and rejoined the Wallace party on 6 and 9 September respectively. The ambush at Villaines cost the lives of only three members of the Wallace party – Lt David Leigh, Signalman Ronald McEachan and Tpr Leonard Rudd – and two others, Lt Dodd and Cpl Walsh, were captured. Walsh subsequently escaped; Dodd survived captivity.

Farran and his men knew none of what had gone on after they quit Villaines, of course, but one can imagine that as they drove through the night – at little more than walking pace – towards their final objective in the Forêt de Châtillon there was a general feeling of having had more than enough for the moment. Just after dawn, however, the party found itself halted by a closed level-crossing gate outside the village of Boux-sous-Salmaise. Before Farran could order a general retreat into cover, a goods train some twenty wagons long appeared around a curve in the track. The party, drawn up along the road parallel to the tracks, waited until it drew level, and on Farran's signal opened up with every Vickers K and Bren which could be brought to bear, peppering locomotive and goods vans with a mixture of incendiary, tracer and ball ammunition at point-blank range. By the time the locomotive had travelled a few hundred metres down the track and creaked to a halt it was leaking steam from myriad holes, the wagons were ablaze from end to end and two rather unfortunate German sentries riding in the guard's van and too surprised to respond, lay dead. Farran watched with some amusement as the French engineer descended from the locomotive, surveyed the scene, shrugged resignedly and walked away, before ordering the gates opened so that his column could proceed on its way.

Even then the day's programme of events was not concluded. Farran's column approached the Châtillon forest from the south-west, crossing the main N71 road (and soon afterwards the Seine, little more than a stream at this point) at around breakfast time. An hour or so later they reached the village of Beaulieu and just beyond it the column stopped, the lead jeep with Farran's second-in-command, Capt Jim Mackie, aboard having come unexpectedly upon a radar installation in a clearing. Even as Mackie and Farran were assessing the situation, machine-gun fire broke out and the SAS's guns replied in what was to be a short and fruitless exchange. Farran ordered a withdrawal, and the small column skirted the installation. Farran learned later from prisoners that they had been taken for an advance party of the American 3rd Army (the vanguard units of which were still at least eighty kilometres away to the west), and that the radar installation was blown up in consequence, the crew beating a hasty retreat towards Langres. They were to be unlucky, running into a patrol from the Hardy party in the northern part of the forest, losing most of their vehicles and taking many casualties.

Farran and Grant Hibbert met up in the early afternoon of 24 August, to the latter's amazement – he simply could not believe that a column of British soldiers in uniform, travelling in what were clearly military vehicles, bristling with machine-guns and some of them pulling trailers, could possibly cross 250 kilometres of enemy-occupied territory in less than four days. Farran was more worried by the depletion the fight at Villaines had wrought on his party; instead of the hundred men he had planned would make up the combined Wallace/Hardy party, he now had barely more than sixty, with a score of vehicles rather than almost twice that number. In the event, the reduction in the party's size was not to have any great bearing on its effectiveness, though one may imagine that the loss of many experienced men, at least four of them officers, was felt profoundly.

Although he had mounted a few small offensive operations, Hibbert had stuck largely to his brief, and had established concealed supply dumps in a number of locations in the forest, all of them well away from the campsite set up on 19 August. Farran decided they should now quit that location and establish a new combined base. That night there was a further resupply drop – Farran's first experience of one under operational conditions – from two aircraft, all the containers being safely recovered. The next two days were taken up in servicing the vehicles and weapons, the men of the original Wallace party soon recovering from the emotional and physical stress of their journey, and on 27 August the enlarged party commenced offensive operations in earnest, patrolling the main roads around the forest while Farran and Hibbert set out to meet the leader of the *Maquis* Claude at Aignay-le-Duc. Col Claude (Claude Monod), who according to Fleetwood-Hesketh 'commanded all the FFI in Burgundy' impressed Farran, but he found himself agreeing with Hibbert that a loose liaison between the partisans and the SAS was all that could be expected to pay a dividend. Also at Aignay was Johnny Wiseman, from the satellite Houndsworth base he had established nearer to Dijon, despatched to advise Claude of the changing situation in the Morvan and to alert him to the prospect of wider-reaching patrol activity from that quarter.

That night the RAF flew a mission to insert two additional drivers, Cpl West and Tpr Joachim Kalkstein, a Polish Jew who had served with Farran in Italy. Wise landed safely, but Kalkstein died, apparently as a result of acid eating through his parachute's static line, causing it to part instead of pulling the parachute with its pack free from the jumper's harness, allowing the rigging lines attached to the harness and finally the canopy to deploy. There was no provision for manual release using a parachute of this type, known as the Model X or statichute, introduced in 1940 and a major improvement over the earlier type, which deployed the 'chute from a pack which remained on the parachutist's back. Up to August 1948, just forty-two fatal accidents occurred with the Model X out of well over half a million training drops made at No. 1 Parachute School – less than one in 12,000. Statistics relating to operational losses due to equipment malfunction are not available, for obvious reasons. Trooper Kalkstein was buried in the communal cemetery in Recey-sur-Ource.

Patrols were being sent out each day now, but on 29 August the chance for a more sophisticated operation presented itself when Hibbert learned from *résistance* contacts that there was a significant concentration of German troops at a farm named La Barotte, close to the town of Châtillon, and Farran decided to reconnoitre with a view to attacking. In the event, a telephone call to the mayor of Châtillon produced the information that the force had now left La Barotte, but that the main garrison at Châtillon was in the process of being relieved by a force of Panzer Grenadiers from Montbard, and that at that moment, only around 150 troops, with twenty vehicles, were in the town, housed within the precincts of the Château Marmont, set in a spacious park. Farran, accompanied by Hibbert and a young lieutenant named Dayrell Morris, who had been the first man from the operation to touch ground on the night of 26 July and led the Squadron's 3in mortar team, set off in a jeep to investigate, Hibbert eventually scaling a cliff to a vantage point from which he could look down into the château itself. The presence of a British jeep in Châtillon caused a considerable stir, and the reaction of the townspeople meant that it was only a matter of time – and probably scant minutes – before the Germans were spurred to investigate, so Farran signalled to Hibbert to return and turned the jeep around, leaving town by the main Dijon road rather than by the back lanes by which he had entered. He had just turned off this road and on to a minor road in the direction of Beaulieu, which parallels the N71 for some distance, when a convoy of four trucks passed along the main road, heading for Châtillon; he reversed the jeep and went after them, hoping to catch them at the junction, at Aisey-sur-Seine. In the event, the trucks were stopped by an ambush, and by the time Farran arrived there was a fierce firefight in progress, the German troops – they proved to be *feldgendarmerie* – having dismounted from the vehicles and giving as good as they were getting from a small Resistance group armed with Brens and rifles. Neither party seemed aware of Farran's arrival upon the scene, and he achieved perfect surprise, the three SAS officers opening up with Vickers Ks, setting three trucks alight and adding considerably to the death toll.

There was another (rather drunken, says Farran) meeting over dinner with Col Claude that evening, at which the *Maquis* leader agreed to Farran's suggestion to mount a joint operation against the German troops in Châtillon the next day, if the SAS would provide petrol for enough trucks to move the five hundred men such an attack would require. Farran agreed readily, and a truck was despatched to the Wallace base to fetch the petrol there and then. The assault parties were to be in position at first light, and Farran and Hibbert returned to their parachute-fabric tents in a glow of anticipation.

Farran's plan was straightforward: to control the junction of the two main roads leading out of the town, south to Montbard and Dijon, and north to Troyes and Chaumont; set up the 3in mortar in a position from which Morris could lob bombs into the château; occupy the minor road junctions around the town centre and send Bren-armed parties in a sweep around through the back streets, to assault the château from the north. The movement phase went off without a hitch and at 0700, by which time Sgt Young had cut the telephone cables, Lt Morris began to drop mortar bombs, some four dozen in all, into the château precinct at the leisurely rate of about three per minute, changing the point of aim frequently. He still had ammunition in hand when a convoy of trucks arrived from the direction of Montbard, and suddenly the jeeps at the southern road junction had a fight on their hands. The lead vehicle of the convoy was barely twenty yards away when Sgt Vickers' jeep's machine-guns opened up, setting fires in the first five trucks, two of which were carrying ammunition which began to cook-off in the heat. By now the fighting had spread right through the town and into the woods beyond, where Lt Jamie Robertson had set up his Brens to form a stop group; Morris's mortar ammunition was all expended, and Farran sent him and his crew to reinforce the positions in the town centre, where the parachutists were hardest pressed, a column of German infantry having sortied from the château and made its way down into the town. It was some two hours, Farran says, before he acknowledged that the promised *maquisard* reinforcements were probably not coming, and he began to think about withdrawing his men before events took a turn for the worse. He stepped out into the open, acknowledged with a wave a pretty girl in a red dress, who had been cheering them on from an upstairs window since the firefight started, and fired two Very lights, the signal to break off the action.

The withdrawal went relatively smoothly until Hibbert, in command of the foot party, met up with around sixty of the promised five hundred partisans, gathered on the town's small airfield, adjacent to the Dijon road. He agreed to lead them back into the town, sending a runner after Farran, who had gone on ahead to the RV on the outskirts with most of the vehicles, to ask him to launch a supporting attack. On balance, this was probably a mistake, for the Germans were thoroughly stirred up by now, and still outnumbered the Allies, even after the partisans were taken into account. Almost immediately, Hibbert's party came under fire from an armoured car; he managed to subdue it, but by that time additional German troops had come up, and he was hard put to extricate his men from a walled garden. By then, however, Farran had returned with his jeeps and was in control of the main road intersection to the south once more, just in time to halt another convoy of eight vehicles coming up from Montbard.

Quite inexplicably – he certainly offers no explanation in his own account of the action, and the after-action report is uncharacteristically terse on the subject, saying, 'Major Farran found that the maquis would not penetrate deeper than the outskirts of the town, so he made a lone raid with his foot party …', which actually tells us nothing – Farran then decided to circumnavigate the town on foot, with a small party which included Lt Michel Pinci and Sgts Robinson and Young. Perhaps an hour later, after having caught sight of small numbers of scattered German troops and taken care not to engage them, they found themselves in a narrow lane leading down to the Troyes road, where, rounding a corner, they came upon a pair of German machine-gun positions, sited so as to cover the road itself and thus with their backs to them. Farran admits that he simply did not know what to do, and the little party retreated to the cover of a garden to think things over, and then, 'Lt Pinci begged a bottle of wine, bread and cheese from a French cottage, so we had lunch.'

Frankly, the most sensible thing would probably have been to have left the two machine-gun positions to their own devices – they were not threatening anybody, since there were no Allied troops to their front – but Farran did not see it that way. In the event the SAS patrol crept back down the lane, which was steep-sided with high banks, and opened fire on both posts, and immediately came under very heavy submachine-gun fire from troops whose existence they had not even suspected, and whose locations they could not pinpoint. All they could do was run for it, bursting through the front door of an adjacent house and straight out the back, down a bank on to the canal towpath and away, as fast as their legs could carry them. They crossed the canal at a lock, and then headed well away from the town, climbing through a ploughed field towards a crest where a thin hedge ran. No sooner had they reached it than they came under fire from two more machine-guns, and went to ground, with only the furrows as protection. Farran admits in his writings to feeling more tired than he had ever known, knowing that only by moving would he save his life but scarcely able to do so. Even Sgt Robinson, who was wounded in the leg, was moving faster than he was, he says, adding, 'Never have I been so frightened and so incapable of helping myself.' Eventually they reached the safety of dead ground, and later were found by Jim Mackie, who took them, aboard his jeep, to the farmhouse from which they had contacted the mayor the day before, where Farran dressed Robinson's wound before transporting him to Col Claude's *maquisard* hospital at Aignay-le-Duc.

Farran says he was told that over a hundred Germans had been killed in what was styled the battle of Châtillon, with many more wounded, and that nine trucks, four cars and a motorcycle combination had been destroyed (and the official report follows that estimate); SAS losses amounted to one – Tpr Bill Holland, killed in the fighting in the centre of the town (where a monument to him was later erected) – and two wounded. Sgt Vickers was awarded the DCM for his actions at the crossroads.

Somewhat strangely, for it gives every appearance of being comprehensive, and by his own admission the author stayed 'in close touch with [Claude] all the time', Fleetwood-Hesketh's report makes no mention of the agreement to mount a joint SAS/FFI attack on Châtillon, though he does mention the operation itself, almost in passing, saying, 'They [2 SAS] got right into the town and shot a number of Germans and destroyed some German transport.'

The point has been made elsewhere that an offensive operation of this sort was almost precisely what Farran should *not* have been undertaking; although Wallace had somewhat different objectives to the operations we have examined so far, Farran's instructions were still clearly to concentrate on lines of communication and to harry the retreating German forces, not to become involved in set-piece battles, with or without Resistance elements. Instead, Farran permitted himself to be seduced into an entirely inappropriate 'adventure'. He realised his mistake soon enough, excusing himself (but only later) by saying that he 'partly blame[d] the action … on the quantity of red wine consumed' at his dinner with Claude, adding that the latter probably thought it was the drink talking and did not take the plan to attack Châtillon seriously, which probably accounts for him not having shown up. The action had little tactical (and no strategic) value, and it could, of course, have been costly for the men involved – it is frankly amazing that the disparity in the casualties each side took was so great – but, to paraphrase the Service's motto, success excuses all the risks taken, and Farran escaped official criticism. The official Wallace report calls the operation 'well conceived and brilliantly executed', but since it was written to Farran's orders, that is hardly surprising.

He was at least responsible enough to recognise that the outcome of the attack on the Châtillon garrison would be enhanced security operations in the area where the SAS were believed to be based, and the next day, 31 August, he led the party to a new location south of Auberive in the Forêt de Montaubert, and that same night received a supply drop which included two jeeps and fifty-two containers; the following night four officers, including a doctor, and two ORs plus four additional jeeps arrived, all landing safely. The strength of the party now stood at seventy-seven effectives, with eighteen serviceable vehicles, and Farran decided to split it into three components. He would lead a column of nine jeeps east and operate in the Forêt de Darney (though he actually penetrated rather further than that, as far as the Moselle at Épinal); Hibbert would remain in the area in which they were currently based for three days more and then move a short distance to the east to operate in the vicinity of Bourbonne-les-Bains, while Lt Michel Pinci would command what is sometimes referred to as Operation Robey, a two-section party which would operate on foot (and in such vehicles as they could obtain) in the area around Chaumont, an important town with around 20,000 inhabitants which stands astride a major crossroads some forty kilometres north-west of Châtillon. It would appear from the decision to split his party in this way that Farran had either been told or had divined that he would receive no further additional vehicles.

Operation Robey was to achieve little and its mission was short-lived. Pinci's party, composed of four officers and nineteen ORs, was ferried to its new operational area the next day. There is no record of its activities over the few days following, save to say that the men soon moved south, towards Auberive, where Jedburgh team Bunny was based, so as to gain access to its radio, having none of their own. A priority was to find vehicles of some sort, it seems, for on 7 September Pinci is reported as leaving 'for an extensive recce to Troyes and Paris to find transport', though he also wanted to try to secure the services of an armoured car detachment. In fact, he had met Capt Fleetwood-Hesketh, the PWE Liaison Officer who had dropped in to the Hardy party but had operated chiefly in the Côte-d'Or. Hesketh drove Pinci to Paris, and got him a meeting at SHAEF HQ with General Joinville, who promised that a detachment from General Leclerc's Second Armoured Division was on its way to the area, and the pair returned via Châtillon, which had just been liberated. They spent two days trying to persuade American and French armoured units to come to the assistance of the FFI in the town, which was in danger of being retaken (elements of the latter arrived in the nick of time), and then parted company, Pinci, in a requisitioned car, to return to his patrol.

Their only significant success had come while Pinci was absent, on 8 September, when an ambush was mounted on the road between Châtillon and Chaumont using three trucks borrowed from the local *Maquis*. Four large half-track personnel carriers crowded with troops fell into the trap, and casualties were heavy. Lt Pinci returned on 11 September driving the unmarked civilian car; that same afternoon, he was killed in a 'blue-on-blue' air strike by Allied fighter-bombers. Leadership of the party was taken over by Lt Walker-Brown who was able to achieve very little before being overrun by Leclerc's division when it arrived in the area on 13 September. The situation was not improved by the attitude of the leader of the Auberive *Maquis*, 'Captain Max' (whose affiliation is not recorded, but can probably be assumed to be FTP), and particularly his relationship with Col Claude. Max proved to have an agenda of his own, and according to Walker-Brown, 'shooting incidents were reported between this and other more orthodox Maquis groups'.

During what the official report describes as Phase Two of the operation, the two motorised Wallace columns would follow different but parallel routes. Both were running into the zone between the American 3rd Army, advancing eastwards in a broad front but momentarily stalled, largely because it had outrun its logistical support and supply lines, and the American 7th Army which had landed on the Mediterranean coast in Operation Dragoon and advanced up the Rhône and then the Saône valleys at almost unimaginable speed. This fairly narrow gap, which would soon be squeezed out of existence, was packed of course with most of the German forces fleeing France, and the sheer density of them on the ground was to make Operation Wallace difficult and eventually unsustainable, but for the moment it was still possible to move, and Farran, having delivered Pinci's party to its new operational area, set out eastward on the evening of 2 September.

The first obstacle confronting Farran's party was the main N19 road between Langres and Vesoul, and it was a full twenty-four hours before the column succeeded in finding a suitable crossing point, but by the early hours of 4 September Farran had found a temporary leaguer in the woods above the village of Bize. The next morning Lt Carpendale and Sgt Young returned to the highway and both executed successful ambushes, and by early afternoon the column was on the move again, towards a campsite near Passavant-la-Rochère in the southern part of the Fôret de Darney, some twenty kilometres to the north-east. The party operated from this base for the next two days before Farran detached Chips Carpendale to make a protracted reconnaissance in the direction of Épinal and particularly to observe the German defensive positions along the River Moselle.

Meanwhile, Farran himself had made contact with a well-organised but untried *Maquis* band composed largely of boy scouts, which had its headquarters near Grandrupt-les-Bains, close to the forest's eastern

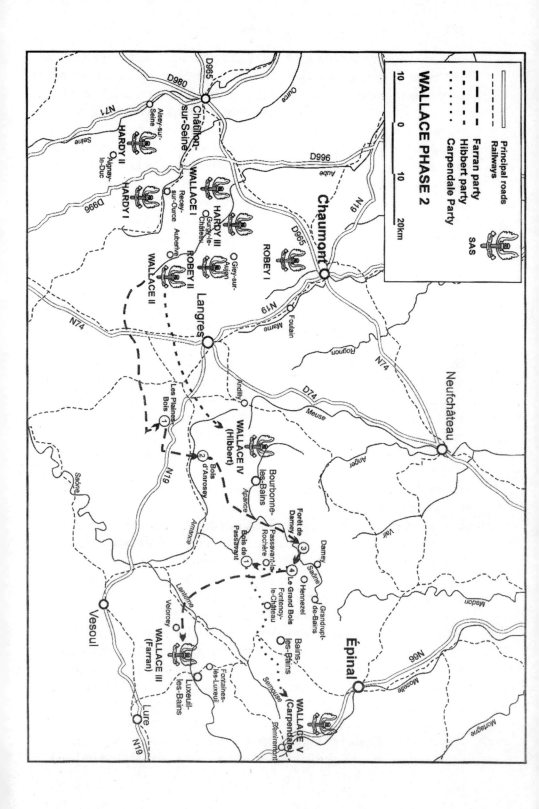

margin. Farran says that he decided to call in a resupply mission to a DZ these boys had selected and cleared, largely to give them experience, even though the ground was actually far from ideal (it was too small, and lined with woodland; any canisters which went astray would therefore be difficult to recover quickly). In the event, the drop consisted not only of supplies but also of Lt Gurney, L/Cpl Challenor and Tpr Fyfe, together with a single jeep. Men and vehicle landed safely, but many of the containers did, indeed, go astray, and some had not been recovered before dawn. Farran admits that at that point he and his men retired to the perimeter of the DZ to eat breakfast, leaving the *maquisards* to try to recover the remainder, and tells how his meal was interrupted by the arrival of one of the boys with a report of a battalion of German troops supported by light armoured vehicles closing rapidly on the DZ down the single access track which led into it from the east. Farran initially thought there was no way he could extricate his men and vehicles, and took up a defensive position hull-down in the centre of the zone, but then spied a possible route to the south-west, through a coppice of young saplings, and burst through them 'like fear-crazed elephants in the jungle', leaving the *maquisards* to exfiltrate through the forest. As soon as the jeeps reached a position of comparative safety, Farren detached two pairs, under Hugh Gurney and Sgt Vickers, to circle around and attack the German column in the rear, hoping by this means to take the worst of the pressure off the boy scouts; both parties were soon in action and both reported a measure of success at no cost to themselves, thanks largely to their having achieved complete surprise.

Farran and his men returned to the campsite in the forest, intending to lie low while the inevitable search-and-destroy mission passed them by, the self-imposed inactivity broken only by small parties issuing to mine the roads and the arrival of two French mechanics who worked in the German motor workshops at Bains-les-Bains, come to repair the clutches on two of the jeeps (burned-out clutches were commonplace, especially on those vehicles which pulled trailers). Carpendale returned on 9 September having mounted two successful assaults on German elements but with bad news as to the situation along the river, where a German brigade was occupying strong defensive positions south-west of Épinal, while there was dense traffic on the highway between there and Remiremont. Now that his column was complete once more, Farran decided to move campsites prior to a resupply drop – the last he could expect before he moved into the Belfort Gap – scheduled for that night. During the move the party narrowly avoided a German force which evidently was still searching for them, and which had diverted to burn the village of Hennezel; Farran's men lay low until dark and then, knowing that the Germans were unlikely to leave the road under such circumstances, retired southwards on forest tracks with no further incident. Although the DZ scheduled for that night's operation was scarcely five kilometres from the German position, they felt secure enough to light the beacon fires which would call the aircraft in, and were rewarded by a major resupply, six aircraft dropping two jeeps and the other three men who had returned to the UK via the Houndsworth base, and close to a hundred canisters and panniers containing fuel, supplies, clean clothing, mail, cigarettes and even a few very welcome bottles of whisky.

Two jeeps were damaged next day, Carpendale's suffering a smashed sump, which put it out of action. Cpl Bird's jeep towed it to Passavant, where the two vehicles and their crews remained when the rest of party cleared the area before daybreak, heading south-east now, and crossing the Saône. Before the end of the day it became clear that German troop concentrations were so thick on the ground that further movement would be very difficult indeed. Sure enough, when Gurney led a small reconnaissance party out of that night's campsite – an unsatisfactory location in a too-small patch of woodland – he made contact almost immediately and had to withdraw, bringing the Germans with him. The party, unable to move after the three leading jeeps had became inextricably bogged down on the only track out of the wood, passed a frightened but ultimately uneventful night in totally inadequate cover, with German troops sometimes no more than a hundred metres away and a convoy later estimated at over two thousand vehicles passing down the adjacent road, man-handling the vehicles away the next morning and eventually finding a more satisfactory leaguer in the forests north of Luxeuil-les-Bains. Until this point, despite having been in contact with superior German forces on a number of occasions, since leaving the Forêt de Châtillon Farran's party had taken no casualties. That was to change the following day, when Hugh Gurney's jeep confronted a small German convoy in the village of Velorcey. Gurney opened fire on the lead truck with his twin Vickers at close range; the truck, which contained ammunition and demolition charges, exploded almost immediately, wrecking the jeep and throwing Gurney clear, straight into the line of fire of a machine-gun, which killed him outright. Lt Birtwhistle had marginally better luck when he attacked a column of horse-drawn vehicles near Fontaines-les-Bains, knocking out five and killing thirty before effective machine-gun fire wrecked one of his vehicles and severely wounded the three men aboard. Only Jim Mackie's small party, which set out to ambush vehicles near Luxeuil, escaped unscathed.

By now, Farran tells us, he could hear American artillery away to the south but was effectively pinned down by the sheer weight of German traffic on the roads. All he could do was retreat deeper into the forest, and was very glad he did, for within hours the position he had occupied was taken over by a battery of 8.8cm guns, which commenced firing on the advancing Americans. Hurriedly the SAS troopers began to dig in, knowing that a response would be forthcoming as soon as the American guns came within range. Relief finally came on 16 September, when the German battery withdrew and *maquisards* contacted by Farran and his men came to lead them to the spearhead elements of the American 7th Army.

Carpendale and Cpl Bird, the former's jeep now repaired, had left Passavant on the morning of 12 September and were in trouble within less than an hour, when they ran into a party of German cyclists at Fontenoy-le-Château, but managed to extricate themselves. They found that their plan – essentially, to link up with Farran as soon as possible – was impractical due to the sheer weight and volume of German traffic on the roads, and over the next week (save on the evening of 16 September, when they took advantage of the general confusion to attack a large convoy of horse-drawn vehicles, between Belfontaine and Ramirement) they had to content themselves with attacking isolated vehicles while their fuel supply dwindled. On 19 September, by now almost immobilised, they met an American reconnaissance unit, and subsequently rejoined Major Farran's party.

Hibbert, meanwhile, had turned his attention to a large fuel dump at Foulain, near a canal dock, which he had reconnoitred on 14 August and called in as a target for aerial bombardment. The bombers never came, and now he decided to take matters into his own hands. Together with a group of *maquisards*, a small SAS party entered the dump, which is reported to have been only lightly guarded. They loaded around 5,000 litres of fuel aboard the partisans' lorries, and then proceeded to lay charges to destroy the rest, variously estimated at from 100,000 to 500,000 litres; the resulting explosion and fire were seen and heard many kilometres away. Hibbert's party then set out eastward; he detached Lt Morris and his section, in two jeeps, to take a different route, expecting to meet up with him at Larivière-sur-Apance on 6 September, but Morris almost came to grief when he ran into a party of

Germans who had taken refuge in a grain silo, and the two vehicles came under heavy fire. As his driver tried to turn, the jeep overturned, trapping Morris beneath it; the driver, who had been thrown clear, managed to free him and then gave covering fire while the second jeep came up and joined in, silencing the German machine-gun and driving the enemy troops under cover, whereupon the upturned jeep was righted and the pair beat a hasty retreat.

It was 7 September before Morris rejoined Hibbert, and by that time it was becoming clear that any thought of moving further east would have to be abandoned; Hibbert, Lt Robertson, SQMS Puttock and Sgt Linton had all taken out raiding or reconnaissance parties in the meantime, with good results, particularly on Robertson's part, and by the time Morris turned up they had identified an important target: a train consisting of petrol tankers, in a siding next to the station at Andilly-en-Bassigny. This time, however, the target was heavily guarded, effectively surrounded by machine-guns dug into protected positions, and Hibbert, after a second reconnaissance, concluded that it would be impossible for him to assault it, even with 3in mortars, and called it in as a bombing target, but once more, nothing came of it. By the night of 9 September, when a resupply mission was scheduled, the party's own fuel supplies were dangerously low, and it came as a severe disappointment to learn that due to a mix-up at Station 1090, Hibbert's party had received the containers destined for Pinci's party, which, of course, contained no petrol. It was two nights before a further resupply could be arranged, and meanwhile the party mounted local patrols with some success, the area being still swamped with retreating Germans. Unfortunately, Tpr James Downey was accidentally killed on 11 September during one of those missions.

From then on, the concentration of German forces in the area increased day by day, and Hibbert's party's activities became more and more restricted. Eventually, like Farran, they found themselves virtually pinned down, and it was with considerable relief that they were finally overrun by American forces on 17 September.

Within two days of being stood down, Farran's column was heading westward, bound for Paris and a week's unofficial leave financed by the last of the operational funds, having spent almost a month behind enemy lines, destroying close on a hundred vehicles and causing perhaps 500 casualties at a cost of seven killed, seven wounded and two captured, plus sixteen vehicles lost.

Operation Wallace was a very demanding affair, the prototype of a new sort of mission. It was certainly fortunate in having Major Roy Farran, widely accepted as one of the SAS's most talented field commanders, as its commanding officer; with the exception of the attack on Châtillon, which was an all-hands effort anyway, he sensibly took a back seat in most small operations which, despite the degree of self-criticism on this score in his autobiography, was precisely the right approach to adopt. He himself singled out Jim Mackie and Grant Hibbert for particular praise (Hibbert was subsequently promoted major, and led a squadron during the later operations in Germany), and it is clear that Wallace had a very strong 'senior management team'. However, Farran was to criticise some of his junior officers, without naming names, as being too inexperienced to be expected to command men of the stature of his own; he blamed their lack of training, not their characters or will, but was to state, in his observations and comments on the operation, that this had imposed restrictions on him:

> Lack of previous training made it necessary for the jeeps to move from one area to another in large parties under experienced officers. If sufficient troop leaders of high quality, reliability and experience had been available, I believe that more damage could have been inflicted on the enemy by widely dispersed troops, only regrouping periodically for resupply. Three jeeps could have penetrated to areas impossible for a party of nine. A firm base is not necessary for jeeps and it is better to maintain mobility by aiming at complete independence of troops without being tied to dumps. This, of course, is contrary to our previous ideas when we thought that jeeps should always operate from a fixed base where refitting and refueling could be carried out ... It was not always easy to find a forest large enough to conceal a base for nine jeeps. On the other hand there was always plenty of small woods quite adequate for concealing a troop. A troop could move daily with the greatest ease, but the movement of a squadron column was always fraught with grave risk.

Farran's terminology is perhaps misleading: a troop – three sections plus HQ, and thus more than thirty officers and men – could hardly be mounted on three vehicles; it would seem that for 'troop' we should read 'section', and for 'squadron', 'troop'.

Would the operation have been more effective if it had been launched earlier? Certainly the situation was more fluid in early August than it was to be later in the month, after the battle in Normandy was lost and won, especially in the congested approaches to the Belfort Gap, but against that we have to set the fatigue factor; it is by no means certain that Farran's men would have been sufficiently alert after two or three more weeks of what was, after all, a very precarious existence to have maintained the vigilance necessary to have remained out of what could have been very serious trouble. (One may observe that most of the personnel of Operation Houndsworth were in occupied territory for much longer, but we should perhaps bear in mind that they were in a single location, were present in greater numbers, and were in constant touch with very strong partisan elements the whole time, and be wary of making a non-valid comparison.) We can perhaps leave the last word on that subject to Roy Farran himself:

> I believe that our operations were most effective during the last two weeks in the area of the Vosges. Although, during this time, the enemy was very sensitive to our attacks and made our life very uncomfortable, I take this as proof that he disliked our presence more there than in other regions. During this period we actually knocked out a smaller number of vehicles, but our patrols covered a wide area and knocked out important vehicles from large convoys.

RUPERT

The next operation for which 2 SAS personnel were briefed, Operation Rupert, had familiar objectives – to set up a base deep in occupied territory, well to the east of Paris in the area around St-Dizier in the Haute Marne from which railway lines and roads, this time those running eastwards from Paris through Châlons-sur-Marne (now Châlons-en-Champagne) and St-Dizier or Bar-le-Duc to Nancy and then on through the Moselle into the Rhineland, could be attacked, as well as arming local partisan bands. It was to be inserted very late, and it was hampered as a result.

Rupert was actually planned in advance of D-Day for insertion in mid-June, but was delayed, apparently after SFHQ objected to the presence of uniformed Allied personnel in the area which, it felt, would lead to unacceptable levels of reprisals. Brian Franks himself seems to have been involved with the negotiations between SAS and SFHQ over the insertion of the Rupert party, and ran foul of Major Nicholas Bodington in the process. Bodington was deputy head of SOE's F Section. Paris correspondent of the *Daily Express* newspaper before the war, he was an early recruit to SOE and was inserted into France on a number of occasions to act as a trouble-shooter. Bodington was due to be inserted into Rupert's operational area himself in July 1944, and eventually, and very reluctantly, agreed to make arrangements for the reconnaissance party's reception. Instead, and without any apparent justification, he radioed back that it would be 'criminally sadistic to send SAS men to this area', so determined was he to keep uniformed parachutists out. Bodington was eventually unsuccessful, but he did delay the party's insertion. (Bodington's activities in the Haute-Marne are well documented, and it seems his concerns were honestly held. He personally led two partisan units in the liberation of the *département*, according to Michel-André Pichard, de Gaulle's Director of Military Operations, and also arranged the FFI's arms supplies.)

A small advance party of seven men from 3 Squadron (also known as G Squadron), 2 SAS, under the command of Major Felix Symes and with Lt Ian Grant as second-in-command, together with a two-man Phantom party, was eventually despatched on the night of 22 July to identify a suitable location for an operating base, but sadly, while circling in an effort to locate the DZ, the Halifax carrying them ran into severe turbulence. The pilot descended through thick cloud with a low base altitude and crashed into a wooded hillside near the village of Graffigny-Chemin with the loss of most of those on board.

Due to the periods of the moon, it was ten days before a replacement reconnaissance party could be inserted, on 4 August. The phases of the moon placed an important restriction on the nights on which SAS parties which were to be dropped 'blind' could be inserted. The last week of July 1944 was a moonless period, but by the first week of August the moon had waxed enough to provide a bare sufficiency of light to enable the pilot to identify the target area, and insertion flights began once more. There was a further consideration related to night flying: the extent of the hours of darkness. Overlord had had to take place close to the summer solstice, when nights are at their shortest, and that put a limit on how far the RAF and USAAF's aircraft could penetrate occupied territory under cover of darkness. This was not a consideration in missions to the area behind the Normandy battlefield, but it was in those which were to be carried out in more distant areas, such as Rupert and more particularly Operation Loyton, which we shall examine in due course. No considerations seems to have been given to 'staging' missions at airfields closer to hand – in Kent, for example – rather than directly from the Wiltshire/Gloucestershire area, probably for the simple reason that a two-stage mission would have used up too much aircraft/aircrew capacity at a time when every sortie by every aircraft was vitally important to the main battle.

The second reconnaissance party consisted of eight men, and was under the command of Lt DV Laws. They made a good landing in a ploughed field near Bailly-le-Franc, hid close to the DZ through the following day, then moved out that night in a north-easterly direction to locate a suitable DZ for two further sections, sending for them in the scheduled radio transmission on 7 August. In fact, it was the night of 12 August before they were dropped, and this time the insertion was not so successful – one stick was dropped from a height of 2,000 feet (550 m) and was spread out over a considerable distance in consequence, and as a result of packing detonators alongside plastic explosive (an all too common failing), both panniers of demolition supplies were lost. Two container parachutes failed to open and three kitbags broke loose during the descent. In all, the only supplies which arrived in usable condition were items of spare clothing.

Laws ordered the two sticks, under Lts Cameron and Marsh, to lie-up in the Bois des Moines and then operate independently, and moved with his own party into the Forêt du Der. He was soon in touch with a small partisan band, mostly escaped PoWs and Russians, but also including three deserters from the *Wehrmacht*. The after-action report gives no details, but simply says that some of the *maquisards*, contrary to orders, attacked a German staff car; this resulted in a sweep of the woodland in which the men were hiding, and that, in turn, led to a skirmish in which five of the enemy were killed and two partisans wounded. Laws prudently cleared the area, and began looking for a suitable DZ for the Squadron HQ. They were to have been inserted on 20 August, but in the event only one of the aircraft found the DZ and identified the signals, and only Capt Walters, Lt Maynard and a signaller dropped. It was three days before the RAF could try again, but by this time there was a significant amount of traffic on the roads, moving east, and Laws put the attempt off again. Eventually, on the night of 24 August, Major Michael Rooney, the squadron's replacement CO, arrived, with the veteran SSM Bob Tait, a jeep and a driver. The insertion was uneventful, save that the jeep actually landed on high-tension electricity cables, shorting them out and breaking them but remaining undamaged itself (Rooney's 'chute brushed the same cables, and he fell heavily but was unhurt).

Rooney set off immediately on a scouting mission into the Argonne, to the north, leaving Laws to wait for another party of three sections under Lts Arnold, Fletcher and Gibbon, promised for the following night; only Arnold's stick was actually inserted, and then failed to make the RV and was out of touch for a week. At this point, the mission was split into five separate parties, none of which numbered more than a dozen and a half men; none of them was in close touch with any other, there was no central base and supply dump, they had just one vehicle (which Rooney had appropriated), no particularly good contact with the Resistance and none as yet with an SOE organiser or a Jedburgh team. Two of these were inserted into the Haute-Marne: Bunny, on 18 August and Stanley on 1 September; Bunny's operational area was in the very south of the *département*, and its after-action report indicates that it worked in conjunction with an SAS unit, described only as consisting of 'four lieutenants and about twenty other ranks', around Auberives and Langres from about 6 September. (This was actually the Robey party from Operation Wallace.) Stanley, also in the south, had no contact with any SAS party. Eventually, the day before he joined up with the advancing Americans, Rooney met up with Jedburgh teams Benjamin and Bernard, who were operating together in the Meuse, after losing Benjamin's Jedset during their combined insertion on 20 August. It immediately became clear that the SAS and the Jedburghs had both called in resupply missions to the same DZ, and it was decided to handle the operation together. Later, Rooney (who makes no mention of this encounter in his report) cancelled it without consulting the Jedburghs, which was unfortunate from their point of view, since one of the items they had asked for was a replacement radio. They lost the only set they had a few days later, and were rendered totally ineffective as a result.

Laws had been instructed not to move without Arnold, and thus he, too, was immobilised, and had to content himself with occasional forays in support of the *maquis*, who were increasingly active in the face of a rather disorganised German withdrawal. By 30 August, on which day Capt Walters and a small party ambushed a staff car and killed both its occupants, the local garrisons began to pull out, *Waffen-SS* troops amongst them killing civilians and firing villages on their way, while the *maquisards* did their best to harass them. On 31 August, Lt Laws made contact with the spearhead elements of the advancing American 3rd Army, the vanguard of which had reached Nancy on 29 August. Meanwhile, by now south and east of St Dizier, Cameron and Marsh's sticks, very short of ordnance throughout, were able to mount two sabotage operations, cutting railway lines in two places, before they, too, met American forces. Marsh himself joined up with Lt Pinci's 'Robey' party from Operation Wallace on 10 September, but the association was short-lived, that party being stood down in its turn on 15 September.

Major Rooney's small party consisted of himself, Lt Maynard, SSM Tait, a trooper and two signallers, accompanied by two French guides, one of whom promptly sat on the Jedset and wrecked it, leaving the group out of contact with Moor Park. Rooney sent the unfortunate Frenchman back to Laws, to collect his spare radio set, but in the meantime could do little, although he did manage to ambush a small car carrying two junior officers, a sergeant and a private soldier, killing them all. In fact, Rooney was able to use a *Maquis* radio the following

day, and heard from Franks that no additional personnel or further
resupply would be forthcoming, on account of the proximity of the
Americans, who were all around him. He linked up with an element of
7th Armored Division on 28 August, having been in the field something
short of five days, though his small group was to remain in the area,
operating as a reconnaissance element for the Americans, until he was
recalled by Moor Park on 10 September.

LOYTON

Operation Loyton, mounted by 1 Squadron, 2 SAS, had as its broad objective the establishment of a chain of small bases from which to attack the routes through the Vosges mountains toward the important Rhine crossing at Strasbourg. It was to be one of the least effective and most costly of all the Brigade's missions, thanks to its timing and to local conditions. Thirty-three SAS personnel who took part in it, plus two members of the attached Phantom patrol and two Jedburghs were to lose their lives, all but three or four of them killed in captivity.

It has been held by some to be significant that the impetus to mount Loyton came from SHAEF HQ and not from within SAS Brigade. This distorts the chain of command out of all recognition and suggests that somehow staff at Airborne Forces or SAS Brigade HQ might have been expected to take responsibility for broad strategic decisions upon themselves, a notion which is not worth contemplating. The impetus came from within Supreme Headquarters, and it was then Airborne Forces HQ's responsibility to hand the order down to SAS Brigade, which in turn selected a regiment (the choice was not exactly wide at this point) with the capacity to turn the requirement into a feasible action plan and then carry it out. There *were* cases where SHAEF (or 21st Army Group, where the operation fell within the greater Normandy battlefield area) passed down a totally unsuitable requirement – Operation Defoe was one of them – but the objectives for Loyton were entirely reasonable, and certainly met the criteria David Stirling and his successors had set for SAS participation.

The problem with Loyton was not one of concept; it was all to do with timing and the inability to react flexibly to changing conditions within the operational area. If Brigade HQ was at fault, it was in not cancelling the operation, desirable as its objectives certainly were, when it became clear that this was simply not the right way to go about achieving them. With the benefit of hindsight it is easy to see that

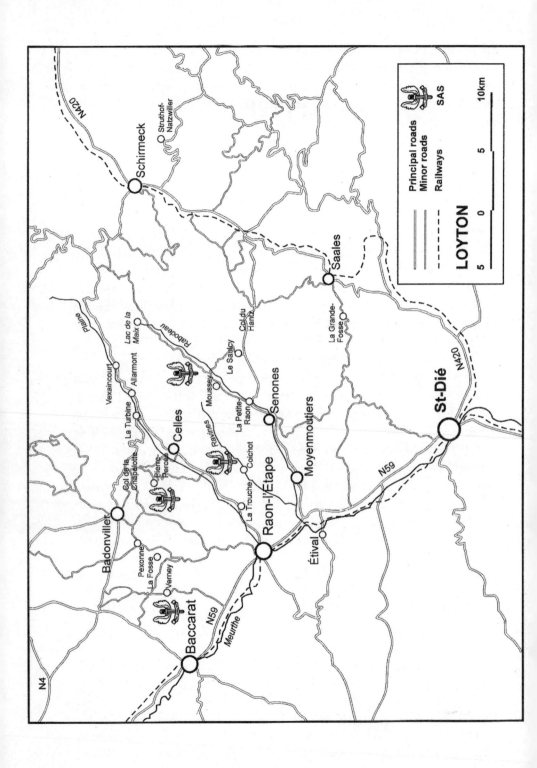

dropping almost an entire squadron of SAS troops into the Vosges mountains, where the Resistance infrastructure was patchy at best, and which was teeming with German troops, was an error. Even the much more adaptable Jedburgh teams were to find operating conditions there almost impossible, and it is worth noting that that which accompanied Loyton was wiped out, with two of its members killed and the third captured. Phillip Warner, in *The Special Air Service*, quotes a participant in Loyton, Capt John Hislop, who commanded the Phantom patrol, as saying that an entire SS Division was withdrawn from the American front 'for the sole purpose of destroying us', and used that very dubious assertion to justify the operation, but there is no substance in the claim.

From the outset the relationship between the SAS advance party and the local *maquisards* was poor; it is accepted that its communications channels to London were extremely restricted and it found the extent of the German presence in the area to be such as to make meaningful offensive operations virtually impossible. Why, then, was the insertion of the main party allowed to go ahead? The operation could have been called off even then, and the advance party told to exfiltrate or lay up and wait to be overrun by the advancing American 3rd Army, expected to arrive within three weeks. (In fact that estimate proved to be wildly optimistic, and formed a further weak link in the planning process. In the event Patton's advance stalled on the Moselle, and this was to be the root cause of serious problems, for German security forces in the area then had plenty of time to devote to hunting down parachutists.) Operation Instruction No. 38, which defined Operation Loyton, allowed for the possibility of the mission being truncated if the advance party found itself in difficulties:

> The recce party will be followed by reinforcements as required up to one troop [in fact, as we shall see, the reinforcements went astray]. *If this party were successful and targets were available and aircraft supply problems proved easy, permission to increase the party up to one sqn would almost certainly be given.* [italics added]

Those conditions were certainly not met, and it is tempting to speculate that a strong element of bloody-mindedness within the upper echelons of Regimental HQ was at least partially responsible for the operation going ahead anyway, although no correspondence on the subject exists within the files. As we have noted, the process of planning the SAS missions into occupied France required the co-operation of sometimes hostile elements within Special Forces HQ. In the case of Loyton, it is obvious from Lt-Col Brian Franks' correspondence, as quoted in Part One, that he believed he had found clear evidence that SFHQ was dragging its feet, if not being downright duplicitous, just as it had done and been during the planning stage of Operation Rupert, afraid that the presence of an SAS operation in the area in question would upset its own plans. Having achieved the complex task of getting Loyton (quite literally) off the ground, how easy would it have been for Franks to have then gone to McLeod and requested permission to call it off, even if he wanted to, and even though the Operation Instruction allowed for this possibility? It is clear that he certainly did *not* want to, for he had already made the decision to lead the operation himself, even though it involved only one of his regiment's four squadrons. At this point it is fairly safe to say that he was personally committed to it, and that the cancellation option did not even occur to him.

The Vosges mountains run roughly north–south, from east of Saar-brucken to the Belfort Gap, parallel to the River Rhine which is the natural border between France and Germany. While they are not spec-tacularly high (the passes rarely exceed 1,300m (4,000 feet) in altitude, and in the area in which the Loyton party was to operate, half that), thanks to their relative youth in geological terms, they have narrow, winding valleys with steep gradients, and thus form a very effective barrier, particularly to heavy vehicles. On the face of it, that part of the chain in which Loyton's operational area was located, in what is now the northern sector of the Parc National Régional des Ballons des Vosges, should have been ideal for the SAS party's purposes. Wilder even than the Massif du Morvan, the character of the landscape would, the opera-tion's planners believed, have allowed the parachutists' encampments to remain completely undetected by security forces, while the network of minor roads linking the small centres of population would give them relatively easy access to the more major routes and the few railway lines which German forces used to traverse the region.

Had it been possible to have mounted the operation during the last week of June, as those planners envisaged (the plan itself, at least in outline, was drawn up in early May), they might have been right, but by the time the main party was in place, if it could be said to *ever* have been properly in place, in early September, the area was already saturated with German troops including at least three of *Sipo-SD*'s *Einsatz-Kommando* units, which were tasked with hunting down partisans and parachutists, and not a few very active and now increasingly desperate and therefore extremely dangerous French collaborators, who together would make life very difficult indeed for the men of 2 SAS. We may recall that the two jeep-mounted elements of the Wallace party, when they arrived in the area due west of Loyton's the week after its main party arrived, would find it almost impossible to operate in any meaningful way for that same reason, and that the Kipling party would be similarly constrained when it took over the Houndsworth area at the same time.

In fact, for all Franks' protestations in the aftermath of Loyton that the mission was two months too late, had anyone stopped to consider the ground rules for inserting combat groups by air that deep inside occupied territory, it would have been obvious that the notion of commencing Operation Loyton in June, or even July, was actually a pipe-dream. The RAF advised SAS Brigade in mid-May that the first date it could contemplate inserting an advance party at such a distance, given the need for the aircraft to return to friendly airspace within the hours of darkness, was the night of 3 August. Coincidentally, that was the very date on which SHAEF issued a revised operational requirement for a mission to the Vosges to the Brigade, and that same day McLeod issued Operation Instruction No. 38 to Lt-Col Franks, laying down the requirements for Operation Loyton. It is interesting to note that the attitude of SAS Brigade vis-à-vis the Resistance had clearly changed out of all recognition since mid-June, for the prime purpose of the mission, McLeod ordered,

> was to co-operate with resistance groups at first in clandestine and later in overt offensive action in attacking enemy communications, installations, airfields and general harassing of the enemy. Also to assist resistance groups in becoming organised and in their training.

By an ironic twist of fate, unlike those in the Morvan, which Fraser's Houndsworth party had been instructed to keep at arm's length, the resistance groups in question were to prove extremely untrustworthy; Franks called them 'totally incompetent ... well infiltrated with informers and with no fighting spirit', and the Loyton party would perhaps have fared much better if it had followed the original guidelines and left them severely alone.

The summary of the after-action report makes great play of the importance of operating against the main railway lines running into

Strasbourg. In fact rail traffic in France in general was already reduced to a trickle. Few trains were derailed during the course of the mission, one of them by an element of the Loyton party which had been inserted in entirely the wrong location, and which then operated independently. And as we shall see, a satellite party, dropped away from the main operational area and tasked primarily with rendering the main Paris–Strasbourg line unusable were actually beaten to the job by the Germans.

Franks was instructed to insert a reconnaissance party of ten all-ranks as soon as possible after 5 August, but in the event, priority was given to the replacement advance party for Operation Rupert (q.v.), and it was the night of 12 August before the Loyton advance party of five SAS ORs under Capt Henry Druce and a French captain named de Lesseps, who used Goodfellow as his *nom de guerre*, plus a Phantom patrol under Capt Hislop and the ill-fated Jedburgh team Jacob, fifteen men in all, were inserted to the east of Raon-l'Étape, near the village of La Petite-Raon. The drop was not a complete success; in particular, containers of weapons sufficient to arm 200 men, were simply appropriated by *maquisards* under the local leader, 'Colonel Maximum', as a fee for the use of the DZ, while the radios were lost, according to the SAS after-action report, and this 'delayed reinforcements by a further nineteen vital days'. When Druce did send for reinforcements, the message was apparently confused with another received the same day, and when the party, ten strong, under Major Peter le Poer Power, 1 Squadron's commanding officer, was inserted, on the night of 27 August, it was dropped some forty kilometres out of position. Power's party was dropped with Jedburgh team Alastair, the report of which says the insertion took place three nights earlier. Power's party set off eastward in the general direction of the Loyton area, but it was 18 September before some of them were able to make contact with other members of the Loyton party. The remainder, four men under Lt Alastair McGregor, a veteran of the Italian campaign, spent much of the intervening period trying to mount sabotage operations along the St-Dié–Luneville railway with very little in the way of explosives or accessories, living on what they could beg from local inhabitants. On the verge of exhaustion, they managed to link up with an American unit on 8 October.

Druce's party seemingly split into three groups (the Jedburgh team accompanying one of them), and managed to evade for four days, but on 17 August, on wooded high ground north of the village of Moussey, the group led by Capt Goodfellow either ran into, or was betrayed to, a

German search party. In the course of the firefight which followed, Sgt Robert Lodge DCM (his real name was Friedlaender) and Tpr Wallace Hall of 2 SAS, together with Sgt Seymour, the Jedburgh team's radio operator, were captured, the latter after he had fallen behind the main body of the party due to a dislocated big toe he suffered on landing.

Sgt Lodge's body was later taken to Moussey and given over to the village priest, who was told that the man had taken his own life before he had been captured; however, Abbé Achille Gasmann, when he examined the body, found a gunshot wound to the back of the head and bayonet wounds in the stomach. Tpr Hall, taken with Lodge, was later seen alive at the concentration camp at Schirmeck, about twenty kilometres away to the east, in the direction of Strasbourg; he is believed to have been killed between Schirmeck and the nearby larger camp at Struthof-Natzweiler. His body was never recovered.

Sgt Seymour, who tells us in his report that he was abandoned by the *maquisards* who had been told off to escort him, and fought alone with Bren, carbine and pistol until his ammunition was expended and he was forced to surrender, was the only man captured during Operation Loyton to survive. He was also taken to Schirmeck, and in his report, made post-war, he says he was threatened and deprived of food, but not physically maltreated during his interrogation there by *SS-Obersturmbannführer* Wilhelm Schneider, although he had been earlier, at the time of his capture. He was later taken to Strasbourg, from there to the holding centre at Haguenau, some way to the north, then to Dulag Luft, the interrogation centre and transit camp for downed aircrew at Oberürsel near Frankfurt-am-Main, later to a succession of PoW camps, and finally was forced to participate in one of the 'death marches' around eastern Germany in the final months of the war, in the course of which so many Allied PoWs died.

Sgt Gerald Davis of the Phantom patrol led by Capt Hislop seems to have become separated from the others somewhere near Vexaincourt, also on 17 August, and by 20 August was clearly in a bad way. He approached a farmer at St-Jean-le-Saulcy early that morning, asked for food and was refused, and then approached the priest, Abbé Clément Colin, who not only turned him away but also denounced him to *Sipo-SD*'s *Einsatz-Kommando* Schöner, housed in the nearby Château de Belval. His body was found in the spring of 1945, in the hills above Moussey, and the SAS team which investigated war crimes perpetrated on regimental and attached personnel conjectured that he had been taken back to the area from Schirmeck, where he had also been interrogated by Schneider, ordered to reveal the location of a *maquisard* camp, and was shot when he refused to do so.

Brian Franks' twenty-three-strong element of the main party landed on the night of 1 September. Druce had been able to extricate himself and the remains of his group from the immediate area of Moussey, and was in position to receive the main party, at a DZ near Veney, on the far side of Raon-l'Étape, but any sense of satisfaction he and they may have experienced at that small success was very short-lived, for the affair turned into a chaotic and ultimately murderous farce when members of rival partisan groups, who had turned up at the DZ unannounced and certainly uninvited, started rifling through the containers, appropriating weapons and ammunition along with other supplies, eventually opening fire on one another, either in confusion or simply in open fighting over the spoils, though there are persistent reports of the *maquisards* having been infiltrated by an informer, who began shooting to draw the attention of German troops. Druce is supposed to have killed this man with a pistol shot to the heart, but Franks makes no mention of any such incident in his after-action report, simply saying that the confusion was caused by the presence of escaped Russian PoWs who spoke German and were taken for Germans in the darkness. Franks and the rest of the SAS party eventually gave up and left them to it. Major Dennis Reynolds and fourteen more men arrived at a new DZ about four kilometres east of Veney on the night of 6 September; by that time Franks had ordered a move away from the *maquisards* who had been so troublesome during his arrival and shifted camp to the area of Pierre-Percée, above Celles, but the general situation had, if anything, deteriorated even further. As the after-action report summary puts it, 'the story is one of constant moves and German search parties, of shortage of food and German reprisals against those farmers who gave assistance', in an area which was very pro-German to begin with, and where the collaboration of members of the public with British soldiers would have been patchy, even without the certainty of harsh punishment if it were discovered. Three men from Reynolds' party, Sgt Michael Fitzpatrick MM and Tprs John Conway and John Elliott, did not link up after the insertion. From evidence gathered post-war, it seems that Tpr Elliott fractured his femur on landing, and the others carried him to a farm named La Fosse. They remained there until 16 September, when they were taken prisoner by a *Sipo-SD* unit, *Einsatz-Kommando* Wenger, seemingly after having been betrayed by a Frenchwoman who was working for the Germans. They were brought back to the farm three days later and shot, and their bodies were partially burned in an outbuilding; their remains later were interred in Moussey churchyard, along with those of many of their comrades.

If conditions were bad when Franks and Reynolds arrived, they soon got worse. The weather that autumn was cold and wet, and resupply missions were rare thanks to the combination of poor flying conditions and local difficulties, while the mood of the population was unpredictable and the German presence strong and strengthening. As the summary of the after-action report has it:

> The ... history of the Loyton force is rich in examples of the difficulty of sustaining a base on the back-stage of a battle in an area where ordinary security forces are augmented by B echelon and reserve troops ... Resupply ... was made more difficult by German picketing and difficulties of movement out of the area to reach other targets were correspondingly increased. The arrival of six jeeps and crews on the night of 21 September [in fact, three jeeps and six men were droppped on the night of 19 September, and three more vehicles and fourteen more men two nights later, all of them to a DZ just to the north of Moussey, to which the entire party had by then returned] did not add fluidity because after one or two sorties they were traced to their base and eliminated as a mobile force,

though this 'elimination' seems not to have finally taken place until the second week in October according to the War Diary. In fact, the jeeps were never a great deal of use during Operation Loyton. Most of them arrived in poor general condition and required a considerable amount of work to bring them up to serviceability, and they seem to have suffered more than their fair share of the usual defects such as weak gun mounts, and that did not improve the men's opinions of them. Loyton also seems to have suffered from much more than its fair share of defective everyday equipment and ordnance, and Brian Franks was highly critical of Station 1090 in consequence. The men who were dropped with the jeeps proved somewhat unsatisfactory, too; many were very recent recruits to 2 SAS who had little training, and Franks was quite scathing in his criticism of their having been sent into action in this way. The list of faults he found bears repeating:

(a) Carbines – Some ... were literally solid with rust and had to be buried.

(b) Ammunition for Vickers K was bent and dented and would certainly have caused a stoppage. It had to be sorted out round by round ...

(c) Vickers magazines – All were dirty and carelessly loaded.

(d) No oil was sent for jeeps. One jeep was only half full.

(e) No fittings for extra petrol tanks were included.

(f) A number of defective Bren magazines were sent.

(g) Thompson SMGs were sent but no magazines.

(h) Training bombs were sent with the Bazookas.

(i) Eureka sent without batteries.

And added that:

Four out of six jeep [machine-gun] mountings were useless owing to the welding going before the guns were fired ...

Of the men he said:

Some of the men sent with the jeeps as final reinforcements were quite unsuitable. They arrived very nervous and were either so scared as to be useless or so confident that they were extremely careless. Most of these men were recent recruits who were clearly not of the right type and had not had sufficient training. This operation showed very clearly that both officers and men who had not had previous battle experience were very nervous, and inclined to spread this disease amongst others. The experienced men were good and could almost always be guaranteed to get away with it.

The new base Franks had established near Pierre-Percée on 5 September lay six kilometres to the east of Pexonne, on the hillside overlooking the valley of the River Plaine, (which actually takes its name from Celles, the small town below Pierre-Percée), north and west of the Val de Senones in which La Petite-Raon and Moussey lie. It was from here that the first offensive raiding party, led by Lt Marx, sortied, to operate against vehicles using the secondary road which crosses the Col de la Chapelotte some kilometres to the north. Marx and his men mined the road and disabled two *Wehrmacht* trucks, but soon ran into a German patrol and became engaged in a close-quarters gun battle. They were able to withdraw without casualties, and some hours later ambushed a third truck, but towards the end of the afternoon they bumped a security force.

During the course of the firefight which followed, the party was split; Marx and six men managed to clear the area, and returned to the camp at Pierre-Percée, though it seems that they may have betrayed its location in the process, for the next day it was attacked and the Loyton party was lucky to be able to exfiltrate without loss, save all its stores.

In search of a safer site, Franks ordered a move across the valley and into the hills to the south-east, to return to the vicinity of Moussey, where the situation seemed to have calmed down. The move seems to have been made on foot, in small groups, and probably took the best part of two days – the distance is not great, but the terrain is punishing. An RV was established at the Lac de la Maix, in the hills north-east of Moussey and some distance from the village. One of the men, Tpr Maurice Griffin, became separated from the rest during the move, proceeded to the RV alone and was captured near the lake on 10 September. Griffin was taken to Schirmek camp the following day then transferred to Rotenfels, a small holding centre near Rastatt between Baden-Baden and Karlsruhe, when Schirmeck was evacuated on 22 November. He was shot at neighbouring Gaggenau on 25 November, along with other captured SAS men, the leader of the Jedburgh team Jacob, Capt Victor Gough, and downed Allied aircrew.

Griffin was not the only one captured during the move. A five-man party under Lt James Black, comprising Cpl Harry Winder and Tprs James Dowling, Len Lloyd and James Salter, which Franks had sent out in an attempt to ambush a patrol of some thirty German troops who were advancing on the party's laying-up place, subsequently also lost its way while crossing the valley. Franks' report places the sortie on the morning of 11 September, but other accounts suggest it may have been a day earlier, and that on the evening of 10 September Black's patrol sought refuge at one of the many small sawmills in the Val de Celles, the Scierie de la Turbine. Here it encountered the trio of men who had become separated from Lt Marx's section, Sgt Frank Terry-Hall, Cpl Thomas Ivison and Tpr Jack Crosier, who had last been seen 'running like hell up a track towards La Chapellotte, pursued by SS troops and Alsatian dogs', and who had also had instructions to fall back on the lake. Unfortunately, these men had been betrayed by an informer (later named by Major Eric Barkworth as Gaston Mathieu) who reported their presence to a *Sipo-SD* detachment at Raon-l'Étape. The precise chronology of events is unclear, and there are unresolved problems with conflicting accounts and inconsistencies (such as why they had remained at the sawmill instead of making their way to the RV at the lake), but according to a reconstruction of events made by Barkworth and his small investigation team, post-war, a mixed unit of German SS and SD personnel and *Miliciens* was despatched on 15 September to arrest the men and in the brief firefight which resulted, Black was wounded in the leg. There is some evidence that Sgt Terry-Hall evaded and was not captured until later, but the French couple who ran the sawmill were both killed. The men were taken to Raon-l'Étape, and eventually reached Schirmeck, seemingly on 18 September. The following morning all eight left the camp, apparently en route for Strasbourg, where they were to be interrogated by Schneider. Although he denied it, Schneider is believed to have asked his superior, *SS-Standartenführer* Dr Erich Isselhorst, to have them shot, which instruction was carried out, probably at or near St-Dié on 20 or 21 September. Their remains were later recovered and buried at the Allied war cemetery at Durnbach in Bavaria.

By mid-September, Operation Loyton had achieved very little, and had lost sixteen of its participants, but the two weeks which followed were rather more positive, and the main party was even able to undertake more offensive action, though in truth the results still came nowhere near justifying the risk of reprisals. In the early hours of 20 September the party received its first vehicles, three of them, together with six more men, and the next day Franks himself led a two-car patrol in the Senones area. Ambushes were laid twice, but came to nothing. He repeated the exercise the following day with similar results, though his report talks of having discovered German armour laying up in woods four kilometres south of the village and the jeeps manoeuvring into a position to launch an attack, which came to nothing.

That night, three more jeeps and fourteen more men, including Capt McGibbon-Lewis and Lt Silly, whom we last encountered during Operation Defoe in Normandy a month previously, were parachuted in successfully. By this time, Franks was expecting a relieving American force to reach the area any day, and the following morning decided to divide his party and instigate more aggressive patrolling, sending Capt Miller and Lts Silly and Swayne with six men to watch the Senones–Moyenmoutier road and allocating most of the other commissioned personnel (himself, Maj Power, Capts Lewis and Druce, and Lts Dill and Manners, who had joined the Loyton party after his somewhat precipitate return from Operation Wallace) to act as jeep commanders (and drivers), the vehicles to work in pairs. Power's and Lewis' cars were in action the next day, attacking a convoy on the main road up the Val de Celles, north-west of Celles itself, destroying three cars and a three-ton truck, but this had the effect of preventing Franks and Dill from using the road to reach the area in which they had intended to operate, where the valley narrows between Raon-l'Etape and Celles, and instead the pair set off across country in the opposite direction, towards Allarmont. This proved to be a one-way journey, the track they used to descend towards the village being impossible to climb again. Worse, a strong enemy force was in Allarmont, and Franks' small party was forced to turn left down the road, towards Celles, intending to lie in ambush near another track which led back up the hillside, and which they hoped to use as an escape route. Dill remained on the road while Franks reconnoitred the track; he found it feasible and returned, but no sooner had the two jeeps positioned themselves adjacent to a straight stretch between two blind bends than a lone German cyclist appeared, and the sounds of vehicles and men could be heard in both directions. One of Franks' machine-gunners despatched the cyclist and was answered by automatic fire from a nearby house, whereupon all the Vickers Ks engaged it while the vehicles beat a hasty retreat towards the track junction. Franks' car never made it; he put a wheel in the ditch, and the jeep overturned. Unhurt, the four men aboard scrabbled for a hand-hold on Dill's jeep, and the overloaded vehicle managed to climb the incline and disappear, only to be confronted by a roadblock consisting of fallen trees just past the point where Franks had terminated his reconnaissance. Pursued by infantry whose fire was fast becoming effective, they had no alternative but to abandon the vehicle and clear the area on foot, later re-crossing the ridge towards Moussey.

Reprisals followed rapidly. On Sunday, 24 September German troops arrived in Moussey in large numbers and arrested all the male inhabitants between sixteen and sixty years of age, a total of 210, and subsequently deported them to concentration camps (from which just seventy returned after the war's end). This was a serious, if not quite a fatal, blow to the morale of both the civilian population and the SAS party, and Franks responded by curtailing patrol activity – which was having very little result anyway – and effectively suspending Loyton, perhaps with the idea of relaunching it should Patton's army succeed in forcing a passage through to the Vosges and changing the general situation there. He also ordered a move once more, to Coichot, roughly midway between Celles and Senones. Local patrols did go out, however, and in the course of one of them, Cpl Boris King (actually,

Boris Kasperovitch), was shot and killed. He was one of only three or four men to die in combat or of wounds received therein during the course of Operation Loyton. There is no clear evidence as to how, when and where the next man to fall, Tpr Frederick Puttick, was captured or killed, but he was seen in captivity at Étival and later at the Château Belval by one of the *Kommando* Wenger's French collaborators, a Milicien named Louis Perdon, and by the Frenchwoman who is thought to have betrayed the three parachutists captured at La Fosse. Anecdotal evidence from the former suggests that Tpr Puttick was taken from Étival and murdered by one of Wenger's men, and that the body was burnt. Tpr Puttick's name is on the Roll of Honour at the Airborne Forces Memorial at Groesbeek in the Netherlands, and his date of death is given as 5 October.

On 7 October what is described as 'the SAS rear party', composed of Lt David Dill, Sgt Ralph Hay, L/Cpls George Robinson and Fred Austin, and Tprs James Bennett and Edwin Weaver, which had stayed behind after the main group moved from the campsite above Moussey to another at Coichot, south of Celles, in order to await the return of a three-man sabotage party under Sgt Nevill, were captured by a Panzer unit, probably after having been betrayed. They were held for two days by the unit which captured them, and then, on the evening of 9 October were taken to Saales and handed over to an *Einsatz-Kommando* commanded by *SS-Sturmbannführer* Hans-Dieter Ernst. They were kept in a cell at the Maison Barthlèmy in Saales, and there were reunited with Sgt Walter Nevill and Tprs Reg Church and Peter McGovern, and with the leader of Jedburgh team Jacob, Capt Victor Gough.

Following Sgt Seymour's capture on 17 August, Gough had continued to operate with his French liaison officer, Capt Maurice Boissarie, who used the *nom de guerre* Baraud. Seemingly, Boissarie was killed during a skirmish at a farm named Viambois on 4 September, and thereafter Gough operated alone, away from the Loyton party, and relied on *maquisards* for support, though he clearly stayed in touch. He was seemingly captured at the end of September or the beginning of October (his last radio transmission to London was made on 18 September, using an SAS set; Franks reported seeing him in the company of Col Maximum on the morning of 30 September), and by the time Dill's party arrived at Saales had already undergone prolonged interrogation, though apparently without having been tortured; he was in good enough health and spirits to have drawn a number of cartoons while he was in captivity, two of which are reproduced in Barkworth's report on the circumstances of his death. Sgt Nevill's small party, which had been operating against transport on the Col du Hantz, had been captured near La Petite-Raon, seemingly on 8 October.

On 15 October, the two officers were separated from the eight men, and the latter were taken some two kilometres to a spot known as La Grande-Fosse, where a pit had already been dug to receive their bodies. They were taken one by one from the truck, stripped naked and shot, and later Ernst reported to Isselhorst that they had been killed while trying to escape. The bodies of the eight men were recovered on 6 November 1945, and were later re-buried at Durnbach. Lt Dill and Capt Gough were transferred to Schirmeck and thence to Rotenfels, and they too were shot at Gaggenau on 25 November. The case was another of those which came under the scrutiny of Eric Barkworth, and in May 1946, eight men, the most senior of whom was a captain named Karl Gölkel, who seems not actually to have been present at the execution, were found guilty of the murder, and were sentenced by a British military court to a total of forty-three years' imprisonment. Four of those men, and three others, were also found guilty of the murder of Lt Black's party, but in that case Barkworth was able to deliver more concrete evidence to the court, and Griem, Jantzen, Neuschwanger and Wetzel, all of them SS NCOs, most of whom were suspected of having been at least involved in other murders, were sentenced to death and shot at Werl Prison in September 1946.

Another parachutist, Tpr Selwyn Brown, who had been the detachment's cook, was seemingly also captured on 7 October, between Senones and Moussey, when he mistook a German vehicle, probably a *Kübelwagen*, for an SAS jeep. Brown was not handed over to *Einsatz-Kommando* Ernst with Dill's party, but to *Kommando* Wenger at Étival-Clairfontaine instead, and subsequently arrived at Schirmeck, where he found himself in the company of Lt James Silly and Tpr Donald Lewis, who were captured trying to cross the River Meurthe, both of whom had also been briefly confined at Étival. Once again, it seems that the officer was separated from the ORs, but this time both he and they were returned to the units which had captured them and were murdered by them. Tprs Brown and Lewis were seemingly killed on 16 October, at a farm known as Le Harcholet, and Lt Silly on 22 October at a sawmill named the Scierie Barodet near Moyenmoutier. The remains of all three bodies were later recovered, though those which were reliably assumed to be Lt Silly's, discovered in the cellar of the sawmill, were unrecognizable after having been burned, and he was identified from circumstantial evidence; all were buried in Moussey churchyard.

> The position now was that rations were very short indeed – approximately one box of 24 hr rations per man. We had no explosives and the likelihood of a re-supply drop appeared negligible. The Allied line appeared static and the weather which had been bad enough before was now worsening. I decided to end the operation and instruct parties to make their way to the American lines as best they could. I gave an RV near the Celles valley, where I would be for the next 48 hours.

The party was to be divided into five groups for the purpose, one led by Franks, one by Capt McGibbon-Lewis, the third by Lt Silly, the fourth by Lt Marx and the last by Lt Swayne. During the course of the exfiltration Lt Silly and Tpr Lewis were captured, as described above, and two more men were killed in action: Lt Geoffrey Castellain, who had actually led one of the Operation Pistol parties (q.v.), and had made his way, along with four men, to join up with the Loyton party on 1 October, died at Raon-l'Étape of wounds he received in a firefight with a German patrol on 12 October, and on 20 October, one of the Phantoms, Sgmn Peter Bannerman, was killed. They, too, were buried at Moussey. Majors Dennis Reynolds and Anthony Whately-Smith were captured at La Trouche, near Raon-l'Étape, on 30 October, together with a Frenchman and woman who had been helping them. Reynolds had been wounded in hand and head during an attack on a truck, and had been unable to move before that date; Whately-Smith had remained behind to look after him. The two men were removed to Schirmek on 5 November, and when that camp was evacuated on 22 November, to Rotenfels, they too were shot at Gaggenau on 25 November. Those members of the Loyton party who exfiltrated successfully linked up with American forces between the Moselle and the Meurthe rivers.

In addition to the main party and Major Power's stick which went astray, there was a further element of Operation Loyton, a ten-man unit under the command of Lt Joseph Rousseau (a Canadian; seven of the nine ORs in the party were actually Frenchmen from 3 or 4 SAS), which was dropped on the night of 9 September, well to the north of the main operational area, some ten or twelve kilometres west of

Sarrebourg on the edge of the Forêt de Réchicourt. This party was tasked with operating against the main N4 road and the railway linking Sarrebourg with Nancy (and thus Paris with Strasbourg). There was a delay between numbers five and six exiting the aircraft, and as a result the stick was split into two. From the map references the two groups gave in their reports they were probably no more than 500 metres apart when they dropped, but the two halves were not reunited until over a week had passed. The groups were entirely unbalanced; Rousseau's contained three NCOs, the other was made up entirely of troopers.

Rousseau's party laid up through the first day and then set out that night to cut the railway, but discovered that the Germans had already made a thorough job of that. It then turned south-west, in the general direction of Raon-l'Étape and still moving only by night, reached the vicinity of Repaix, near Blamont, by the early morning of 13 September. There Rousseau contacted the village priest, who hid the men in the church tower over the next five days. On 19 September they heard from the curé of Domèvre, the other side of Blamont, that advance elements of the American 3rd Army were in the vicinity, and that the missing five men had been located and would be brought to Repaix. Cpl Pichon was detailed to wait for them, while the remainder of the party went in search of the Americans. The next day the four operated with them, and by the afternoon were close to the village of Igney. Entering the village, they were fêted, but in the excitement, no one noticed that German infantrymen had returned in strength. The Americans withdrew without informing Rousseau, who made for the woodland on the edge of the village. In the process one man, Tpr Centolle, was wounded, and Lt Rousseau and L/Cpl Galmard were both captured. Joseph Rousseau was later either shot or died of wounds he sustained in the action, at Avricourt; since he was buried in a marked grave, the latter seems more likely. His remains were subsequently reinterred at the Allied War Cemetery at Ranville in Normandy, next to his brother, who died on 7 June. L/Cpl Galmard was reported to have been shot at Foulcrey, some kilometres away.

The other group lay up for three nights and then started south-westward; it spent the night of 15 September in a wood near Frenonville, just a kilometre from Repaix. The reports diverge at this point, Tpr Reichenstein, who wrote the second group's, stating that they met up with Cpl Pichon on 17 September, and were in action just minutes later when three German trucks loaded with ammunition passed and they attacked, destroying them. They then moved off to Autrepierre, where they met up with an American armoured unit. At 0200 that night, Reichenstien records, the M4 Sherman tank beside which they were sleeping was attacked by German infantry armed with rocket-propelled grenades; they were driven off 'leaving behind a German steel helmet, a gas mask (property of *Gefreiter* Bender), and an SAS jumping jacket (i.e. a Dennison smock) with D.E. Reynolds written on the collar', which is a not inconsiderable coincidence. The depleted stick then moved to Lunéville; it is not recorded whether it subsequently rejoined the main Loyton party before being stood down.

PISTOL

Immediately after the first element of the Loyton main party had been inserted, it was decided to mount a further operation in the area to the north, to the east of the River Moselle between Metz and Nancy. The plan called for four sections to be dropped and for each to split into two groups of between six and eight men, to operate independently; in the event, the D party was not to be inserted. The four Stirlings carrying the men left Keevil on the night of 15 September, the after-action report summary tells us, and three pilots believed they had found their allotted DZs and dropped their sticks. 'Between 12th and 17th Sept five attempts were made' to insert the last party, it says (which hardly squares with the date given in the summary's own first paragraph). 'Unfavourable weather reports only permitted 3 flights and these were unsuccessful as ground fog and cloud conditions made it impossible to recognise the DZ.' In fact, only one of the three parties which were dropped, the A party, was anywhere near the intended target area and it was separated into two halves which landed roughly a mile apart. The B party missed its DZ by twelve kilometres, and one of its members never linked up with the rest; Tpr Christopher Ashe was captured by German troops (it is not known whether they were *Wehrmacht* or *SS* personnel) a week later, on 23 September, south of Bitche, perhaps twenty kilometres from where he had landed. He was taken first to Strasbourg and placed in the rue du Fil prison, and four days later was taken to Schirmeck. It is believed that he was moved to Rotenfels with the others on 22 November, and that he, too, was shot at Gaggenau on 25 November. The C party landed some twenty-five kilometres off target, and its leader, Capt Scott, broke (or perhaps badly sprained; accounts vary) his ankle.

In fact, the parties were to be split into more and smaller groups than had been planned, a total of ten, with between two to five members. Each small party submitted an after-action report, and they are some of the most detailed and least formal of all the documents preserved from this period. A representative example states: 'In the evening we set off in a southerly direction and came upon some SAS boot tracks in a lane leading to a farm. We followed these tracks in the hope of meeting some of our party but as we approached the farmhouse we saw a couple of Germans having a meal so we retired and hid until they had gone.' (The so-called 'commando soles' were distinctive; this and many other reports from other operations made the point that they gave away the presence of SAS troops all too easily.) The reports tell a fairly uniform story of minor hardship and discomfort, of hiding in ditches and sleeping in woods, fields and hedges in weather which, in that equinoctal season, was predominantly wet (some reports speak of men being soaked through from the time they were inserted until they encountered American troops at the end of their mission), frequently too close to German troops for comfort and occasionally in firefights, though few of them were consequential.

In direct contrast to Loyton, the Pistol parties had no brief to contact, let alone operate with, local partisan groups; this had both advantages and disadvantages, of course, but it is noteworthy that the casualty rate from Pistol was very light in comparison to that from Loyton, and also that the men captured during the latter were, with the exception of Tpr Ashe, treated properly, as prisoners of war. The downside of the situation was that the troops were on their own, without any form of support, and few were to be resupplied. This, coupled with the fact that not all the containers and panniers dropped when the men were inserted were recovered, meant that they were short of both rations and ordnance right from the start. 'The food problem was surmountable by small parties', the after-action report summary tells us, but as was the case with Lt McGregor's Loyton party, the shortage of explosive material would certainly have hampered attempts to mount sabotage operations had other factors not combined to curtail them.

In all, perhaps a dozen small missions were undertaken, fully half of them by Tprs Clowes and Nicols after the pair had separated from the rest of the B party. Not all were successful, and the confirmed results from all the parties' operations make a short list: one concrete pylon carrying a high-voltage power line; a cattle train and a shunting engine derailed, and three vehicles immobilised by tyre-burster mines. To set against that, the casualty list was short, too; as well as Tpr Ashe and Lt Castellain, there was to be one more fatal casualty, for Lt Ronald Birnie, who was taken prisoner together with two other men in his party, was later killed in an air raid while in PoW camp. Two more of Birnie's party were also captured. Capt Scott, who had somehow managed to walk some fifty kilometres or more on his damaged ankle, and had brought his men to within reach of the Americans' positions, instructed the men in his party to leave him behind when they ran into a security patrol, was captured and spent the remaining months of the war in a PoW camp, as did Lt Darwall and Cpl Melvin, taken prisoner near St-Avold. Some of the parties crossed into American-occupied territory quite early on – five men from the A party, who had had to abandon all their kit when surrounded by a German search party, were out for barely five days – but Darwall's party remained in enemy territory until well in to November, having found a relatively safe laying-up place and a ready source of food, and its other three members linked up with friendly forces towards the end of the month. This was exceptional, however, and most of the parties came in during the first week of October.

Part Four

3 SAS (3e RÉGIMENT DE CHASSEURS PARACHUTISTS)

DICKENS

Operation Dickens, mounted by a reinforced troop from 1 Squadron, 3 SAS, was the first occasion on which 3 French Para went into action. It got off to a poor start when the reconnaissance party which consisted of a British liaison officer, Capt Burt, from 2 SAS, and Lt Étienne Poisson, together with Jedburgh team Harold, was dropped some thirty kilometres north of the chosen location in the Forêt de l'Absie, on the night of 15 July. Some of the party landed directly in a village, the Jedburgh team leader, Major Whitty, actually in the baker's yard; most of such equipment as was recovered was useless, and the Jedburghs were out of direct contact with London for three weeks in consequence. The loss was eventually made good only after a local *résistant* bicycled to meet 'Samuel' (Amédée Maingard, the Bulbasket party's SOE contact in the Vienne), some hundred kilometres away, with a pre-encoded message for him to transmit; a Jedset was then dropped to the SAS main party on 7 August, and delivered to the Jedburgh team.

To make matters worse, Lt Boutillon's advance party, which included the operation's own signallers, which was dropped two nights later, was inserted not in the alternative DZ in the Bois d'Anjou, which was twenty-five kilometres due east of Cholet and some way north of the reconnaissance party's actual location, but an even greater distance north, near Chemillé in the neighbouring *département* of Maine-et-Loire. It was scattered in the process, though that did not prevent its commander from calling in an air strike on a train full of SS troops standing in Chemillé station, with 'excellent results', the following day. As a result it was some time before the two advance elements reached the Bois d'Anjou and a full week before the first element of the main party, the 'HQ stick', could be inserted. It was followed by two sections more on each of the following nights, and by the morning of 28 July the entire party of fifty-six ORs and six officers, under *Capitaine* Georges

Fournier, was finally in place. There was no doubt in the minds of the participants that this delay rendered the operation less effective than it might otherwise have been.

There exist two reports on Operation Dickens in the archives; Burt's was made independently of the operational commander. The two are thus complementary, although there are inconsistencies. The latter's (and it includes additional reports from the leaders of each section or stick), is little more than a chronology of events, while Burt's report analyses the operation's strengths and weaknesses in some detail; he was to be very critical of what he saw as the failings of the higher echelon to support the party adequately, and of the Jedburgh team to co-operate in virtually any sense. The report of Jedburgh team Harold exists too, of course, and since its defining paragraph states that its mission was 'to act as a link for the SAS with their organisation in England and transmit their messages for them' and 'to aid them as much as possible', it comes as rather a surprise to discover that it mentions the SAS party only occasionally during the first week, and just once thereafter, and then critically, charging that it 'seriously hindered our work by attempting to organise resistance groups themselves [sic] without being qualified to do so, or informing us'. In this case there seems to have been a complete lack of meaningful communication between SAS and Jedburghs.

Even with the entire Dickens party in place, it was still almost a week before offensive operations commenced – one should bear in mind that the area the party was briefed to cover extended to three full *départe-ments* and totalled some 18,000 square kilometres; getting individual sections dispersed into the areas in which they were to operate, on foot and without drawing attention to themselves, which was the first step, was a time-consuming business. The first party into action was that led by *Sergeant-Chef* Gervais, detached to operate in the area between Clisson and Cholet; it was in position by 4 August and began operations against the permanent way and signal installations that same night. Gervais's section was to attack railway targets a score of times until 22 August, and then turned its attention to the roads. On 7 August Fournier's own HQ section, allocated the area around the town of Niort, went into action; the railway lines towards Parthenay and St-Maixent were cut in two places each, and the next night those towards La Rochelle, Saintes and Fontenay received the same treatment, the operations being repeated as required over the next three nights and sporadically thereafter; other sections were dispersed around the region (which made communications, both between sections extremely difficult and between all but the HQ section and Moor Park impossible) and carried out similar activities.

In all, the Dickens party was to cut railways eighty-three times, causing eleven derailments and destroying twenty locomotives (in particular, Burt reports two trains packed with troops having been derailed at speed, and three more totally destroyed by the RAF), and by 23 August Fournier was able to report that 'no more trains passed in this area', though by then his men had also begun to mount effective ambushes on the roads and continued to do so until 7 September (and occasionally thereafter), when Niort was liberated. During this phase, the HQ section alone destroyed some thirty vehicles and captured half a dozen more, together with around 400 prisoners, 500 personal weapons and 600 tons of ammunition and stores, with large numbers of enemy personnel killed and wounded. Fournier records one fatal casualty of his own – Pct André Schmidt, at Montravers on 27 August. A requisitioned vehicle in which he was travelling drove into the village in ignorance of the presence of some 800 SS troops; he fought until his ammunition was expended and then, wounded in head and stomach, was taken into captivity and killed out of hand (according to Burt, who notes that the Dickens party suffered a total of four fatalities. Only two can be traced, Schmidt and Pct Joseph Hadj, who died, also at Montravers, on 22 August).

After 7 September, Fournier, by now reinforced by a considerable number of newly armed FFI volunteers (he put the figure at around 500), was ordered to organise the northern sector of the perimeter around the important naval base of La Rochelle, which, like Lorient and St-Nazaire, was to remain in German hands until the end of the war in Europe; he remained there until 25 September, when he moved to St-Nazaire, and handed over command to Lt Boutillon, who ran the operation until the Dickens party was withdrawn to Épernay to rest and recuperate. The German forces in control of La Rochelle attempted to break out in strength on a number of occasions, but were contained each time. During this period the men of 3 French Para fought as 'regular' infantry, in more-or-less fixed positions; whether this was proper employment for men who had demonstrated their ability to work in small parties in enemy-held territory is moot (and that very point was made in the Brigade's War Diary). The Dickens party was joined at La Rochelle by the Samson party (q.v.), on 13 September, and some days later the Moses party arrived, and set up a base to the north-west of the area, inland from St Brévin-les-Pins, just across the mouth of the Loire estuary from St-Nazaire, where there was a large concentration of German troops largely penned in behind the Atlantic Wall defences which stretched from Paimboeuf to Pornic. On 20 September Fournier took the Samson party and his HQ stick to join them. He himself was wounded in a skirmish at the Moulin-Rouge near Frossay on 27 September (and one of the Samson party, Pct Dunyac (or Dunyack) was killed, as were fourteen enemy personnel) and before the end of the month the party was back at La Rochelle, in time to help repulse an attempted break-out in the Charron sector on 5 October.

There is an inconsistency between Burt's and Fournier's reports; it concerns an event which the former states took place on 9 August (but which other sources, including the Brigade's War Diary, indicate actually happened two days earlier), to which Burt refers in passing and Fournier not at all, which is somewhat surprising given that it involved the main campsite of the party, in the Bois d'Anjou, being 'overrun', in Burt's words, 'by over 900 SS from Cholet'. Frustratingly, he supplies no further information save that at the time the majority of the men were 'dispersed in small parties carrying out its various missions'; he was not a witness to the event himself, having succumbed to the curse of Philippeville – a bout of malaria which kept him out of action for a week, hidden in the house of a *résistant* – and that may account for the discrepancy in the dates. One of the other Dickens party reports, that of Lt Boutillon, makes brief mention of the affair. Boutillon relates that he received a parachutage of arms and supplies for the Resistance and 'During the day [seemingly 6 August] a [*Maquis*] truck containing arms was captured by the Germans, next day the base was attacked by 1,800 Germans. Our losses were 1 man from the resistance ... and Lt Poisson wounded. German losses were 84 killed, 164 wounded (report by German Capt.).' This seems rather unbalanced until one reads the somewhat fuller (for once) entry in the War Diary, which explains that 'on 7 August the base was attacked by SS troops, but the base party managed to avoid capture or casualties [sic], though the enemy, who spent many hours firing at each other, suffered ... extraordinary losses ... caused entirely by their own action'. Fournier was absent at the time; his report of 11 August states 'Went in search of men at Bois d'Anjou as I had had no news of them since operations started [on 7 August], and found them on 14 August.' The next day, he says, he moved his base to the 'farm of Deux Chênes near Amaillaix'; no such location exists, but there is a village named Amailloux, ten kilometres north of Parthenay, around which town activities were concentrated for the rest of the month, and Boutillon refers to regrouping at a farm named Brands, near Amailloux, after the attack on the Bois d'Anjoux base.

The more important aspects of Burt's report concern the lack of support he felt the party had received from certain quarters. He clearly had little respect for the FFI, noting:

> These proved more of a handicap than a help. They frequently shot up our vehicles and wounded half a dozen of the detachment including one officer. There appeared to be no control – divided counsels and rival leadership. As a result [sic] Harold was unable to provide us with the assistance we were led to believe that we should get and uncoordinated activity by small groups of FFI were a serious embarrassment. There can be little doubt that our base was attacked as a result of information obtained by the enemy from our local FFI where keenness did not compensate for their lack of military training or discretion.'

One has the feeling that he did not actually expect much more (or much better) from the FFI, but the Jedburghs, with whom he was inserted, were a different matter, and he clearly viewed their performance with contempt, dismissing them as non-co-operative and even obstructive. Their failure to provide communications channels, as laid down in their orders, he found particularly lamentable (though it is difficult to see what they could have achieved without a functioning radio set). For his part, the Jedburgh leader, Major Whitty, had a similar contemptuous view of the SAS party, and was particularly incensed by Fournier's willingness to arm FTP (Communist) partisans. Later, despite his promises to do so, Whitty consistently failed to arm partisan bands associated with the Dickens party, even from a consignment of forty-four tons which was landed from two Royal Navy destroyers, HMSs *Kelvin* and *Urania*, at Les Sables d'Olonne, along with four more Jedburgh teams, on 28 September.

As for other Allies, Burt had a scathing but somewhat whimsical attitude to those elements of the US Army he observed at first hand ('Regular US Army forces refused to cross the Loire,' he said): 'Odd USA rubber-necking parties were occasionally encountered about and after this date [mid-September]. They were not combat troops but attached to paramilitary organisations of various kinds. Their occupation and delight appeared to be "committing liberation" in the various small towns through which they passed.'

Burt's greatest regret was the party's lack of adequate transportation, particularly jeeps:

> After two weeks on the ground it was clear that for operations against enemy columns which were beginning to stream away through the network of excellent roads the fire power and mobility of the jeeps would have been invaluable particularly in those parts of the country where the "bocage" – the system of small fields surrounded by banks and hedges with sunken lanes running through them – afforded unrivalled conditions for hit and run tactics.

And he adds in his general observations: 'The absence of jeeps ... was heart-breaking when the enemy was milling around the roads offering magnificent targets. It is no exaggeration to say that the detachment could have killed or captured thousands instead of hundreds.' We may note that the three jeeps destined for Dickens as part of Operation Newton, which could have been with the party from 21 August, just when they were needed, were diverted to join the Americans far to the east, and wonder why that was.

Burt also bemoaned the late insertion of the party, and the extra delay caused by the reconnaissance and advance parties being dropped in the wrong places:

> Without detracting from achievements of the detachments in the very least degree, I am convinced that they could have done infinitely more damage had they arrived in the area earlier. By the time they started operating a large amount of enemy reinforcements including armour and guns had already passed over the Loire ... The movement started ... soon after 'D' day with an average of 30 trains a day going up to Nantes, Angers and Saumur. The fact that the detachment succeeded in bringing all rail traffic to a standstill in little over a week is an indication of the amount of interference it could have caused by this means alone.

He was perhaps being a little disingenuous; to have had the sort of effect he was talking about, the Dickens party would have needed to be inserted on the night of 5 June, along with Bulbasket, and there is room to doubt that it could possibly have been as effective as it was under the more difficult conditions which applied then. However, he does make a valid point, and one may justifiably ask why consideration was not given to inserting a (French) SAS party into the Vendée/Maine-et-Loire region immediately after the invasion was launched, especially in view of the fact that SHAEF knew full well that the routes through that region would be of enormous importance to the enemy. It might have suffered losses – compare Dingson/Samwest (q.v.) – but that would surely have been a risk worth running in view of the possible advantage to be gained; we may note that 3 SAS was unemployed at the time. In his report Burt notes that there was little information available about the situation (i.e. the Resistance) in the area, there having been 'widespread arrests of suspected heads of resistance in February'. If there had been discussion as to the relative merits of operating in the Vendée/Maine-et-Loire region as opposed to the Vienne/Deux-Sèvres, that alone might have swung the balance in favour of Bulbasket.

McLeod was certainly aware of the need to mount an operation in the Vendée a month before Dickens was actually launched. He wrote to Browning at HQ Airborne Troops on 26 June:

> From the point of view of morale it is important to employ some of 3 French Para Bn as soon as possible. At present there is a gap on the Southern flank of the German Army which is covered by neither SAS nor Resistance: viz. the Vendée.
>
> I suggest one squadron should be employed in this area at once with the main objective of cutting Lot 4 [the line through Parthanay] and all railways to the west.
>
> This will allow 1 SAS in the Bullbasket area to concentrate on Lot 2 and Lot 1 and lateral lines from SE.

Burt was full of praise for Fournier ('easily the greatest contributing factor to the success of the operation') and his officers and men. He said:

> I do not think that British troops would have produced the results in the time. The mere fact that they were Frenchmen gave them a great advantage in obtaining local assistance, in moving about in civilian clothes [much of the operation, at least up until 7 September, seems to have been carried out in civilian clothes] and in knowing whom to approach and whom to avoid. This was particularly valuable in view of the breakdown of the FFI organisation.

As we have noted, the Dickens party was reinforced by the smaller two-section Samson party, also from 3 SAS and under the command of Capt Michel Leblond, which had been inserted a considerable way to the south, close to Limoges, on 10 August, and which had moved steadily north-westward, joining forces with Capt Jean-Saloman Simon's Moses party, which had replaced the Bulbasket party, on the way. As the area emptied of German forces, the combined Dickens/Samson/Moses party was further strengthened by the four sections which had undertaken Operations Marshall and Snelgrove. The various parties kept their original identities and were wound up at different times; Moses, whose men had been in the field since the first week of August, ended on 4 October and the Dickens party was withdrawn on 7 October, some ten days after Operation Samson terminated. All the parties from 3 SAS later assembled at Épernay, just south of Reims, to begin further operations in the Low Countries.

MOSES, SAMSON, MARSHALL
AND SNELGROVE

Only in two cases were SAS Brigade operations in France refreshed: when most of the Kipling party was sent into the Morvan to replace the Houndsworth party, and when Operation Moses took over from Operation Bulbasket. The latter substitution was the second operation mounted by 3 SAS. The Moses advance party was dropped to a reception arranged by John Tonkin, the Bulbasket CO, on 2 August; it comprised Capt Jean-Saloman Simon, the mission's commander, Capt JE Cameron, a liaison officer from 2 SAS, and six others including a signals party. When the two Hudson aircraft which repatriated Tonkin and most of his men landed at the Bon Bon LZ on the night of 6 August they brought in three more officers and eight ORs; two officers and twelve men arrived by parachute the following night, and two nights later the Dakota aircraft which evacuated the rest of Tonkin's party brought in another officer and seven men, bringing the Moses party up to nine officers and twenty-eight ORs, plus the signallers. An additional officer was inserted a week later.

Reports on the operation were submitted by Capt Cameron and by Capt Simon and some of his deputy commanders; as with Operation Dickens, the latter tend to be chronologies, but this time the former submitted an interim account, short on analysis but offering a snapshot of the situation as it was on 21 August, and then an update on 27 September.

By the third week of August, Cameron tells us, the Vienne was largely clear of enemy and in the hands of the FFI, save that there was a large concentration of German troops – he put the number at 10,000 – at Poitiers, and perhaps another 5,000 at Châtellerault; these were the men – and a few women, junior *Luftwaffe* personnel from the air bases in the area – who were to make up the Elster column (q.v.). The total number was certainly much higher than Cameron's estimate; when the column capitulated it was made up of 754 officers and 18,852 ORs, and by then it had already lost significant numbers in its journey across the country. The railway line Paris–Limoges (via Châteauroux; 'Lot 1') was out of action, but the Paris–Bordeaux line (via Châtellerault and Poitiers, 'Lot 2') was still in use, despite repeated operations by Bulbasket parties and *maquisards* to cut it. The main west–east road through the *département*, from Poitiers to Le Blanc, was under FFI control, as was the road from Poitiers south-east to Limoges, but traffic was heavy on the route north from Poitiers to Châtellerault. Local enemy activity, he says, had diminished to next to nothing over the period since he had arrived in the area but Cameron was not optimistic about the FFI's ability to prevent a determined breakout from Poitiers and Châtellerault towards the east, save it were reinforced by effective close air support. In the event, the Elster column was to be channelled through the area by way of the main roads, prevented from fanning out across the countryside by partisan activity, and eventually drove itself to a standstill between Châteauroux and Issoudun, but not before a massed attack by USAAF P-47 Thunderbolts, on the morning of 2 September, to the east of the Creuse crossing at La Roche-Posay, administered a virtual *coup de grâce*, destroying something of the order of 400 of its vehicles, said Cameron; other reports were more conservative, talking of around 150 vehicles of all types destroyed. The credit for having arranged this close-support mission went to the leader of Jedburgh teams Hugh and Hamish, William Crawshay and Robert Anstett, who had flown to London specifically to press for it.

The Moses party had shifted to the north by now, and was based some fifteen kilometres south-east of Châtellerault so as to be able to operate in the area between Poitiers, Châtellerault and Le Blanc though it was also still targeting the 'Lot 2' line both north and south of Poitiers. With one captured German truck, two cars and two light trucks, and the one remaining jeep which had been dropped to Bulbasket, which was now coming to the end of its useful life, it was short of adequate transport, and its resupply seems to have been poorly handled, with many of the aircraft dropping on fires lit hopefully by partisans and others, without bothering with verification signals.

By the end of the month, when it had moved twice more, north-eastward on both occasions, its attention had largely switched to blocking the main roads to the east, and on 29 August it demolished the bridge across the Creuse at Lesigny; the next night, FFI detachments destroyed the bridge at La Haye-Descartes and the minor crossing at Leugny, channelling the traffic towards La Roche-Posay, where a bridge remained intact. Clearly there were still stragglers (at least) moving through the area, for Simon reports ambush parties being active every night until 5 September, especially on the routes leading to La Roche-Posay. By the following day the last remnants of the German Army had pulled out of Poitiers and Châtellerault, and the stragglers were making their way to Châteauroux (the city had been 'liberated' by the FFI on 27 August, but had been reoccupied without too much trouble two days later), clearing that city on 9 September. That same day Lt Plowright's patrol of four jeeps, which we last encountered doing very little to assist the Haggard party, arrived from the east, and Moses moved in to the outskirts of Châteauroux, where it linked up, the following day, with the Marshall and Snelgrove (q.v.) parties which had been active around the city for some time. Lt de Sablet's four jeeps arrived on 11 September. Had his and Plowright's vehicles been available earlier, they might have been of more use, but as it was, the movement of German forces west of the River Cher had already slowed to a trickle and offensive operations in the Indre had virtually ceased.

The Moses party remained in the Châteauroux area, where it was later joined by the parties from the other operations 3 SAS mounted further south in west-central France – Samson, in the Haute Vienne, Snelgrove, in the Creuse, east of Limoges and Marshall, further south in the Corrèze. After the Germans had quit the Indre they were despatched to the coastal region, where they joined forces with the Operation Dickens party and the FFI, struggling to maintain a restrictive cordon around the port of La Rochelle, which continued to be under German occupation, as did an enclave further north, on the southern shore of the Loire estuary. The five parties from 3 SAS all took on missions in this area just prior to being stood down.

The first of the southerly operations, and the third 3 SAS had mounted (Operation Derry, an account of which will be found within that of Operation Dingson, began on 5 August), was Operation Samson, in the Haute Vienne, focused on the important city of Limoges. The mission was inserted on the night of 9 August as a single group, under the command of Capt Michel Leblond, with one *Aspirant* and four NCOs, together with Jedburgh team Lee, by a pair of Keevil-based Stirlings, dropping on to a DZ named Framboise, south-west of Eymoutiers. Once again the Jedburghs, as well as running their own operation in support of the *Maquis*, were to provide the communications channel for the SAS party, and so it was no doubt doubly vexing to learn that the Jedset which the team leader, Capt Charles Brown of the US Cavalry, had packed in his leg bag was smashed on landing, and that the spare, in a container, had gone the same way. It was probably more than doubly gratifying, then, to learn that another container, loaded aboard the aircraft by mistake, which landed intact, held the kit and radio of Major Robert Montgomery, leader of team Tony, which was scheduled be inserted to work with team Harold in the Vendée, some days later.

The Jedburghs and the SAS party moved south-westward to the vicinity of La Croisille-sur-Briance, on the edge of the Forêt de Châteauneuf, where the SOE F Section representative, Philippe Liewer ('Hamlet', known as Major Charles Staunton), organiser of the Salesman circuit, had his base. The next night the Samson party joined up with the OSS Operational Group Percy Red. Together with a local partisan band the parachutists laid an ambush for an armoured train which had been assembled to reopen the line between Limoges and Brive-la-Gaillarde, to the south. The ambush went wrong, seemingly by the purest ill chance, for the next morning, as the train approached the scene, it stopped, the driver having spotted a cable, unseen by the ambush party in the darkness, lying across the track. A man was sent to investigate, scouted the area and noticed something suspicious; he was allowed to leave, and returned with an LMG team. In the firefight which followed, the leader of Percy Red, Capt William Larson, and two men from 3 SAS, *Caporal-Chef* Christophe Savey and *Soldat* André Menardi, were killed, and one SAS trooper, Saveur Touret, was taken prisoner (he was subsequently released from Limoges prison after the city had been liberated). The armoured train returned whence it had come, unharmed and the track was later blown; other reports say that the bridge at Pouget was demolished, cutting the line definitively.

The situation in the Haute-Vienne at the time was protean; the Germans held St-Léonard-de-Noblat and the nearby wolframite mine (wolframite is the principal ore of tungsten), as well as Limoges. While the *maquisards* virtually controlled the rest of the *département*, they could not prevent large, well-armed patrols or convoys travelling the main roads, particularly that between the two garrisons. The Resistance groups were predominantly FTP, and Staunton had earlier made a policy decision to co-operate with them fully, over the protests of the non-Communists. The Jedburgh team leader made no objection to this, while the SAS, as usual, paid no heed to the politics and were simply ready to assist anybody who wanted to kill Germans.

During their first week in the area, the SAS team worked alongside Percy Red, the Jedburghs and the FTP *maquisards* to demolish a steel trestle bridge which carried the Limoges–St-Léonard road over the River Vienne, with the object of cutting the link between the two garrisons, and then dug anti-tank ditches and laid mines on the N20 north of Fombelaux, the latter in response to a report from London that it was one of the routes the German 159. Infantry Division, then still in south-western France, was taking in an effort to escape the huge pincer formed when the Allies landed in Provence.

Throughout that week, attention was firmly fixed on the efforts to persuade the garrison at Limoges to capitulate, rather than try to fight its way out of the trap the city was fast becoming. As well as the *Wehrmacht* and a relatively small number of *SS* and *SD* personnel, Limoges was home to a large detachment of French *Gardes Mobiles* and *Gardes Mobiles Reserve*, some twenty-six squadrons in all, a total of 3,000 men according to some reckonings. Already, certain (non-Communist) elements of the Resistance had been in informal negotiations with the commander of this detachment, and though the talks were set back considerably on 18 August, when a car full of *maquisards* armed with machine-pistols and apparently intent on driving through the centre of the city and shooting any German on sight, interrupted a parley in most dramatic fashion, they were ultimately successful, and over the next two days the Pétainist paramilitaries simply melted away, leaving the approaches to the city, which they had been detailed to guard, undefended. The next step, persuading the Germans either to capitulate or go quietly, would not be so straightforward; it was eventually accomplished by a team comprising the American and French Jedburgh officers, Major Staunton and a representative of the FFI chief, but by the time the deadline for capitulation arrived, it was discovered that the majority of the Germans had managed to leave the city and reach St Léonard, having succeeded in repairing the damaged bridge; with them was the garrison commander, *Generalmajor* Gleininger, arrested (and later shot) by the *Sipo-SD* as a reward for his having agreed surrender terms. A total of 341 prisoners were taken, however, the vast majority of them (264) Russians, and the only shots fired in the liberation of Limoges were sporadic *feux de joie*. The role of the SAS party in this phase of the operation was restricted to providing security.

By 22 August Limoges was clear of Germans, and five days later, during which time the city's airfield was returned to working order, the

Jedburghs, OG Percy Red and the Samson party moved westward, in the direction of Angoulême, where the N10 had become the main artery for German northward movement. There was a plan to cut the road near Fenêtre, about ten kilometres north of the city, on 29 August, but the traffic was simply too heavy to allow an ambush party to get into a suitable position, and it was abandoned. Two days later the SAS party and the OG separated, and this time both were able to cause considerable damage to the last convoys to leave Angoulême before the city was liberated on 1 September. The recombined party then returned to Limoges, and was redirected, almost immediately, to the Vienne/Indre region, arriving in the vicinity of Le Blanc on the evening of 3 September. The following day, having been directed to a *route départemental* through the Brenne marshes which large numbers of Germans were using in an attempt to move from Châtellerault towards Châteauroux, the combined party mounted a set-piece attack on the Château de Claveau, where a group had taken refuge, Percy Red providing covering fire while the Samson party made the assault. For the next ten days they operated north and east of Le Blanc, venturing as far as the limit of the Indre, harassing elements of the retreating German Army south of Issoudun. When the last of the stragglers had been mopped up, on 13 September, the Samson party was ordered to the Vendée.

The Marshall and Snelgrove parties were inserted into neighbouring adjacent *départements*, Marshall in the Corrèze, Snelgrove in the Creuse (the two operations are often lumped together; it may be no coincidence that their code-names were the two components of the name of a chain of department stores in London's Oxford Street and elsewhere). In *Airborne Forces*, Otway notes that the Marshall and Snelgrove parties 'carried out very successful ambushes showing great courage, sometimes of almost too reckless a nature, in their attacks on heavily armed German troop trains and convoys'. In fact, that was not really the case (though their courage was certainly not in doubt); by the time they were established in their operational areas, the *Maquis* had come to dominate the situation, exactly as they had in the Haute Vienne, and German forces never moved outside their garrisons except in heavily armed columns which were effectively invulnerable to attack from groups armed with nothing heavier than light machine-guns, PIATs and 2in mortars.

The Marshall party, under the command of Capt Claude Wauthier, with Lt François Collery as his deputy, consisted of two sections and a small headquarters, and numbered twenty-six. It was dropped, together with Jedburgh team James, during the night of 10 August, from Fairford-based Stirlings, to a reception committee arranged by Inter-Allied Mission Tilleul, near Bonnefond, about twenty kilometres north-west of Égletons. The terrain here, in the north-east of the Corrèze, is mountainous (to close-on a thousand metres) and wooded, habitations are sparse and consequently roads are few; it is an ideal area to conceal a guerrilla band. Through the *département*, south-west to north-east, runs the N89, the main road between Bordeaux and Clermont-Ferrand, and in August 1944 this was the only road German forces used; considerable effort had been expended on keeping it open as an escape route across the inhospitable Massif Central. According to intelligence reports, German forces in the *département* were concentrated in Brive-la-Gaillarde (around 500), Tulle (800, though that figure was by now almost certainly exaggerated), Égletons (300, including around 50 SS) and Ussel (150). The Brive detachment had a dozen 2cm cannon, that at Égletons some 3.7cm anti-tank guns.

On 13 August Wauthier reviewed the situation with the Jedburgh officers, Lts John Singlaub and Jacques Le Bel, who used Leb as a *nom de guerre*; Major Jacques de Guélis, the leader of Mission Tilleul, and Flt/Lt André Simon, his deputy (both had dual French and British nationality, and shared a reputation as being somewhat anti-Gaullist). The mission had been in the area for something over a month; French sources suggest it had singularly failed to establish a good relationship with the right-leaning *Armée Secrète* – de Guélis had established his headquarters alongside the FTP, which was by far the strongest Resistance group in the region and became much stronger thanks to its proximity to Tilleul; it got almost all the arms the mission requested from London – and as a result there was considerable tension. The Jedburgh team report tells a different story, however: Tilleul, it said, had chosen the Brive AS detachment as a conduit for arms and equipment, but its leader had kept for his own use virtually everything passed on to him, and the other AS groups in the area suffered in consequence. Whatever the truth of the matter, the N89 had been cut in two places between Tulle and Égletons, and once between Égletons and Ussel by the time the Marshall party arrived and each of the four garrison towns had been invested, Égletons, the closest to the SAS base, by the FTP and a strong contingent of *Corps Franc* from Tulle.

Before Wauthier could formulate a plan of his own, the FTP commander at Égletons informed him that he intended to attack the garrison (despite having nothing heavier than Bren guns), and the following morning, 14 August, FTP forces launched an assault quite independently of the Tulle faction, and without even informing it of their intentions. All the precipitate action achieved was to drive the Germans from the town into a stone-built trade school with deep cellars, where a strong defensive position had been prepared. First the Jedburgh team and then Wauthier, presented with a *fait accompli*, opted to come to the FTP's assistance, but things took a decided turn for the worse in mid-morning, when a trio of Heinkel He.111s dropped bombs at low level, and were followed by a trio of Focke-Wulf FW.190s which strafed the partisans' positions with cannon and machine-guns. Ground attacks continued over the next four days, and one Heinkel was downed by a Bren gun in the hands of SAS Sgt Robert Rundwasser. In the almost continuous firefight throughout that first afternoon, an SAS sergeant, Alphonse Zemb, was killed, and another wounded, although these, together with the American Jedburgh officer, Singlaub, who was hit in the face by bullet fragments, were the only casualties the Allied forces sustained in the battle for Égletons.

That night, according to the Jedburgh team (the SAS report makes no mention of it) Wauthier sent a message to London asking for an air strike on the school the following afternoon at 1700, and laid his plans around it. It never came, and the assault Wauthier had intended to send in in its wake had to be cancelled. From here on, the available reports start to diverge very markedly; at some points Wauthier's (which is only one page long in any event; the Jedburgh team's report for the same period covers eight pages) quite inexplicably turns to pure fantasy. He tells us: 'As the paratroopers (i.e. his men) engaged at Égletons with the FFI could not dispose of the enemy garrison in the school, 3,000 incendiary bullets were fired by Brens, setting fire to the roof of the building. The whole building was soon ablaze and the garrison had to surrender.' The incident to which he is referring here is actually an assault on *another* beseiged school, this one at Ussel; at the time the nearest SAS trooper was no closer than thirty kilometres to Ussel. And as we shall see, the garrison at Égletons never did surrender, no matter how many reports to the contrary there were, nor whence they came.

Wauthier leaves us in limbo between 14 and 17 August; we must, therefore, turn to the Jedburgh team's account to fill in the missing days as best we may. Singlaub says the SAS troopers went into action on 15 August (and has high praise for their fighting abilities), and that Wauthier called in the air strike on 16 August. That same evening the AS at

Ussel assaulted the school there, with the result noted above, and later Singlaub left Égletons to attend negotiations for the unconditional surrender of Tulle and Brive. In fact the latter's garrison had already capitulated, and that of Tulle would follow the next morning.

The defenders at Égletons, however, showed no sign of wishing to capitulate, and were still putting up a determined fight on the morning of 17 August, and the reason for that soon became clear: a column of 2,000 Germans, part of *Kampfgruppe* Jesser (see below), in 150 vehicles, had left Clermont-Ferrand to come to their relief and take back control of Ussel and Tulle. (French sources quote the column as consisting of 295 vehicles, including self-propelled guns and four tanks, with air cover and spotter planes.) Despite attempts to delay or stop it, the column passed through Ussel that evening and arrived at Égletons early the following morning, relieved the school and continued on towards Tulle. Ironically, early that evening the RAF finally responded to Wauthier's request (since reinforced by the Jedburghs) for an air strike, and eight Mosquitoes flattened the school in a display of accurate close air support which would have been most welcome had it come even twenty-four hours earlier. To add insult to injury, an hour before the air raid, the BBC reported that Égletons had fallen to the FFI … Meanwhile, the relief column, travelling by minor roads north of the N89, and harassed by the *Armée Secrète* partisans all the way (it took eight hours to cover the thirty kilometres between Égletons and Tulle), arrived at its destination, found the garrison already passed into captivity, and had no option but to retrace its route to Clermont. In all, the Jedburghs' report tells us, it lost perhaps a hundred men and numerous vehicles during its short incursion into the Corrèze, almost as many as it rescued from Égletons. The partisans' response was degraded early on thanks to false reports, received at Égletons on 17 August, that the Tulle garrison had somehow reconstituted and rearmed itself, and was marching on Égletons; a strong force of *maquisards* promptly headed off down the N89 to try to intecept this phantom column, and were out of contact when they were needed most.

Wauthier tells us that when he heard of the enemy column from Clermont-Ferrand 'advancing to raise the siege', on 17 August, he ordered his men to retreat to Roufiat (of which no trace can be found even in the most detailed gazetteer), and that he later took his second-in-command and three men to Ussel, to warn the leader of the *résistants* there, *Commandant* Duret, of the retreat of the relief column back towards Clermont (since the *résistants* in Tulle, Égletons and Ussel were in touch by telephone, this was quite unnecessary). He tells us that Duret's men subsequently held the column up 'for thirty-six hours between Égletons and the Chavanon Pass', which is east of Ussel, on the border between the Corrèze and the Puy-de-Dôme, and that he and his small party, with a unit of *maquisards*, travelled by a circuitous route to the pass itself, and on 22 August laid a very old-fashioned ambush there, rolling rocks and boulders down on to the German vehicles when they were halted by mines laid on the road below, escaping when their position was attacked by infantry (the chronology has flaws; Jesser and his men did not leave Tulle until the morning of 21 August).

The tracks of the Jedburgh team and the SAS party now diverge, the former going to Limoges and from there into the Creuse. On 24 August, having asked for instructions from Moor Park and received none, Wauthier sought and received permission from the DMR to head north, and joined up with the Snelgrove party at Guéret on the way.

Unfortunately, the Snelgrove after-action report forms just a brief adjunct – one lengthy paragraph – to that of Captain Wauthier, and thus we are forced to try to put additonal flesh on rather bare bones by referring to the account produced by the Jedburgh team which accompanied the mission; doubly unfortunately, that team suffered a mishap during its insertion, actually saw little of the SAS party, and soon left the Creuse in any event, the Délégue Militaire Regional (DMR) believing that it would be more effectively employed in the Dordogne.

The Snelgrove party, under the command of Lt Edmond Hubler, and with S/Lt Marc Mora as his deputy, numbered twenty-four. It was inserted on the night of 12 August, ordered to liaise with the Inter-Allied Mission Bergamotte, which had been in position since 27 June. Bergamotte had a clear field in terms of requesting resupply missions, and had arranged two massive drops of arms and equipment on 4 and 15 July, and as a result the Resistance in the Creuse was well armed. The *maquisards* did not have things their own way, however, for from 15 July German reinforcements in the shape of *Kampfgruppe* Jesser arrived in the area. Jesser's battlegroup was specially trained for 'counter-terrorist' operations and had earlier been operating in the Cantal; it immediately began a most effective *ratissage*, attacking and dispersing the Mission Bergamotte command post on 17 July. It remained in the Creuse for almost a month, causing serious disruption to Resistance operations, before moving on into the *département* of Puy-de-Dôme the day before the Snelgrove party arrived.

Like the Samson and Marshall parties, Snelgrove was accompanied by a Jedburgh team, Alexander; unfortunately, there was a serious misunderstanding in its aircraft. After difficulty in locating the DZ, the RAF despatcher announced that they would dispense with the standard procedure, and that the first man in the stick (the Jedburgh team leader, Stewart Alsop) would drop 'as soon as he saw the lights'. In the event, someone in the rear of the aircraft seemingly glimpsed the lights through the 'joe hole', and flashed on a torch; the next moment, Alsop disappeared; the next man, the radio operator, Sgt Norman Franklin, was momentarily held back, but then he jumped too, and after a short delay the rest of the stick followed him. The DZ they had seen proved to be that of a party expecting canisters. Alsop landed in a tree, some miles away from the rest; Franklin landed in a cemetery and the French liaison officer, Lt René de la Touche, known as Thouville, who had been third out of the aircraft, became hung up on high tension cables. The rest of the party got down without serious mishap, which was fortunate because the DZ was reckoned to be totally unsuitable for parachutists. It was also in the Forêt de St Gilles in the Haute Vienne, some sixty kilometres away from their true objective and adjacent to the area in which the Operation Samson party and Jedburgh team Lee had set up camp just a few days earlier, and their presence saved the day.

Largely thanks to the efforts of Major Staunton, team Alexander and the stray SAS stick reached the Creuse on the night of 15 August, after a remarkably uneventful journey in a *gazogène*-powered truck, and the Snelgrove party was reunited at the Mission Bergamotte command post, some fifteen kilometres east of Bourganeuf. The situation was very much akin to that in the Corrèze, to the south, with the German garrisons in the major towns only able to move outside them with impunity if they did so in considerable strength; the situation within the Resistance movement was a good deal easier, however, since the Bergamotte mission had, uniquely, been able to impose a unified command structure, with partisans of all persuasions, even the Communist FTP, working closely together; in this, the mission's task was eased by the fact that it had been able to arrange for the two huge resupply missions, the first of which saw some sixty planeloads of arms and ammunition flown in.

It soon became obvious that both the Snelgrove party and the Jedburgh team were largely surplus to requirements. Team Alexander left the Creuse on 18 August and moved to the Dordogne (via Égletons, where it spent an uncomfortable night in the combat zone), while Lt Hubler joined forces with the *maquisards* to drive the Germans out of nearby Bourganeuf. Once again, the defence was centred on a school, but this time the Germans lacked the spirit to put up much resistance; they saw off one assault, during which S/Lt Mora was wounded, but by the next morning they had gone, leaving behind them a significant dump of arms and equipment. There was no more for the Snelgrove party to do, and less than a fortnight after being inserted it was on its way north, linking up with the Marshall party at Guéret and then proceeding to the Indre, near Châteauroux, arriving around 4 September. The combined party joined in the general effort to contain and further disable the Elster column, laying ambushes and on one occasion assaulting a command post, and on 12 September entered the city itself. From Châteauroux the Marshall and Snelgrove parties, now linked up with Moses and Samson, moved further west and joined the other elements of 3 SAS in the coastal area; both operations were stood down on 12 October and the men returned to the United Kingdom for a short period of rest and recuperation before being assigned to new operational tasks.

JOCKWORTH, BARKER AND HARROD

The same Operation Instruction No. 40 addressed to 3 SAS which set up Operations Samson, Marshall and Snelgrove in central south-western France (and which for the first time placed the battalion under the overall command of General Koenig and the EMFFI, rather than SHAEF) also targeted German forces on the other side of the Massif Central, in the Rhône and Saône valleys, in three operations designed specifically to interdict movement. The Operation Instruction places both Harrod and Barker – whose after-action reports are combined, leading one to believe that the two were under unified command, the Barker party operating to the south-west of Lyon initially, and the Harrod party further north – in the Saône-et-Loire *département*, and Jockworth on the Loire/Rhône border, west of Lyon. In fact, the Operation Barker parties were dropped to the same location as the Jockworth parties, and seem to have operated independently of, but alongside, them (the two parties also moved camps at the same time, and to the same locations). There is circumstantial evidence to suggest that the two were intended to have been combined, and that there was a last-minute change of plan.

The insertion of these parties coincided with the Anvil/Dragoon landings in Provence on 15 August, and the operational area spanned the German escape route up the river valleys and eventually towards the Belfort Gap. In the event, the Allied northward advance proceeded at such a rate that the parties from 3 SAS inserted into the Lyon/Mâcon area had very little time to establish themselves and form working relationships with Resistance bands before they were overtaken by a veritable flood of fleeing enemy troops; the operations in question were short-lived as a result, with most groups on the ground for at most a fortnight.

The Jockworth party was inserted by Stirlings from Fairford at two locations – one of them (seemingly in error) near Villefranche-sur-

Saône to the north of Lyon, and the others north-east of St-Étienne to
the south-west – on the night of 14 August, the mid-August moon
period providing the first opportunity, given the overriding requirement that the aircraft should be over France only during the hours of
darkness. The SAS party was accompanied by Jedburgh team Jude,
which initially provided its radio link with London but also, and more
importantly, liaised with Inter-Allied Mission Gingembre, oversaw the
arming of the partisan bands in the Loire and Rhône *départements* and
later operated independently to run battle and officer-training courses
on the British OCTU model for the FFI at St-Genis-Laval on the
southern fringe of Lyon, continuing that activity into 1945. Resistance
in the two *départements* was well established, and had received its first
parachutage of arms and material in August 1943. From D-Day onward
it had carried out successful attacks on railway lines and installations,
the Loire partisans being particularly effective in the Giers valley
between Lyon and the important industrial city of St-Étienne (where
many of the *résistants* were of Polish origin), and with the arrival of the
French SAS party it took on a more open and important role.

The stick – a seven-man party led by the operation's commander, Lt
Jean Hourst – which was dropped out of position in the area of Ville-
franche, landed badly; there were no injuries, but much of the material
and personal kit was either lost or destroyed. During the next day it made
a journey of eighty kilometres by truck to the area of St-Symphorien-sur-
Coise, to the south-west of Lyon, where the other two parties, together
with Jedburgh team Jude, had been dropped, narrowly avoiding a confrontation with a train full of German troops at Ste-Foy-l'Argentière on
the way. (Two sticks from Operation Harrod/Barker dropped on to the
St-Symphorien DZ that night, a third stick was dropped at the same location the night after, and another at St-Martin-la-Plaine, near
Rive-de-Gier and less than twenty kilometres away, on the night of 17
August. The 3 SAS after-action report places these two latter parties in
Operation Harrod/Barker, but a French nominal roll – not always reliable, admittedly – includes them with Jockworth, the report of which
makes no specific mention of them, though it is clear that the stick which
dropped on the night of August 15 took part in Jockworth's first operation, at L'Arbresles.) Over the next three days Hourst made contact with
local *maquisard* bands, and on 19 August launched a joint operation with
an FFI company at L'Arbresle to attack railway installations there, with
some success. Hourst and his men were less fortunate over the next five
days, when they reconnoitred the main N7 road which links Lyon with

Paris by way of Moulins, the Loire valley and Montargis, and laid ambushes repeatedly without result, but on the return journey to L'Arbresle they met a convoy of five German trucks, all of them displaying Red Cross flags and panels, and immediately came under heavy small-arms fire, which they returned, eventually destroying three of the vehicles and killing ten, and capturing a truck and three prisoners, together with some arms and ammunition.

On 25 August the party moved to Grezieux-la-Varenne, due west of Lyon, regrouped, (and reinforced to a total strength of forty, but from where it is not clear; one of the Barker sticks may have been put under Hourst's command) and was supplied with heavier weapons, particularly 3in mortars and .5in machine-guns, in an air drop. On 29 August, by which time the Germans were in wholesale retreat up the Rhône valley, the party decamped to Thurins to begin joint operations with partisan bands around nearby Montagny, aimed at cutting the N7 between Givors and Lyon. There was heavy fighting all through 30 August, and the party withdrew from Montagny before nightfall, returning the following morning to repeat the exercise. On 1 September the SAS party made its first contact with advance elements of the French Army advancing from the south, and the following day was able to occupy Givors, which was now empty of German forces; it then moved up to Brignais, fifteen kilometres further north and no more than that from the centre of Lyon, which was still occupied in strength. From then on, the fighting was house-to-house, for which the relatively lightly-armed SAS and *maquisard* forces, unsupported by armour and heavy weapons, were not ideally equipped, and they started to take casualties, six of the SAS soldiers being wounded, some seriously. The arrival of more and more Allied troops from the south, well supplied with tanks and self-propelled assault guns, improved the situation rapidly, and by the morning of 4 September, Lyon was in French hands. The following day Hourst and his men paraded before General De Lattre de Tassigny, the commander-in-chief of *Armée B* (later the 1st French Army), the French component of the force which had landed in Provence; Hourst, by now promoted to captain, was awarded the Croix de Guerre, and the unit as a whole received a citation. On 8 September the men went on leave prior to being assigned a new task.

If the insertion of the Jockworth party went somewhat awry, it was text-book correct compared to that of Harrod/Barker. These were nominally separate operations (though like Marshall and Snelgrove, they are generally considered together), and were supposed to have been inserted starting on the night of 8 August. Three Stirlings left Fairford that night (French sources say 11 August); all the aircraft failed to find their objective and on the return journey one of them, carrying the HQ party of 1 Troop, 1 Squadron, 3 SAS was apparently shot down by anti-aircraft fire from the vicinity of Cherbourg (there is no indication in the reports whether the aircraft was hit by land-based or naval AA guns, but it was almost certainly a 'blue on blue' incident; the port-city and its environs had been in Allied hands since 27 June) and crashed into the sea some ten miles off the coast, killing two, Cpl Roger D'Astis and Pct Daniel Selles, and injuring three badly enough for them to require hospitalisation in Cherbourg. A party of sappers under *Aspirant* Philippe Akar, and a six-man stick under *Sous-Lieutenant* Jacques Dreyfus were inserted at 'Savilly-sur-Crosne' (in all probability Savigny-sur-Grosne), about fifteen kilometres south-west of Chalons-sur-Saône on the night of 12 August. These two groups were to work apart from the main bodies, chiefly in the area between Paray-le-Monial and Montceau-les-Mines, though they linked up with other elements from time to time, and for the sake of convenience we can call them the western group. Four sections (called Sticks 1, 2, 4 and 7 in the 3 SAS report) and the HQ party of 2 Troop, together with Jedburgh team Anthony, were dropped near Salornay-sur-Guye, some forty kilometres north-west of Mâcon, on the night of 13 August; two more sections left the UK on the following night but failed once again to find their objective and returned, but Sticks 5 and 6 were inserted successfully near St-Symphorien, together with most of the Jockworth party, and were joined there by Stick 8 the following night, 15 August. Stick 3 and the Squadron HQ were dropped at Lamure, seemingly on the DZ where Hourst's Jockworth party had been inserted by mistake, on the night of 17 August; this was the former's fourth attempted insertion and the latter's third – a record for SAS operations during World War Two.

In all, ten fighting sections, the engineering section and three smaller HQ sections, under the overall command of *Commandant* Pierre Château-Jobert (known as Yves Conan, who had been named by General Koenig as commander of all FFI units in the area), the commanding officer of 3 SAS, were inserted, together with the two Jedburgh teams. All of them, except for HQ, 2 Troop, plus some of the survivors from the aircraft downed on the night of 8 August, who were dropped on the night of 22 August (and a ten-man party under *Sous-Lieutenant* Jacques Zermati, which dropped at Messey-sur-Grosne, five kilometres from Savigny, on the night of 27 August), were on the ground by the morning of 18 August. By that time some of the first groups to have been inserted had already been in action a number of times and the operation had already suffered its first combat fatality when Sgt Roland Panloup of Stick 4 was killed in an assault on a bridge while supporting the western group. Akar's report states that this was an attempt to demolish 'the railway bridge at Galuzot' (Galuzot is now a suburb of Montceau-les-Mines; the bridge in question carries the line over the Canal du Centre), supported by 'Lieutenant Porot's stick' (Jean-François Porot commanded Stick 4) and a *résistant* group. The German garrison at Montceau had been warned of this attack, and around 300 heavily-armed men were in position to repulse it. They suffered disproportionate casualties but forced the assaulting party to withdraw. Akar's sappers worked closely with Resistance groups, and naturally enough concentrated on demolitions; their most successful missions involved cutting the Paray–Charolles road on 27 August (the charges they laid caused craters eight metres wide and three metres deep); that between Paray and Monceau (by demolishing the embankment separating the road from the Canal du Centre, which runs alongside it) and that between Paray and Volesvres, on 30 August. All the roads in question were out of action until well after the area had been liberated.

Sgt Panloup was one of thirteen SAS fatalities during the course of operations in the Mâconnais (and more were wounded, some of them seriously). Most – six men from Operation Newton plus Capt Christian Boissonas, who led Stick 2, and Parachutists Robert Barkatz and Roland Lombardo, detached from Zermati's party to operate with them – died at Sennecy-le-Grand on 4 September, when they tried to liberate the town and were met by a German detachment which proved to be very much more formidable than they had estimated (see below). The other men killed were Parachutists Marcel Sanchez (named as Sancere in the 3 SAS report), who died on 18 August in a skirmish while Stick 4 was patrolling the Forêt de la Ferté, south of Chalons-sur-Saône; Jules Lebon, who was a member of Picard's patrol from Operation Newton, and who died at Gratoux, between Montceau-les-Mines and Le Creusot on 2 September, and *Aspirant* Georges Lyon-Caen (almost certainly a *nom de guerre*, though no other is recorded), who had served with 3 French Para since 1943, mortally wounded while leading Stick 2 during a skirmish at La Chapelle-St-Martin, near Sennecy, on 22 August.

Such Operation Harrod parties (i.e. Sticks 1, 2, 3, 4 and 7) as were in the operational zone were in action every day from 15 August, often alongside elements of the FFI, in an area which extended northward to the southern limit of the Côte-d'Or and took in the important industrial towns of Montceau-les-Mines and Le Creusot, and westward as far as Paray-le-Monial and the right bank of the Loire. Their operational area was thus contiguous with that of the Houndsworth parties to the north and – nominally, at least – with the Haggard parties to the west. Their foci of activities were the main N6 road running north from Lyon towards Dijon, and the railway which parallels it, and the N70 which links Mâcon with Paray and Digoin. Conan had his headquarters at Lugny, and the Harrod party was divided, the better to cover the objective, with Sticks 1 and 7 ('the southern group') to the south of Tournus and Sticks 2 and 4 ('the northern group') to the north. The report of the leader of Jedburgh team Alan, a British captain named Cannicott, says that Cmdt Conan 'was exerting no real influence in the region' and that, in consequence they ignored him – and seemingly the SAS party as a whole – and joined a *Maquis* battalion instead. The report of the French liasion officer, Captain Robert Toussaint (who operated under the *nom de guerre* of Galraud) states the position rather differently; according to him, he took command of the *Maquis* battalion, with Cannicott as his second, on Conan's orders. The unit occupied itself with the stretch of road and railway between Lyon and Mâcon, and took a significant part, together with the French 1st Armoured Division, in the heavy fighting which resulted in the liberation of Villefranche-sur-Saône on 3 September. Unfortunately, since Alan operated independently of the SAS parties, its reports shed little additional light on their activities. Jedburgh team Anthony was also detached, and its leader, Capt Stasse, who went by the *nom de guerre* of Duprez, was given command, by Cmdt Conan, of a *Maquis* batallion operating in the Paray–Monceau area. Like that of Alan, its report has little to say about the activities of the Harrod/Barker parties.

The southern group, under the overall command of Lt Marcel Coste, were particularly successful on the N6 just to the south of Tournus, at a point where the road ran through a patch of woodland. Here, on 20, 21, 23 and 29 August they ambushed convoys, destroying a total of thirty-five trucks and an armoured car, and killing, wounding or capturing well over three hundred. They also mounted ambushes elsewhere on the road and cut the railway line repeatedly. The northern group, under Capt Christian Boissonas, maintained the same sort of

level of activity in its sector, and later, minus its leader, who died at
Sennecy, moved to the west, in the direction of Montceau-les-Mines,
cutting the road and railways linking the town with Paray-le-Monial to
the south and reconnoitring in preparation for liberating it and its
satellite, Blanzy. When the majority of the Harrod parties were temporarily stood down, on 4 September, these two sticks continued their
operations and led strong elements of the FFI which drove the occupying forces out, two days later, before moving further north to Autun, to
repeat the exercise there. Stick 3 operated initially in the Mâconnais
and later with the Barker parties further south.

The Harrod parties were supplemented on or about 31 August by
eight jeeps from Operation Newton (q.v.), the two groups of four being
allocated to the sector between Montceau and Chalons (Picard's patrol)
and along the N6 (de Roquebrune's patrol). The latter, in particular,
proved very effective, and in an ambush and strafing operation carried
out on 1 September on the Mâcon–Dijon stretch of the N6, killed and
wounded perhaps 150. Three days later, on 4 September, the patrol
became involved, along with elements of Operation Harrod, in an
attempt to liberate the town of Sennecy-le-Grand, fifteen kilometres
south of Chalons. Sennecy and neighbouring Sens had already been the
scene of a number of more-or-less successful ambushes, and that may
have given the SAS party a sense of false security, for it seems that no
preliminary reconnaissance was made. This time the situation was very
different; some French accounts put the number of Germans in the
town at 3,000 (that may be an exaggeration, but others are even more
far-fetched, describing de Roquebrune's patrol as taking on an enemy 'a
thousand times stronger'), and when the SAS party – de Roquebrune's
men in their armed jeeps at its head, and others, plus FFI elements, in
requisitioned civilian transport – entered it, the firefight was very
intense. A brief report by one of the survivors of de Roquebrune's party,
Pct Bailleux, talks of the French killing four hundred and wounding
three hundred more, and destroying at least thirty vehicles, many of
them horse-drawn, on a first pass through the main street (which is
perhaps 600 metres long), and a French report, which is hardly more
fulsome, states that they then found themselves face-to-face with an
approaching convoy which blocked the road, and turned to retrace
their route. Unfortunately, that gave the Germans in Sennecy time to
regroup, and on the second pass the Newton party, which evidently
placed itself to give covering fire to the other vehicles, suffered six men
killed – Combaud de Roquebrune himself, Jean-Paul Pache, Pierre

Aubert-Stribi, Jacob Benamou and brothers Gilbert and Lucien Djian, plus three from Operation Harrod – and three wounded. The French national monument to the men who died serving with 3 and 4 French Paras, inaugurated in 1984, was to be located at Sennecy-le-Grand, just to the south of the town, where the action took place.

The Barker parties (Sticks 5, 6 and 8, though the latter had earlier been in action alongside the Jockworth party) seem not to have struck their first real blow until 23 August, when they ambushed a small German column on the Roanne–Lyon road, destroying four vehicles and killing ten. They joined up with Stick 3 and the Squadron HQ the following day, and the enlarged party turned its attention towards the N6 immediately north of Lyon. Over the next four days they were engaged, alongside FFI elements, in mounting ambushes, both on the main road and on more minor routes, but without significant success – most enemy movement was assembled into large, relatively powerful contingents, impossible to attack with the light weapons which were all the SAS and partisans had at their disposal. Their precise movements are unclear, but they seem to have circled around to the south subsequently and linked up with elements of Jockworth again, south of the city, before the end of the month. Together they moved into the suburbs, and later the centre, of Lyon from the morning of 3 September, by which time enemy forces in the city had largely dispersed, though there was sporadic fighting, chiefly with *Milice* units. They occupied the town hall and the telephone exchange briefly, before handing them over to elements of the French Army. Operations ceased on 4 September.

After a brief period of rest and recuperation locally, 1 Squadron regrouped, and on 14 September left for the Doubs, where, like the men of 2 Squadron inserted to carry out Operation Abel (q.v.), they briefly acted as reconnaissance elements for American units recently arrived in the area before being stood down again on 24 September.

NEWTON

By the time Newton was launched, 3 SAS was already heavily committed, with Operations Dickens, Marshall and Snelgrove, Moses and Samson under way, and the Harrod/Barker and Jockworth parties about to be inserted; from the outset it was conceived as a means of providing some of those parties with armed jeeps and 'during movement to bases', the parties' orders stated, 'every effort will be made to avoid contact with the enemy and no offensive operation will be undertaken from any base until the remainder of the jeeps have been gone for at least 24 hours.' A paragraph in Operation Instruction No. 42 of 15 August, which defined Operation Newton itself, sheds light on the decision to infiltrate the vehicles overland rather than drop them from aircraft, and indicates that it was a lack of very basic resources which dictated the decision:

> No parachute apparatus can at present be spared for allotment to 3 French Para Bn, nor can the jeeps be landed by glider or aircraft before the next moon period, and then only in small numbers.

If we set this alongside the inadequate number of jeeps dropped to the Houndsworth and other parties, we can probably conclude that even at this fairly late stage there was actually a serious shortage of the relatively simple equipment needed – after all, there was certainly no shortage of jeeps, and it was always possible to find an aircraft, though perhaps not immediately. This is somewhat surprising, since jeep deliveries by air had actually commenced two full months earlier, and had proved to be immediately successful, the number of vehicles destroyed in the process notwithstanding.

In any event, a total of nineteen jeeps were allocated to Operation Newton, split into five patrols, one vehicle of each of which would tow a trailer. Three of the vehicles were destined to reinforce Operation

Dickens, south of Nantes, eight for Moses in the Vienne and eight for Harrod, north of Lyon. At the discretion of the officers commanding Moses and Harrod, some of the vehicles earmarked for them could be passed on to Samson, Marshall and Snelgrove, and Barker or Jock-worth, respectively. They crossed the Channel by surface transport and landed at Courseulles in Normandy, and then proceeded towards Nantes by way of Mayenne and Laval. All were then to have made for the Dickens base near Cholet; the sixteen jeeps which were to have gone further into still-occupied France were all to have proceeded to join up with the Moses party near Le Blanc, and then the eight destined to join Operation Harrod would make their way to the area around Chalons-sur-Saône via the Marshall and Snelgrove operational area, north of Limoges.

The orders seem to have been changed while the operation was under way. On arriving at Nantes on 18 August, instead of joining the Dickens party, *Aspirant* Jean Valayer's patrol of three jeeps was detached to operate as the advanced reconnaissance element of the American drive eastward of Troyes into the Moselle valley; two four-car patrols under Lt de Roquebrune and *Aspirant* Picard were to join Operation Harrod as planned, but via a northerly route which took them up the Loire valley, into the Yonne and from there to the area south of the Houndsworth area, which was entirely sensible. Lt de Sablet and *Aspirant* Plowright's parties of nine vehicles – where the additional jeep came from is a mystery – were still ordered to reinforce the Moses party, but rather than heading for the Vienne by the most direct route, they too proceeded up the Loire valley, and crossed the river at Briare on 28 August; they then headed south and west and based themselves with Lepine's Haggard party for up to ten days, seemingly losing one of their jeeps in the process, before proceeding.

The Operation Instruction stated that American troops had already 'crossed the Loire at Nantes, and are believed to have occupied Angers', but that proved to be an optimistic assessment. They had *reached* Nantes, as early as 10 August, and got to Angers the following day, but had certainly not crossed the river in any strength. The strategic priority, of course, was to drive eastward to enclose the Falaise Pocket, and nothing was to be gained – though much could have been risked; the German counter-attack at Mortain, on 7 August, was probably still much in the Allied commanders' minds – by crossing the Loire at this time. When the Newton party arrived at Nantes, late on 18 August, it was clear that possession of its southern part, across the river, at least, was still being disputed. In fact, the Germans had not yet entirely conceded possession of the northern part, either, and in the early hours of 20 August Valayer's party was involved in a brisk firefight in support of FFI elements. It may well be that the party's inability to penetrate past the line of the river in this sector at this time was the reason for the change of plans for Operation Newton; it seems that S/Ldr Smith, an RAF officer attached to the SAS Brigade, who had earlier operated with 4 French Para in Brittany (see Operation Dingson/Samwest) and who was now in charge of this phase of Newton, concluded that the chances of them reaching the Moses party at that time were slim, and redirected them, though that does not explain why the group earmarked to join the Dickens party, which was close at hand and desperate for the vehicles, was deprived of its three jeeps, which were then allocated to American forces which were literally falling over them.

Aspirant Valayer's patrol left Nantes on 21 August and followed the north bank of the Loire well past Orléans; at Châteaurenard, twenty kilometres beyond Montargis, they were assigned to an American reconnaissance unit. From then on they pushed eastwards in the forefront of the advancing armoured divisions, and by dawn on 3 September were within sight of Nancy, the capital of Lorraine. At this point the advance bogged down, and after some days of a sort of combat for which they were not at all suited, and which saw them pitted against Pf.Kpfw. VI Tiger tanks and cost them two of their vehicles, they were withdrawn to rest and refit. Somewhat curiously, Valayer gave all the men seven days leave on 13 September, and even more curiously four of them – Cpl Moraglia and Pcts Azem, Couget and Loï – chose to spend it in the United Kingdom, and not in the fleshpots of London, but at Fairford camp! They hitched a lift on a supply plane, were in London by the evening of 14 September and back in Gloucestershire the following day.

On the morning of 19 September they presented themselves at the Fairford Orderly Office, only to be told that there was no prospect of them returning to France for at least a week, and that they could busy themselves around the camp in the meantime. This was evidently not to their liking, and so they resorted to back-channels, and managed to get themselves on an aircraft bound for Brussels out of Aldermaston on 21 September. There they obtained a jeep, and set off in the direction of Paris, but within half an hour they had turned the jeep over at eighty kilometres an hour, seriously injuring Azem, and it was two days before

Moraglia and Loï continued their journey, reaching Luneville by way of the French capital on the evening of 24 September. There they found no sign of Valayer or any other members of 3 SAS, and instead joined up with a unit of American armour. Together with several armoured cars, their jeep fell into an ambush on 28 September; Moraglia was wounded in the leg and was evacuated to Toul the following day. By 5 October he and Loï had returned to Paris once more, and had restarted their search for news of Valayer and the rest of the patrol when, quite by chance, they met *Soldat* Flinois, who had been with Picard's patrol; he was able to tell them the squadron's current location, and they rejoined on 9 October. Of the doings of Valayer and the rest of the patrol in the meantime, there is no record, but it may perhaps be surmised that the replacement vehicles were not forthcoming, and that the remaining members of the patrol had made their way to link up with other members of the battalion.

The activities of the remainder of the parties which carried out Operation Newton are covered in the accounts of Operations Haggard and Moses (the Plowright and de Sablet patrols) and Operation Harrod (Picard and de Roquebrun's parties).

ABEL

The Frenchmen of 2 Squadron, 3 SAS, who went into Britanny towards the end of the fighting there in order to mount Operation Derry (q.v.) were withdrawn after a fortnight, rested from 18 August to 22 August at Vannes and then returned to the United Kingdom. There they were rearmed and re-equipped, and issued with Operation Instruction No. 45 for a mission in the Doubs *département*, which borders on Switzerland north of Lac Léman (Lake Geneva) and Lac du Neuchâtel, to assist the FFI, specifically in the double objective of blockading the international border to prevent German forces finding refuge in neutral Switzerland, and closing the Belfort Gap between the Vosges mountains, to the north, and the Jura, to the south. There is documentary evidence which shows that originally this mission was to have been mounted by 2 SAS. The area is heavily wooded, with hills rising to around a thousand metres in the south. The Belfort Gap had already become the focus for most of the German forces fleeing France, but the resistance there was particularly well organized; one can get some idea of the importance attached to resistance activities in the area from the fact that no less than seven Jedburgh teams were also sent there, three of them having been dropped originally in neighbouring *départements*.

The SAS squadron was to be inserted in two groups; Capt Pierre Sicaud, the commanding officer, together with his HQ Section, the W/T section and the three combat sections which made up 1 Troop were to go on the night of 26 August, and to be reinforced by 2 Troop the following night. In the event, the insertion planned for the night of 26 August went wrong; three of the four Stirlings carrying the men returned to the UK after encountering a very heavy storm in the Paris region, and only two officers, *Aspirants* Puy-Dupin and Ghurko, and twelve ORs, all the former's section and three of the latter's, were actually dropped, to a well-lit and well-manned DZ near the small village of

Montéchéroux adjacent to the Fort de Lomont where the large, well-armed *Maquis* led by Major Paul (an American OSS officer, Ernest Floege) was based. Two days earlier the *maquisards* had liberated Montéchéroux, and had followed it up on 26 August by taking Villars-les-Blamont; while these were no more than small villages, their liberation was important to morale, and the partisans were in very high spirits. In consequence, the parachutists were in action within little more than twelve hours of their feet hitting French soil once more, supporting the FTP *Maquis* Tito in an attack on a German post near the Swiss frontier, at Dannemarie, the following evening. After a firefight lasting an hour, during which significant casualties were inflicted on the fifty-strong defending force, the result was still inconclusive, and the French forces pulled back, but the next morning the Germans were found to have abandoned the post.

That night the remaining members of the first group – the HQ Section with the commander and 2i/c; the signallers; *Aspirant* Anspach and his section, plus the remaining men from Ghurko's, together with a French volunteer only recently returned from the region, who acted as local liaison – were inserted, along with Jedburgh team Brian, which operated independently. They were dropped from too great a height and were widely dispersed as a result, most landing well outside the DZ, across a wooded hillside; it was 1000 the following morning before the last stragglers were rounded up. Sicaud had discretion as to whether the second group should be sent in immediately, but the delay in inserting his own party had a knock-on effect and it was to be the last night of the month before more men were sent, and then only one section out of the remaining three actually made it. It was the night of 5 September before the Abel party was complete, and by that time Sicaud and his men had already taken part in heavy fighting and sustained losses.

By the end of August, the Germans had definitely given up any hope of doing more than escaping from France with as many of their men and as much of their *matériel* as possible intact. In the Doubs, they had certainly abandoned all but the main roads leading toward the Belfort Gap and the open plain leading down to the Rhine beyond. In the Abel party's operational area this meant the D437 from Pontarlier to Montbéliard, and in particular the stretch of the road which parallels the river which gives the *département* its name, from Maiche to Pont-de-Roide via St-Hippolyte, all of which were in German hands. Sicaud decided to concentrate on Pont-de-Roide, which had a German garrison numbering perhaps 300, armed with machine-guns and mortars. Even with a substantial portion of the 700–800 armed and (at least partially) trained *résistants* Major Paul had in the area, this objective would still prove to be beyond Sicaud's capabilities, but on 29 August he launched an assault on it, a section armed with Bren guns and a 3in mortar providing fire support from high ground to the south-east of the town while partisan forces attacked from that direction and the three sections from 1 Troop under *Aspirant* Puy-Dupin, which had forded the Doubs two kilometres downstream, advanced along the west bank. Sicaud soon zeroed his mortars in to the German barracks and had fired four effective rounds when a bomb exploded in the mortar tube, killing *Aspirant* Jean-Marie Ravalec, *Caporal-Chef* Mattei and *Caporal* Bischoff. As Puy-Dupin and his men approached the town, they came under fire from a convoy on the eastern bank as well as from the town itself, and made no further progress, and though the FFI contingent on the eastern side of the river pushed on almost to the bridge which links the two parts of the town, under cover of the Bren team, Sicaud ordered a withdrawal. When Pont-de-Roide was eventually taken, it required an infantry battalion supported by artillery.

Over the next two days, the SAS troopers laid ambushes on the D437; Sicaud achieved nothing, but Puy-Dupin's party, after a thirty-six-hour wait, opened fire on a truck and a car packed with German infantry, killing or wounding twenty-five. During the night of 31 August the remainder of the party was despatched from Fairford, but again, two of the three aircraft failed to find the DZ and returned with their passengers aboard, and only *Aspirant* Duno's section was actually inserted. As a result of the poor showing of the ambush parties, Sicaud concluded that the Germans were no longer using the D437 for major traffic, and after requesting permission from Major Paul, he decided to move his men north-westwards some forty kilometres, to the northern flanks of the Montagne du Lomont, and focus on the N83, which links the larger city of Besançon with Belfort directly and with Montbéliard via the N463, which leaves the major road at L'Isle-sur-le-Doubs. It was south-west of this latter that Sicaud concentrated his forces, and when Duno's section returned from a comprehensive reconnaissance on 3 September, it was decided to mount an ambush near the twin villages of Hyèvre-Paroisse and Hyèvre-Magny, five kilometres from Clerval, moving into a *Maquis* camp at Crosey-le-Petit for the purpose. The SAS party arrived there on the evening of 4 September; unfortunately for Sicaud, this group was outside Major Paul's control, and was directed instead by a somewhat shadowy figure calling himself Col Belin, and the local FFI leader at Crosey refused to go along with Sicaud's plan until he had cleared it with him. This meant a delay of at least twenty-four hours, and in the meantime, Sicaud decided, he would try to link up with the advance guard of the French *Armée B*, which had already pushed past Besançon. He found a *groupement tactique* from the *3e Régiment Tiralleur Algérien* (3RTA; a light infantry regiment) supported by a squadron of armoured cars of the *6e Spahis*, west of Baume-les-Dames, and was instructed by the commanding officer, Lt-Col Goutard, to concentrate on taking Clerval, where the N83 crosses the Doubs.

Sicaud returned to Crosey and discovered that his second-in-command, Lt Tupet-Thomé, had already left for Clerval; when he caught up with him he was in the process of laying an ambush east of the village on the N83 towards L'Isle-sur-le-Doubs, to act as a stop-force for FFI units which had looped around Clerval with the intention of attacking from the north and west. In fact, when the FFI attacked they encountered little opposition, and by mid-morning of 5 September the village was cleared. Tupet-Thomé began to construct defensive positions in case of a German counter-attack, while Sicaud retraced his steps as far as Pont-les-Moulins, near Baume-les-Dames, where the French Army's HQ was now situated. He made a situation report, rounded up supplies of ammunition and then set off for Montéchéroux, where the final two sections of his party under Lts Quelen and Rosset-Gournand were expected that night. He got there at midnight, some two hours before the aircraft were due, gave instructions to his signallers, who had remained with Paul's group, that the newcomers were to be directed to Clerval, and then returned to Pont-les-Moulins.

Meanwhile, the situation at Clerval had deteriorated rapidly; soon after Sicaud left, the village came under fire from German armour, and two petrol tanker-trucks, which Tupet-Thomé had incorporated into a barricade at the point where the railway crossed the main road, exploded, killing two men of the FFI and two parachutists (Sicaud names them in his report as Camy and Clement; it is unclear whether these were *noms de guerre* or simply nicknames, and other sources give their names as Antoine Durand and Robert Seruguet), and seriously wounding the French liaison officer of Jedburgh team Brian, Capt Roger Cretin, who was also present. Despite being both outnumbered and outgunned, the combined SAS and FFI defence held out on the left bank of the Doubs, and even managed to destroy a Pz.Kpfw. IV tank with a Gammon grenade, but were forced to evacuate the following morning.

Sicaud left the French HQ at 0600 that morning for Clerval, by a roundabout route. He got as far as Anteuil, on the slope south of the village, where fighters of the *Maquis* Tito were in action alongside FFI elements against German infantry supported by armour. Learning that Tupet-Thomé was in the process of falling back on their position, and that it was then proposed that they would withdraw in turn to Crosey, he set off for the DZ, hoping to catch the new arrivals before they left for Clerval. In fact, he found them just short of Montéchéroux, setting up an ambush at a crossroads, having been told that German armour was in the vicinity. By this time, units of *Armée B* had begun arriving from the south-west, up the D437, and he left Quelen and Rosset-Gournand to consolidate their position, to return to Crosey, where he rejoined Thomé and his men who had executed a fighting withdrawal, destroying another tank in the process.

From here on, the situation becomes less clear. Sicaud's report is less comprehensive in the later stages of the operation, and is somewhat at odds with the account compiled by the *maquisards*; consequently, it is difficult to determine exactly who did what, and when. By 6 September, not only had the Allied armies entered the area in force, but they were up against much more serious opposition in the shape of strong elements of 9. Panzer Division. In barracks at Aix-en-Provence at the time of the Normandy landings, the division had been committed to the battle there only at the end of August, and had not been caught in the Falaise Pocket; thus it had been well placed to make a strategic withdrawal to the east as the situation deteriorated. It had been brought up to full strength (seventy-eight Pz.Kpfw. IV and seventy-nine 79 Pz.Kpfw. V Panthers) before Normandy, and while it had taken losses, it was still largely intact at the beginning of September; it was a very formidable force indeed.

Certainly, now that Allied regular forces had begun to deploy, the scope for independent action by the SAS party was very much reduced, and from 9 September on its troops were deployed as reconnaissance units, largely for the US 45th Infantry Division. The morning of that day, however, the men of Quelen and Rosset-Gournand's sections got involved in a firefight at Autechaude-Roide, along with a reconnaissance section from 3RTA. The German contingent there had two Panther tanks plus a number of armoured cars, and put up a stiff fight. Sicaud's report says 'The paratroops, who played the most important part in this action, killed 25 Germans, destroyed two armoured vehicles by means of Gammon bombs, suffering no casualties.' That afternoon, Sicaud encountered an American officer, and by that evening had linked up with the DMR, 'Ligne' (Col Broad).

The following day he was brought to the headquarters of the colonel commanding the 45th Inf. Div.'s spearhead unit, the 179th Infantry Regiment, north of L'Isle-sur-le-Doubs, who asked that all his men be assigned to him, a request which Broad granted. Sicaud's men were allocated, section by section, to American infantry companies; first into action, on 13 September, was Rosset-Gournand's section, told off to reconnoitre Accolans ahead of K and L Companies. They met little opposition, and by 1600 the village was in Allied hands, having yielded up some seventy-five prisoners. The neighbouring village, Geney, would not be such an easy proposition.

It was 15 September before an attack on Geney was mounted, and then it was a full-blown assault, preceded by an artillery bombardment and supported by tank destroyers to provide mobile heavy fire support. More than half the SAS force participated, and Sicaud soon found that their tactics, and those of the Americans, were not exactly complementary. The assault commenced at 1600, and the SAS troops, used to fire-and-movement advance, moved up to orchards bordering the village from the west, while American infantrymen advanced from the south, expecting the artillery bombardment to lift according to the agreed programme; it did, but no sooner were they halted by concentrated machine-gun fire than it began again. For some reason, Sicaud had not been provided with a tactical radio, and thus had no way to contact the American command centre directly. He tried to make his way to one of the tank destroyers, stuck on a ridge in their rear, in order to use its radio, but after twenty minutes he was forced to give up, and returned to Puy-Dupin's section. By early evening the Frenchmen had advanced to the outskirts of the village itself, but then the artillery barrage redoubled, and they began to come under fire from German 8.8cm artillery and heavy mortars sited on the hills to the north of the village, as well as from the Americans to their right. The night passed slowly, and soon after first light the next day Sicaud realised that the Americans were actually pulling back, leaving him exposed on the flank. He held his position until 0900, and then ordered a withdrawal to the ridgeline, holding there until 1945, when the tank destroyer was finally made mobile again, before pulling back to Accolans. In all, the SAS lost four men in the attempt to take Geney – *Aspirant* Pierre Rosset-Gournand and Parachutists Bernard Maguet, Francis Salort and Philibert Young, with a further five men wounded (a fifth man, Parachutist Denis Garros, was lost during a reconnaissance mission near Archettes, two days later). Later, Sicaud estimated that the German detachment there amounted to a full battalion, reinforced by artillery, and with two Pz.Kpfw. V Panther tanks and assorted light armoured vehicles.

Geney was later taken by an American infantry battalion, but by that time, Sicaud and his men had moved some way to the north, to reconnoitre the area around the town of Épinal in the Vosges, an important crossing point on the Moselle river. They saw no more set-piece action, though they were involved in occasional skirmishes, and were withdrawn, and Operation Abel terminated, on 25 September, just a month after the leading elements of the unit had left the United Kingdom.

Part Five

4 SAS (2e RÉGIMENT DE CHASSEURS PARACHUTISTES)

DINGSON/SAMWEST

In addition to the three operations 1 SAS commenced on 6 June, the men of the Free French 4 Para were committed to action in Brittany, whence many of them came, on D-Day. 4 SAS's operations were to have a different basic character from that of Bulbasket or Houndsworth, and had a single objective: to arm, train and lead the local *maquisards* and employ them to prevent the important German garrison in the region reinforcing the Normandy battlefield. The plan called for parties of roughly equal strength to be inserted to the north and south of the Armorican peninsula, and a third, divided into small groups, to be dropped between them two nights later. The battalion being wholly French, there was no conflict of interest with De Gaulle's principles, and after a decidedly shaky start the various elements were to be combined into one of the most successful operations the SAS Brigade undertook during the entire battle to liberate France.

The southern operation, Dingson, was launched in two stages, with no preliminary reconnaissance. A relatively large advance party comprising fourteen men and two officers, Lts Henri Déplante and Pierre Marienne, was inserted in the early hours of D-Day in the hilly heathland of the Landes de Lanvaux to the north of the city of Vannes, which is situated on the lagoon-like Gulf of Morbihan on the Biscay coast of the peninsula. The two sticks duplicated each other, and this proved a wise precaution, for Marienne's stick was dropped wide of the DZ, actually on to a German hilltop observation post. Four men, including the signallers with all their equipment, were captured by *Feldpolizei*, one of them, Emile Bouétard, being killed in the process. The remainder of Marienne's party was reunited with Déplante's only on 8 June, and soon thereafter met the FFI commander in the Morbihan *département*, 'Colonel Morice' (Maurice Chenailler), who had ordered the mobilisation of the Resistance *batallions* of Ploërmel-Josselin, Vannes, Auray and Guéméné-sur-Scorf, a total of some 3,500 men, the previous day.

Chenailler had established a base at a farm known as La Nouée (also rendered as La Nouette), adjacent to a DZ known as 'Baleine' ('Whale'), two kilometres west of the village of St-Marcel. This DZ had been in regular use since February 1943, and was practically invisible except from the air, being ringed by high hedges; why it was not used to insert the SAS advance party is unclear. For four nights from 9 June additional paratroopers and around 150 containers of arms and ammunition were dropped on Baleine, and on 13 June the biggest supply operation in Occupied France thus far saw twenty-seven Stirlings drop 700 containers there (Jedburgh team George reported resupply drops 'every night for eight days'). By 17 June, when it received its first *parachutage* of four jeeps – these, and a further four dropped to Operation Bulbasket that same night, are thought to have been the first operational deliveries of motor vehicles by parachute – the SAS party numbered sixteen officers and 171 troopers under the command of the regiment's CO, *Commandant* Pierre Bourgoin (known as 'Le Manchot', being short of a right arm, lost in the fighting for Tunis), plus the three members of team George. Some (French) reports suggest that George and Frederick, which was inserted with the northern SAS group, were hasty replacements for two other teams, members of which had clashed with Bourgoin, apparently over politics, but there is nothing to confirm this in either of the Jedburgh teams' after-action reports; George's report does mention the very cold welcome it received from the French SAS party at Fairford, however, even though its French liaison officer, Captain Raguenean, had previously served with Bourgoin, and that its departure was delayed by twenty-four hours. The team leader, an American captain named Cyr, said:

> Our first impression was not good. There seemed to be a strained feeling between Jedburghs and SAS, the latter did not seem to recognise our value to them and rather implied that we were a nuisance and a burden. SAS feared interference by outsiders in a role which they wished to carry out themselves.

Relations between the SAS party and team George soon improved, as Captain Cyr's after-action report reveals:

> We soon found out that the SAS was an original unit, with no rules or regulations. Officially they were taking orders from someone. Actually they were taking orders from no one. They had their own planes

and their own supplies and their own ideas. They worked in the field as SAS and as Jedburghs [presumably this means that they were both engaged in offensive operations and training and arming the partisans]. However, by no means did they ruin the show, in fact they worked wonderfully … owing to a great deal of diplomacy our relations became more and more friendly. We came to a point where perfect co-ordination was established between Jedburghs, SAS, BOA and French organisations from London. *We never forgot that we were under* Cdt *Bourgoin's command …*' (Italics added).

This contrasts with a reported conversation between Major Wise (leader of Jedburgh team Frederick, see below) and a (British) SAS liaison officer, S/Ldr Smith, in which the former asserted that he was *not* under Bourgoin's command. This was contrary to the 1 June amendment to Browning's Operation Instruction No. 1, addressed to Commander, SAS Troops (Rory McLeod), which said, 'The two Jedburgh teams will, for Operations Dingson and Samwest ONLY, as a special exception, be put under your command' (the emphasis here is in the original). Reading between the lines, it looks as if the problems teams George and Frederick encountered with the French at Fairford stemmed from the attitude of Frederick's leader to the SAS.

During the 13 June *parachutage*, a stick of containers went astray, and landed in the village of La Chapelle-Caro, north of St-Marcel, one of them actually hitting the railway station; that confirmed German suspicions of the presence of an important *Maquis* concentration in the area, which had been aroused earlier when newly armed *maquisards* had become bold enough to start attacking German troops in nearby towns, in daylight (though a French report states that a unit of *Feldgendarmerie* arrived at the DZ while the containers were being collected, and that precipitated the battle which followed).

Such a large body of men, with about as much discipline as an average holiday fairground crowd, was impossible to conceal, of course. At around 0800 on 18 June, two light vehicles carrying eight members of a *Feldgendarmerie* unit blundered into a sentry post on the outskirts in the south-east sector of the area west of St-Marcel where the SAS and Resistance forces were assembled. One car was destroyed by a PIAT bomb, and three men from the other were killed or wounded, but one managed to make good his escape. About an hour later the base was attacked from the same direction by a wholly inadequate force of around 125 German infantrymen (who advanced behind a shield of around a score of civilian hostages, according to French reports). They were driven off with few casualties on either side but within hours a second assault saw a battalion from the 275. Infantry Division, reinforced by armoured cars, artillery and 300 paratroopers – a total of perhaps a thousand men – attacking from two sides. French casualties were surprisingly light, considering the force arrayed against them, largely due to the timely intervention of a formation of fighter-bombers, probably Republican P-47 Thunderbolts from US 9th Air Force's 404th Fighter Group (though one report says they were Mosquitoes) which was called up by radio. The aerial bombardment and strafing held up the assault – although it was actually considerably less effective than it might have been, for by then much of the enemy assault force was hidden from the air in woodland – and allowed most of the men to disperse. The dead included seven of the original Dingson party, the leader of one of the Cooney parties (see below), and a score of partisans, with sixty wounded. Fifteen were captured, including three members of the Samwest party (see below), and were executed at St-Marcel five days later. In the aftermath of the attack on the Dingson base, Ukrainian and Georgian troops fighting with the *Wehrmacht* combed the countryside, executing anyone they deemed suspicious, including four more SAS troopers, and burning whole villages indiscriminately.

The majority of the 4 SAS troopers scattered to act as cadres for the newly armed *Maquis* bands, while Capt Déplante was detached with a party of forty men to set up a relief base, Grog, near Pontivy, some thirty-five kilometres to the north-west, to act as a receiving and distribution centre for further supply drops (which included clothing, boots and rations, as well as more weapons and ammunition). All contact was lost with Jedburgh team George in the process; it resurfaced some time later, having migrated south to the *département* of Loire-Inférieure (now Loire-Atlantique) and continued to operate there under very difficult conditions, and was eventually extracted amid some speculation that it had actively disobeyed orders by leaving its assigned operational area in the Morbihan. The accusation was found to be baseless – the team was out of contact with London and with Bourgoin's headquarters, and had simply made shift to try to improve the situation in the neighbouring *département* after learning that there were many partisans there but no organisation; George was later reinserted south of the Loire.

Long before the Dingson party came under attack, the second

French operation in Brittany, Samwest, had already been dispersed. The Samwest advance party, of sixteen troopers under Lts André Botella and Charles Deschamps, which was again made up of two duplicated sticks, had also been inserted by a pair of Fairford-based Stirlings in the early hours of 6 June, nearer to the north coast of the peninsula, in the Duault forest south-west of Guingamp, about eighty kilometres away from St-Marcel. They were joined by the main party, some 100 strong and under the command of Capt André Leblond, together with Jedburgh team Frederick (one of the rare tri-national teams) on 9 and 10 June. By the following day the Samwest base had become a focal point for every would-be *maquisard* in the area, and this certainly created a security risk. Leblond said in his report:

> The farming population helped us a great deal over transport of containers and over food.
>
> Their goodwill was unbounded and even a little embarrassing, for there was a continual procession of visitors – sightseers and wellwishers – around the base.

It also appears there was the added complication of bad blood between FTP and AS factions, who began arguing over arms distribution, though what happened next had nothing to do with factional squabbling:

> For fear that some enemy agents might slip in, I gave strict orders to forbid sightseers access to the base, but those orders were indifferently carried out as the paratroopers tended to fraternise with all the world, without distinction or mistrust.
>
> On 11 June I had a man called Jean arrested, who had been denounced to me the previous evening as a former Militia-man and black marketeer, and also a Mme. Blondet, a commercial traveller whom the patriots denounced as an enemy agent.
>
> The former was a Parisian, who contradicted himself three times under cross-examination, and who had a plan of the base on him; the woman had worked in the Soldiers' Home at Rennes, and was carrying a note of the names of St Servais, Tybourg and St Nicodème, three villages close by the base. After questioning them closely, and consulting S/Ldr Smith and M. François [a partisan leader], I decided to have them shot and this was done at 2300 hrs.

This is the only verifiable case of an SAS officer ordering the execution of French traitors, though certainly *maquisard* bands closely associated with both the Bulbasket and Houndsworth parties, and perhaps with others, carried out executions, sometimes under the eyes of SAS troopers. The Jedburgh report states that while the woman was shot, the man was 'daggered'.

There was more and worse to come. At around 2100 that same evening, two SAS parachutists and a small group of newly-armed partisans, having gone to fetch food from a farmhouse, were surprised by a German officer and two ORs who had stopped to ask directions, 'quite politely', according to Frederick. They shot the officer (five times with a Sten, according to Frederick; twice with a Colt pistol, says Leblond) but the soldiers managed to drag him into the car and escape. At 0800 the following morning, forty or so men from 3. Parachute Division arrived in three trucks, surrounded the farm, shot everyone in sight and set fire to the buildings. However, the farm was less than a kilometre away from the main SAS camp, and Lts Botella and Deschamps asked Leblond for permission to intervene; he was reluctant because of the proximity of the farm to the base, but agreed because of the effect inaction would have had on morale. Even with the benefit of surprise, the intervention was not entirely successful; whereas perhaps ten Germans were killed, the remainder made an orderly withdrawal, leaving two of the trucks and most of the men in overwatch positions while the third vehicle returned to Maël-Carhaix, some dozen kilometres away to the south-west, where the German parachutists were garrisoned. Before midday, thirteen more truckloads of German troops arrived and spread out around the south and south-west of the patch of forest where the SAS troopers and large numbers of partisans were gathered.

Their initial forrays, which were concentrated on the forest rides, were ineffective, but by early afternoon, after still more German troops had arrived, the situation had both escalated and deteriorated to the point where Leblond feared becoming encircled, and gave the order to break off the engagement gradually, retire in small groups and fall back on the Dingson base. The breakout began at 1530, and was completed by 1800; virtually all the survivors of the SAS party escaped, though two corporals, Marcel Ruelle and Daniel Taupin, were taken prisoner, and were later burnt alive in one of the five farms the Germans destroyed in reprisals. Reports indicate that the French got the better of the prolonged firefight; five SAS troopers, including the two taken captive, and four or five *maquisards* died; German casualties were estimated at forty-five killed and twice that number wounded. The main body of the SAS party immediately withdrew to the south-east, in the direction of the Dingson base, though a score of men under Botella's command, some of them, like him, wounded, remained in the locality, where the wounded were treated, and later acted as weapons and tactics training teams under the direction of the Jedburghs. At the site of the firefight, local *maquisards* were able to recover all the material left behind the following day since the Germans were still reluctant to enter the forest. Leblond and his party reached St-Marcel just in time to participate in the fighting of June 18, and Leblond himself was later exfiltrated to the United Kingdom to make a detailed situation report.

That report makes it clear that in his opinion shortcomings in the Samwest party were largely to blame for its failure to establish itself. He wrote [emphasis in the original]:

> First of all an <u>iron discipline</u> must be enforced. Most of our troubles came from undisciplined or imprudent going to ask for food without orders, taking meals at farmhouses and so on. I have the names of two paratroopers (who paid for their lack of discipline with their lives) who were in part at least responsible for the breaking up of Samwest base.

He also had harsh things to say about his troopers' military skills:

> Discipline is not enough. Paratroopers must be first-class infantry and know every single dodge and trick of the trade. Unfortunately, they are nothing of the sort ...

and he admitted in a letter to Paddy Mayne, answering questions the latter had raised following his reading of the report, that some of his men, recruited from the French Navy and Air Force, simply suffered from a lack of basic training in infantry skills.

Leblond was not alone in criticising the Samwest party, and did not escape censure himself. In particular, Jedburgh team Frederick, co-located with the Samwest party since 9 June, blamed him for arming the Resistance bands too soon and failing to restrain them sufficiently. The criticism may have been justified, but frankly it is difficult to see how the SAS commander could have acted more forcefully, given his overriding instruction to operate in support of local elements and not to attempt to take control, when faced with local determination to take direct action against the forces of occupation, especially since this was a policy his own men clearly supported.

According to other sources, Frederick itself was far from blameless; S/Ldr Smith, an RAF officer attached to the SAS, who was dropped into the Samwest DZ with a small French staff to undertake Operation Wash (essentially a liaison mission) and who later operated alongside the Jedburgh team, was to make a quite devastating personal condemnation of Frederick in a report transmitted from the field by radio in late July. He said:

> I have only had full experience of Frederick, and only a slight sight of Felix [q.v.]. The trouble with Frederick is cold feet, a complaint they share with their French colleague Marceaux, the [FTP] head of the Côtes du Nord resistance ... Frederick don't stiffen Marceaux when he wobbles, and they over-concentrate on personal safety. I am confident that Wise and Aguirrec [Major AW Wise and *Capitaine* Bloch-Auroch, alias Paul Aguirec, the leader and liason officer, respectively, of team Frederick] are short of personality, and Marchand, i/c Felix [actually Capt JJ Marchant], may be so too.

The friction between the SAS and Frederick may have stemmed from the latter misunderstanding, wilfully or otherwise, that it was under SAS command; Wise did not and would not acknowledge that, though his own after-action report says, 'Before leaving I had been placed under the orders of Captain Le Blanc [i.e. Leblond; Wise did get the name right subsequently], who formed the Samwest base on arrival.' When Leblond withdrew, team Frederick remained in northern Brittany, and it may well be that Wise began to act independently as a result of his being out of touch with the command element, but he said under the heading of 'SAS Co-operation' in his report that 'We found at first that it was very difficult to work with the SAS as they had ideas about arming the partisans and rather intruded on our job.' That report certainly shows that Wise and Aguirec were very much happier operating alone (it would appear that they also resented the arrival of the Inter-Allied Mission Aloès, see below), and has a distinct air of self-congratulation about it.

The third operation 4 SAS mounted in Brittany involved inserting a substantial number of small *coup de main* parties to target the railway lines linking the region with adjacent Normandy and thereby hampering reinforcement of the defences there. The eighteen Cooney teams, as the parties were called (though their radio callsigns were Pierre 401–418), usually numbered three men, although two had five members, with a junior officer or senior NCO in command; they were inserted on the night of D+1, across a wide area from St-Brieuc in the north, Pontivy in the west, Pont-Château in the south and Rennes in the east. They were dropped from nine Brize Norton-based Albermarles, which carried two parties each. The DZ which Pierre 404 and 405 shared was surrounded by German troops as they landed; the leader of 405, Sgt Carré, was the only one to escape, and one other was killed according to Leblond's report (though other sources disagree). The parties were instructed to avoid all contact with local people for the first forty-eight hours, while focusing on their primary targets, and were then free to tackle targets of opportunity until their supplies were used up, before falling back on the Dingson and Samwest bases. All the parties which remained at liberty (including Sgt Carré, working alone) appear to have cut railway lines, although we cannot be sure since the level of partisan activity was high, and some parties made no written report, but it is clear that the railway system linking Brittany with the rest of France was effectively disabled at a very important juncture. Each party carried an MCR 1 radio receiver, and those expecting to rally on Samwest were seemingly alerted to its having been abandoned and redirected, and most had reached the St-Marcel base by the time it came under attack. There and in the campaign to corral the Germans in the region, ten of the fifty-eight Cooney men died, two of them executed after having been captured.

By D+14, most of the SAS troopers dropped into Brittany had been consolidated into a single large party – though it was physically dispersed into small groups, both for security reasons and to distribute the trained soldiers among the partisan bands to allow them to give weapons training and instruction in basic fieldcraft and tactics – and enough progress had been made in arming the local partisans that a radical rethinking of strategy was necessary. To that end a small additional party known somewhat curiously as Lost (it was to be an unfortunate choice; of the five ORs in the party, three were captured and executed and one was killed in action), made up of personnel from 4 SAS HQ but including Major Carey-Elwes from 20 Liaison HQ, was inserted on 20 June close to the Grog base, to make an on-the-spot assessment of the situation. When the results of Dingson/Samwest were analysed, and the success of the operation became clear, it was decided to exfiltrate Leblond together with Carey-Elwes so that he could report to SHAEF in person. Another representative of SAS Brigade HQ, a Polish lieutenant named Jasienski, was also parachuted into Brittany on a special mission, in this case to contact White Russian conscripts serving with the *Wehrmacht*. Nothing came of the venture. Two more Jedburgh teams were inserted on July 9 – Felix, close to the north coast at Jugon, east of St-Brieuc, and Giles, far to the west of there, in the Finistère, and two more, Francis and Gilbert, inserted east and west, respectively, of Quimper the following night, simultaneously with a party of signallers being dropped near to the Grog base.

Three weeks later, on the night of 3 August, forty-five more SAS troopers together with eleven additional jeeps were landed in as many gliders, just to the north of Vannes, relatively close to Dingson's original operational area. This was a particularly audacious exercise; German forces were no more than 600 metres away, but were kept at bay by the combined forces of the *Maquis* and the SAS party while the jeeps were extricated from the gliders. This was the only glider-borne SAS operation to be carried out, though others, to insert the parties briefed to take part in Transfigure (q.v.), were planned and then cancelled. The arrival of the jeeps gave Bourgoin's large party the mobility it needed to be able to strike east, to link up with the main body of Patton's American 3rd Army; by that time (the third week in August) the Resistance and the SAS combined, without the assistance of regular troops from the invading armies, had effectively cleared large areas of eastern Brittany of German forces, forcing them to fall back towards the important western ports, Brest and Lorient. (Both of these were heavily fortified. The former, isolated and surrounded from 27 August, finally fell to the US VIII Corps' 6th Armoured Division on 18 September; Lorient, also isolated, and an irrelevance by early September, held out right to the end of the war.)

Meanwhile a fourth SAS combat party, this time made up of a total of eighty-five men from 3 French Para, was inserted in three groups from 5 August in northern Finistère, some way north and west of the Grog base, to mount Operation Derry. Its objectives were to safeguard a vital railway viaduct at Morlaix and a bridge at Landivisiau on the Rennes–Brest line. Another viaduct, at Guimiliau, was to be protected by an OSS Operational Group, Donald, while that at La Méaugon, on the outskirts of St Brieuc, was the responsibility of a partisan group organised by Frederick. The Derry party worked closely with (but independently of) the three

Jedburgh teams active in the north of the Finistère, and also harassed elements of the German army still falling back on Brest; exploiting a chaotic situation, the combined operation was able to attain its objectives handsomely, causing significant casualties and destroying large numbers of vehicles, for the loss of four of its men: Jean Briguet, killed at Daoulas on 5 August; Guy Guichard, killed at Landernau on 6 August; Georges Roger, killed at Gouesnou on 5 August, and Lucien Rotenstien, killed at the same location the following day. Derry came to an end on 18 August, and the party from 3 SAS retired to Vannes.

By this time, German Army personnel were assiduously avoiding known *Maquis* centres and most definitely not straying off the main roads; the back-country had become the preserve of the partisans, around 20,000 of whom had already been armed. As a result, the Americans were able to make very rapid progress indeed through eastern Brittany; the lead elements of the US 1st Army, advancing along the north coast from the direction of St-Malo, were in St-Brieuc the following day; Vannes was liberated by 3rd Army on 5 August and the partisans themselves liberated Quimper on 8 August, Jedburgh team Francis making a triumphal entrance into the city. By that time, the situation had become confused. Partisan bands (and not a few men who 'had never set eyes on a true *maquisard*', and known to the real *résistants* as 'twenty-fifth hour men'), trying to obtain arms, lit DZ beacons at the sound of any approaching aircraft, and were often rewarded – some more handsomely than they could ever have hoped; it was not uncommon for supply drops to included parcels of millions of francs in cash, destined to pay partisans and for local ration procurement, and not a few were never accounted for. Equipped with weaponry they scarcely knew how to use, they promptly set out to 'patrol' the immediate area, of course with fairly predictable results. The number of *résistants* killed and wounded in 'blue on blue' incidents is not recorded. In the confusion, first a trickle and then a minor flood of Germans began to try to fight their way east, out of what was fast becoming an isolated pocket. Some were to achieve local success, largely as a result of the shortcomings of American forward elements, but certainly no formed units escaped, many were captured and the rest of the would-be evaders were forced to turn back towards Brest, where a garrison comprised mainly of *Fallschirmjägeren* under the command of General Hermann Ramcke was to put up a determined defence. It is clear that in Brittany, the combination of SAS parties and Jedburgh teams, arming and co-ordinating a large partisan army, had achieved exactly the sort of effect Stirling, for

one, had envisaged when he refined SAS's operating philosophy in
1942.

The Aloès Mission, under the command of 'Colonel Eon' (also rendered as 'Eono' in some reports) but with 'Colonel Passy' (De Gaulle's
protégé, André Dewaverin) in a supervisory capacity, dropped during
the night of 3 August, despite fully half its number never having parachuted before, even in training, installed its headquarters in the village
school in Kerién, close to the original Samwest campsite, and next day
set about organising the distribution of the large quantity of arms
brought in at the same time as Bourgoin's jeeps and generally carrying
out its brief to transfer effective power into the hands of the local
leaders. This was no simple task, for the area extended over four
départements and there were still unresolved issues between different
Resistance factions as well as considerable confusion, not to mention
numerous pockets of sometimes-fierce German resistance; but the relatively small mission – it numbered only thirty, including clerks and
signallers – was soon able to show results thanks to the direct assistance
of three newly inserted Jedburgh teams (Daniel, Douglas and Ronald),
and four which had been in the area since around 12 July (Francis,
Gilbert, Hilary and Horace). Francis was by that time down to two
men; its leader, Major CM Ogden-Smith, was captured, together with
Maurice Miodon, a trooper who had become separated from 4 SAS
after the fighting in the Forêt de Dualt, by a German *Feldpolizei* unit on
29 July. Ogden-Smith was shot in the stomach; Miodon, an arm and a
leg broken by a grenade, fought until his ammunition was exhausted
(allowing the two remaining members of team Francis to escape in the
process), and then announced to the advancing Germans that they need
not be afraid, since he had no more ammunition; he was then riddled
with fire from a submachine-gun and finished off by a pistol round to
the temple. Major Ogden-Smith, by now barely conscious, was also
murdered by a pistol shot to the head.

As early as their second day in Brittany, Aloès members were already
encountering the reconnaissance elements of spearhead American
units (who were always surprised to be confronted by Allied soldiers in
uniform, not having had the slightest idea that Special Forces were
operating in the area), and it soon became clear that the SAS's task in
Brittany was completed. The presence of uniformed American forces
in the area gave General George Patton the germ of a reason to interest
himself in the interface between the FFI and 'regular' Allied soldiers.

Ostensibly concerned that American infantrymen, trigger-happy through fear of snipers, would shoot first and ask questions afterwards if confronted by armed civilians, Patton's staff asked SFHQ to instruct Jedburgh teams to ensure that local leaders sent out unarmed liaison teams to make contact with advance US Army elements, and General Omar Bradley later went so far as to request Koenig to order all partisans to hand in their weapons as soon as their area had been cleared of Germans and fighting had ceased. That was definitely a step too far, and Koenig's response was perhaps predictable – he was answerable to General de Gaulle, not to Patton or Bradley; Resistance fighters were soldiers, *French* soldiers, and thus would carry arms whether they were actively engaged in combat operations or not; he was in the process of fielding a mission (Aloès) which would be charged with organising them into disciplined units as part of its broader responsibility to exert direct control over all Resistance operations, whether involving uniformed personnel or those dressed in civilian clothes, throughout Brittany, and set up a viable government there. An ugly stalemate was only avoided thanks to the speed with which subsequent events unfolded.

During the course of its operations in Brittany, 4 SAS lost sixty-five men killed, of whom more than a third – twenty-five – were illegally executed after having been captured, many of them wounded, most of them in the Dingson/Grog area. In all, after a somewhat shaky start, Pierre Bourgoin's 4 French Para proved itself arguably the most effective force the SAS Brigade fielded during the period of the liberation of France (though the official view was that 2 SAS's Operation Hardy/ Wallace won that palm. It is difficult to see why; it was a successful mission, certainly, but it had nothing like the strategic impact of Operation Dingson). It is worth quoting part of General Dwight Eisenhower's *Report by the Supreme Commander to the Combined Chiefs of Staff on the Operations in Europe of the Allied Expeditionary Force*, if only to show how attitudes at the very top of SHAEF, at least, changed, vis-à-vis the SAS and the Resistance:

> The overt resistance forces in (Brittany) had been built up since June around a core of (French) SAS troops … to a total strength of some 30,000 men. On the night of 4 August the Etat-Major (EMFFI, but actually the Aloès Mission) was despatched to take charge of their operations. As the Allied columns advanced these French forces ambushed the retreating enemy, attacked isolated groups and strong

points and protected bridges from destruction. When our armor had swept past them they were given the task of clearing up the localities where pockets of Germans remained and of keeping open the Allied lines of communication. They also provided our troops with invaluable assistance in supplying information of the enemy's dispositions and intentions. Not least in importance they had, by their ceaseless harassing activities, surrounded the Germans with a terrible atmosphere of danger and hatred which ate into the confidence of the leaders and the courage of the soldiers.

SPENSER

By the middle of August, Operation Dingson, which had occupied all the resources of 4 SAS since soon after D-Day, was virtually over; the small groups from 4 French Para which had played such an important part in turning the Breton partisans into an effective army began to reassemble and soon headed east towards Rennes, and a detachment of six jeeps and around a score of men escorted Allied intelligence officers into Paris on 25 August, the day the city was officially liberated. After a brief rest period and further reinforcement the force, now enlarged, undertook Operation Spenser.

The first organised action of Operation Spenser, on 26 August, saw a reconnaissance mission launched deep into what was to become the heart of the new mission's operational area, in the Loire valley, southeast of Orléans. Lt Gabaudan, who was entrusted with the assignment, was able to penetrate as far as Pouilly, between Briare and Nevers, and reported a significant concentration of German forces there. Their task seemed to be to safeguard the river crossings, particularly those at Nevers, La Charité and Decize, which would be required if the very large numbers of German troops still in west-central and southwestern France were to be able to withdraw to a position where they might conceivably be of some use. The main body of the Spenser party, which by now numbered thirty-eight officers and 279 other ranks from 4 SAS, including a significant number of *résistants* recruited into the regiment, mounted on fifty-four jeeps and a number of trucks, began to move on 29 August, eastward via Le Mans to Orléans and then along the general line of the Loire.

The forward elements of 1 Company arrived in the outskirts of Briare on 31 August, and (briefly) occupied Sancerre the next day, returning definitively on 3 September. They were joined at Briare by 3 and 2 Companies, in that order, over the next few days, later by the newly formed 4 Company and eventually by the HQ Company, which had remained behind in Vannes until enough vehicles to transport it had been repaired.

The majority of 4 French Para's troops ranged widely on the left bank of the Loire, though Capt Deplante's 4 Company crossed the river and reconnoitred east as far as the limits of the Houndsworth operational area, hoping to link up with elements of 3 French Para which were known to have penetrated from the Chalon-sur-Saône area northwards into the Côte-d'Or (in fact, one platoon had seemingly reached the Lac des Settons, south of Montsauche, and had set up an HQ there, though there is no confirmation of that from 1 SAS sources). Ambushes were laid on all the major roads crossing the area, although with poor results after the first few days, and large numbers of stragglers were rounded up, disarmed and passed into captivity. From the various accounts of Operation Haggard, we have seen that the situation in the Cher, on the left bank, was in fact very confused at this time; many German troops had indeed succeeded in crossing the Loire and were streaming eastward towards the Belfort Gap, to the Rhine and temporary safety, but many more were still in place, cut off, increasingly desperate and thus increasingly dangerous, particularly to the local people. There are many reports of atrocities having been committed, and it was a clear imperative for Bourgouin's men to secure the area as quickly as possible. An incident recorded by Jedburgh team Alec, which was nominally supposed to be in contact with the Haggard party but had long broken that off, gives us a snapshot picture of how they went about it:

> At 1500 hours ... we assembled our forces outside the town. [Les Aix-Augillon]. The forces consisted of 20 maquis and 4 jeeps from the French 4th Battalion parachutists under command of Captaine Larral [actually, Larralde]. We sent two German prisoners in with a white flag to tell the 150 Germans in the town that their position was hopeless as all the roads were blocked. Shortly after the two prisoners returned with the answer. The German Commander was not prepared to surrender. Capt. Larral ordered his jeeps into the town and the two sections of maquis infiltrated into the town on the right and left flanks. The town was cleared in one hour with few casualties to the maquis. [The Spenser party report says one killed, one wounded.] The number of Germans killed was 40 and 18 prisoners were taken.

The liberation of St Pierre-le-Moûtier, twenty-five kilometres south of Nevers, on 11 September, seemed on the surface to be several orders of magnitude more difficult, for the German force in and around the town numbered over 12,000 (though Cmdt Bourgoin's report summary, written the following January, puts the figure at 33,000). However, S/Lt Le Bobinecq, in command of a patrol from 2 Company which was assigned to that area, gathered intelligence which convinced him that they were ill-armed, ill-fed and disillusioned, and he decided to try to trick them into surrendering. A German prisoner sat on the bonnet of his jeep waving a white flag as he drove into the town, and Le Bobinecq convinced the commanders of some elements that he was an advanced party from General de Lattre de Tassigny's *Armée B*, which was then crossing the Loire at Decize. In all, some 2,500 German troops, mostly artillerymen, were persuaded to surrender (Bourgouin says 13,000), while the other 10,000 (20,000) opted to move off in the hope of finding American elements to whom they could surrender instead, and were permitted to follow a prepared route towards Orléans under the surveillance of 1 Company (the Americans were still reluctant to operate south of the Loire, believing the area too dangerous). Le Bobinecq's troop was joined by the rest of 2 Company and by 4 Company that evening, and the prisoners were disarmed overnight.

Clearly, 11 September was a pivotal date in this area. As the day wore on, it became increasingly obvious that all resistance in the Solange, which encompasses part of the *département* of the Cher and more, south and west of the Loire, had ceased, except for isolated pockets of diehards. That same day, 3 Company set off down the Loire towards Nantes, and then swung left to patrol the area between Saintes, Périgueux and Bordeaux. Operations ceased, and 4 Para, save for those elements escorting the Elster column (see below), was temporarily stood down progressively from 12 September.

Perhaps the most significant of the Spenser party's achievements, at least in statistical terms, was to assist in the secure exfiltration into captivity of almost 20,000 German troops – many of them from 159. Infantry Division, which had garrisoned the region closest to the Spanish border, between Dax and Bayonne – who had been frantically trying for weeks to extricate themselves from the trap which south-west France became after the Anvil/Dragoon landings in Provence on 15 August. The surrender of the Elster column, as it was to be known (it was under the overall command of *Generalmajor* Botho Elster) properly speaking falls outside the scope of this work, but it involved many of our cast of players, and a brief account of the events surrounding it sheds an interesting light on the general situation in France in September 1944, and particularly on the attitude of American forces towards their allies.

The ragged column had been making little more than thirty kilometres a night, unable to move at all during daylight hours thanks to the attention it received from long-range fighter-bomber aircraft, and with scarcely half of its strength since it had left Poitiers and Châtellerault, where it had regrouped, on 1 September. It had planned to use three different routes to the east, but was prevented from spreading out across the countryside by partisan bands, co-ordinated by Jedburgh teams and with the invaluable assistance of French troopers from 3 SAS's Operation Moses, and later from the Marshall and Snelgrove parties, snapping at its flanks. In the event it simply ran out of time, the bridges by means of which it had intended to cross the Loire having been taken or destroyed long before even its advance elements got that far east, and its senior officers agreed to talks after it ground to a halt near Issoudun on 10 September. The negotiations which followed involved every Allied formation with any reason to have been in the area, and a good few who actually had none, and each was to claim at least a share of the kudos, and as a result the true history of the affair is somewhat convoluted.

In essence, Elster was willing to surrender, but only to Americans, and the Americans were reluctant to travel south of the Loire. The stalemate was finally resolved by members of various Jedburgh teams and regional FFI leaders, who persuaded the commanding officer of the US 83rd Division, Major-General Robert C Macon, first to send a low-ranking representative, a lieutenant named Magill, to meet Elster at Issoudun, and later to travel there himself, to negotiate.

In the event, Elster secured surrender terms which allowed his men to retain personal weapons including light machine-guns (and thus the ability to defend themselves against reprisal attacks; this was a very real possibility) until they had crossed the Loire into what we may call the American sector. It is clear from a Jedburgh report that Macon, no less than Elster, had an innate distrust of the French; the meeting between the two is described as 'that of two great gentlemen making an agreement only marred by the presence of some troublesome Frenchmen who should not have been there anyway'.

Macon comes out of this looking extremely insensitive, to put it mildly. Capt Courtenay Gosling, the British political officer attached to 1 SAS's Operation Haggard (see above), was involved in the surrender negotiations and later also observed the way the Elster column was treated. He said in his report:

[Macon] told [Elster] to bring his men up through the Cher (now a liberated French department) and surrender to him north of the Loire; to keep all arms and transport, including many hundred bicycles stolen from the French (a specially sore point); and supplied four days' American rations for the 18,000 for the journey. They already had more than enough food and drink taken from the French.

The French, I need hardly say, were furiously indignant about this. They said it was not only an unmerited smack in the eye for them, but would probably lead to unpleasant incidents during the journey, as indeed it did ...

Macon certainly lost no time in claiming the credit for 'capturing' the Elster column, but that proved to be a something of a poisoned chalice. The Americans refused to hand over captured German arms, equipment, vehicles and horses – and even stolen food and drink – to the FFI, which, the latter's representatives argued, were its property at least by right of conquest. This led to American flags being torn down and burned, the appearance of outraged leaders and letters in both local and national (French) newspapers and a very considerable degree of enduring popular ill-will. To add insult to injury, when a proposal was eventually made to allow the French limited access to some of the captured stores, it was in the form of a 'lend-lease' agreement, which meant that the French were actually being asked to buy back items which had been stolen from them in the first place (some enterprising GIs had already taken matters into their own hands, and sold bicycles and even (French) motor vehicles to Frenchmen who had the money to pay for them); and to heap contempt upon contumely, American personnel openly fraternised with Germans and were to be seen handing out chocolate, oranges and American cigarettes to injured German PoWs in the hospital at Bourges while (very) hungry civilian casualties looked on.

The leaders (at least) of 3 SAS's Operation Moses were also in the area at the time of the negotiations, and were later to claim the credit for the surrender of 'General Elster's 18,000 [men] taken 'en masse' owing to our quick action', though without actually specifying what that quick action might have been. 3 SAS's Marshall and Snelgrove parties were involved in the affair, too, at least peripherally; having found themselves effectively unemployed in the Corrèze and the Creuse by the end of August, the two parties linked up (at Guéret) and moved northward together, arriving in the area of Châteauroux on 4

September and operating there in conjunction with FFI elements, mopping up stragglers, for eight days. There were still some rather forlorn fragments of the Elster column in the city when the SAS parties entered on 12 September, and at the request of the newly installed Prefect they were arrested, and SAS troops occupied the public buildings and suppressed a nascent riot.

The rather more tangible participation of 4 SAS in the capitulation seems to have been brought about largely through the efforts of Jedburgh team Ivor; its leader, Capt John Cox, together with the FFI's military commander in the region, Colonel Bertrand, was instrumental in obtaining General Koenig's agreement for the employment of Bourgoin's men in the operation to secure safe passage for the German column, team Ivor's French liaison officer, Lt Yves Dantec (Robert Colin), travelling to EMFFI in Paris, crossing German-occupied territory in both directions, for the purpose. French sources suggest that Elster was subsequently induced (by Col Bertrand) to sign a second surrender instrument, with himself and Cox among its countersignatories. 4 SAS's jeep patrols provided the escort for the German column from Bourges as it was moved out of the Cher and north through Beaugency, where it crossed the Loire and was disarmed, in what was by now a scene of almost complete disorganisation.

Part Six

5 SAS (INDEPENDENT BELGIAN PARACHUTE COMPANY)

BUNYAN, CHAUCER AND SHAKESPEARE

Operation Defoe and the earlier, more successful, Haft were not the only attempts the SAS Brigade made to influence events on the Normandy battlefield. The first elements of 5 SAS, the Belgian Independent Parachute Company, to go into action were dropped into the area north-west of Le Mans, towards Mayenne, on 28 July (twenty-two men under Capt Hazel and Lt Ghys in Operation Chaucer) and 31 July (a further two sections under Lts Debefre and Limbosen, in Operation Shakespeare). Both were tasked with harassing German forces retreating from the west, and both found that their operational plans had, quite literally, been overtaken by events. The bulk of the German forces, made up of the surviving elements of LXXXIV Infantry and LVIII Armoured Corps, had already passed through, and it was only the weak, straggling tail, which in truth was almost more of a liability to German High Command than an asset, save that it acted as a sort of rolling road-block which extended across much of the Mayenne *département*, preventing the pursuing American forces from breaking through as quickly as they would have liked, which remained. The German infantry divisions in particular had already suffered badly, and were very vulnerable as a result; they had lost most of such transport as they had – the countryside was strewn with the bodies of horses and the wagons they had drawn – and certainly could not be considered as a coherent fighting force. This was certainly not the sort of situation to which small parties of very lightly armed men could be expected to contribute significantly.

The Chaucer advance party, under 'Captain Gordon' (Lt Ghys) was dropped on to DZ Caramel on the night of 28 July, and over the next ten days moved slowly towards Nogent-le-Rotrou, its operational area. It reconnoitred as it went and located a suitable DZ for the main party under Capt Hazel, which arrived in shockingly poor order, with much equipment smashed and several injuries as a result of having been dropped at a height of just 200 feet, on the night of 9 August. Over the next four days the party could do little more than watch the German forces retreating in disorder; it laid ambushes, but none was successful. On 14 August it was overtaken by the forward elements of an American armoured unit, which it guided into Nogent, where it linked up with the Bunyan party before withdrawing towards Le Mans.

The Shakespeare advance party, six men under the command of 'Captain Macbef' (Lt Debefre) was inserted (badly, from a very over-crowded Albemarle) on the night of 31 July; two Jedsets and an additional man were dropped to him on the night of 3 August, by which time he had already changed location once, and he immediately moved again towards another prearranged DZ, crossing a main road, a railway line and then the River Loir, in a small boat, between Ruiller and La Chartre, without being detected. On 8 August a larger party consisting of 'Captain Maclean' (Lt Limbosen) and fifteen men were dropped into DZ 'Caramel'. It seems clear that there was a mix-up at the airfield, and that this group were actually to have formed part of Operation Bunyan, and the group dropped to that latter the same night was the real Shake-speare main party. A major *Maquis* resupply operation focused on that same DZ the same night, and as a result the SAS party spent a good part of the next day sorting out their containers from those dropped to the partisans. In the course of removing the weapons dropped to them the *maquisards* were mistaken for Germans and ambushed by another parti-san group. Very little went right from then on. There was only poor transportation available – of four lorries requisitioned, by the second day only two would start, and one of those broke down within 200 metres; as a result, all thoughts of laying formal ambushes were aban-doned. Such small skirmishes as there were came about purely accidentally and were desultory affairs, though one cost the life of L/Cpl Owen (actually, Roger Carrette; many of the Belgians took British-sounding *noms de guerre*). By 11 August, the party realised that it was as likely to encounter Americans as German stragglers, and by the next afternoon the men were resting in Le Mans, where they met up with the Dunhill party from 2 SAS.

Both Belgian parties were extracted, intact, on 15 August; neither had achieved anything of military moment, though after it arrived at Le Mans the Shakespeare party operated under the orders of Airey Neave of MI9 and Capt Coletta of MIS-X, its American counterpart. (MI9 was the branch of British Military Intelligence charged with aiding escape and evasion; Neave himself had successfully escaped from Colditz.) Working alongside the Dunhill party from 2 SAS, it assisted in the rescue of many captured Allied airmen, 152 of whom it escorted into Allied-occupied territory (in a convoy of four buses) when it was itself exfiltrated. It is worth noting, perhaps, that a total of 4,101 Allied aircraft were lost over the greater Normandy battlefield, and even as late as the end of July there were still many airmen held captive locally, often in very primitive conditions; as we have remarked, rescuing and sheltering downed flyers was to be a common task for the SAS parties.

A third Belgian operation, Bunyan, was mounted a good way to the east of Operations Chaucer and Shakespeare, between Chartres and Orléans (and thus into an area adjoining that in which Operation Gain was active), the six-man advance party under 'Captain King' (Lt Kirschen) being dropped into a DZ named 'Toffee' on 3 August. It, too, could do little more than observe initially, but was able to pass details back to Moor Park of two truck assembly areas, each of which held over a hundred vehicles. The main party, when it arrived, on the night of 8 August, consisted entirely of ORs, and had little idea of what it was supposed to do, having been briefed to join the Shakespeare party. Kirschen joined forces with a local Resistance leader, a regular soldier named Jerôme Leveque, and the two performed as well as they could have been expected to under difficult circumstances, engaging in skirmishes which saw a total of perhaps thirty German troops killed, destroying some vehicles (including five trucks and a half-tracked *flakwagen*) and capturing 30,000 litres of petrol, before the Bunyan party was withdrawn, via Nogent, to Le Mans, also on 15 August.

There was one common thread to the reports the leaders of these three operations made – the very poor performance of all but a very few of the local *résistants*, who could apparently always be relied upon to do the wrong thing at the very worst time. This was to be echoed in the reports coming out of the Dickens party, and we may note that some partisan groups in the region to the south, where the Bulbasket party operated, were similarly untrustworthy.

In sum, Bunyan, Chaucer and Shakespeare were mounted too late and were almost completely ineffective as a result, and Operation Dunhill, mounted by 2 SAS, was a complete waste of time, energy and resources too, for exactly the same reason: it was inserted long after any justification for its existence had passed. Bunyan achieved a certain level of success, but seemingly only by accident, if being in the right place at the right time can be so described, and whether it was commensurate with the effort required to mount the operation is open to doubt, while Chaucer and Shakespeare did little more than give their participants a taste of action, which may actually have been the true intention all along.

BENSON AND WOLSEY

As Operation Trueform was being wound up, in the last days of August, two additional missions were inserted nearby, north-east of Paris in the Compiègne–Soissons–Senlis triangle. The first, Operation Wolsey, was actually mounted by Phantom personnel led by Lt C McDevitt, but since the men were members of F Squadron, it was under the auspices of the SAS Brigade, and it will be convenient to describe it here. The Wolsey party consisted of a total of five men, and was tasked with gathering intelligence on enemy movement 'by road, rail or river'. Inserted on the night of 26 August, the patrol met with a mixed reception: some *résistants* were all too keen to help them; others, the majority, wanted nothing to do with them. Living conditions, in a patch of woodland, but without shelter, were difficult; the men were perpetually wet, and thanks to the container with their rations having gone astray during the insertion, never had enough to eat. In all, they were active for five nights, passing back information on troop movements along the N31, which links Le Havre and Rouen with Reims and was thus a main exit route eastward from the lower Seine valley, and the main routes out of Paris towards Lille. During its last few days in France, after the arrival in the region of American forces, the patrol 'helped the FFI (which had become very prominent) in hunting down the few Boche left in hiding', and then fell back on 21st Army Group HQ, where it was stood down.

The second operation, Benson, was mounted by five men from 5 SAS and a French liaison officer from 3 SAS, under the command of Lt Kirschen, whom we last met during Operation Bunyan. After a fortnight back in the United Kingdom, Kirschen was reinserted on the night of 27 August, to the west of the area were the Wolsey party was to operate, near the small town of St-Just-en-Chausée which sits astride what was then the main road between Paris and Amiens. Benson's task was to watch the roads and also to try to pinpoint anti-aircraft batteries.

Its insertion, to an unmarked DZ, was not perfect; the liaison officer and two of the troopers suffered sprained ankles thanks to the unevenness of the ground, and the consignment of a pannier and twenty containers were not recovered (though they were later, by *résistants*, who appropriated the contents for themselves). During its second day in the field, while hiding in an isolated barn, the party was surprised by a German self-propelled gun; a firefight ensued and the liaison officer was wounded, but all managed to evade and regroup. By the fourth day of the operation most of the enemy forces streaming through the area had gone, and on 1 September the patrol met up with an American unit and subsequently retired to Paris.

AFTERWORD

The SAS Brigade's operations in France were effectively wound up with the conclusion of Operations Loyton and Pistol, early in October, although men who had taken part in the former were still in the field until the end of the month.

By then, men of 5 SAS had already carried out operations – Noah, Brutus and Bergbang – on their own soil, and had initiated Operation Fabian, under Lt Kirschen, who had already led two parties in France. Fabian, which lasted a very long time (from 19 September 1944 until mid-March 1945), was tasked with reconnoitring the area around the Belgian–Dutch border, and became involved in the attempts to rescue British and Polish paratroopers who had dropped around Arnhem to carry out Operation Market. Men from 5 SAS were active in eastern Holland during the same period, too, in Operations Gobbo and Keystone.

The first British SAS unit to go into action again was Roy Farran's 3 Squadron from 2 SAS, which was sent into northern Italy to carry out Operations Galia and Tombola (and a few smaller missions with limited objectives) under the command of 15th Army Group; both operations were mounted in the western Apennines, and both, especially the latter, involved significant numbers of partisans.

The French battalions were in action again from the night of 7 April 1945, but this time in a rather different role and in the very different environment of the Dutch–German border. A total force of some 700 divided into sticks of around a dozen men, functioned alongside II Canadian Corps and formed a network of small offensive teams which operated at the very front of the action, effectively preventing German units which were being forced backwards by the main frontal attack ever to consolidate a positon. It was a costly business; as well as twenty-nine men killed in action, a further twenty-nine were captured, and many of them were subsequently murdered.

By this time, Brigadier-General Rory McLeod had handed over command of the brigade to Brigadier-General Mike Calvert, whom we last encountered as an Auxiliary Units organiser, but who had distinguised himself in Burma with Wingate's Chindits in the meantime (McLeod was promoted major-general, and installed as Director of Military Operations at GHQ SEAC at New Delhi, in India).

British SAS units were in action again in Operation Archway, mounted by a squadron from each of the regiments, under the command of Brian Franks. The force, which was entirely mechanised, was tasked with reconnaissance, but also operated, poacher-turned-gamekeeper style, as field police, in the counter-intelligence role. They were the first Allied troops to reach the shores of the Baltic when they entered Kiel, and elements of the force were among the first troops to enter Belsen concentration camp.

The remainder of 1 SAS, under the command of Paddy Mayne, were deployed further south, to act as a reconnaissance element for 4th Canadian Armoured Division. Operation Howard was not a success, largely due to the terrain in north-east Holland – flat, open country, much of it recovered *polder*, criss-crossed by dykes and drainage ditches – being totally unsuitable for jeep operations. Otway tells us: 'The result was that casualties were fairly heavy and the operation unsatisfactory, in spite of the experience and great gallantry of the force commander. SAS troops were not sufficiently heavily equipped for operations of this nature'. It was during the latter stages of Operation Howard that Mayne was awarded the third bar to his Distinguished Service Order. There is widespread and persistent speculation that a conspiracy was joined by certain members of the squadron to concoct reports which would lead to Mayne being awarded the Victoria Cross, it being widely and probably accurately held that he had fulfilled the requirements for that particular award many times during the almost four years he had spent with the SAS. The attempt failed. Just one man serving with the SAS – the Dane, Major Anders Lassen – was awarded the Victoria Cross for actions during WWII. Lassen died leading an assault on a strongpoint during the battle to secure Lake Commachio, in the Po delta, and his award was posthumous.

The Archway and Howard parties were still in the field when news came of the capitulation of German forces, as were the men of 5 SAS, still under the command of Eddie Blondeel who had by now been promoted major. The Larkswood party, which included all the effective strength of the battalion, operated as a reconnaissance force initially, under the control of II Canadian Corps, and later took on field security duties.

Despite the war in Europe being officially over, 1 and 2 SAS were not stood down, but were hurriedly returned to England, re-equipped and despatched to Norway, where they were to spend four months operating as a security force. Calvert returned to the United Kingdom in June, and began lobbying for a role for the Brigade in the war against Japan which, conventional wisdom had it, could continue for years to come; Churchill, who was privy to the Manhattan secret, permitted him to begin planning, even though he was fairly certain the war would be over long before any operation could actually be mounted.

The men of the SAS Brigade were back in barracks (at least nominally) soon after Japan surrendered. On 21 September, formal command of the Belgian battalion was restored to the Belgian Army, the French battalions followed on 1 October and the British formations – by now known as 1st and 2nd Battalions, the SAS Regiment – were disbanded on 4 October. In his letter of that date to Mike Calvert, Field-Marshal Lord Alanbrooke, Chief of the Imperial General Staff for virtually the whole of the SAS's short life, summed up the contribution it had made thus:

> In its short but distinguished history the SAS Regiment has taken part in every campaign from Egypt to the Baltic. It made a fine contribution towards the defeat of Germany, and has not only gained a well deserved reputation, but has also provided a tradition of courage and initiative which will be an inspiration to any troops called upon to undertake similar tasks in the future.
>
> I have no doubt that, given the opportunity, SAS Troops would have played a no less distinguished part in the defeat of Japan, but with the end of the War in the Far East, the requirement for units trained in the SAS role no longer exists.
>
> As you know, the considerable reductions now being made in the size of the Army at home and abroad make it essential to disperse all units for which there is not an active and essential need, and it has therefore been decided, with great reluctance, to disband the SAS Regiment. This will be a great disappointment to you and all ranks of the Regiment, but I know you will understand the need for this decision.
>
> You may rest assured that the valuable lessons gained from the use of SAS troops in the war will not be lost sight of; and it is also

intended to keep a special SAS section in the records at the Airborne
Forces Depot, as a record of the achievements of the SAS Troops.

Did the SAS Brigade justify its existence? The question is an invidious
one, and probably rightly so. Some of those who do have a right to ask it
– the men who served in the Brigade – would answer a wholehearted
'yes', of that there is no doubt, and so would the majority of the Frenchmen (and Belgians and Dutchmen) who fought alongside them. In
financial terms, there is probably no question to answer; the cost of supporting the Brigade in France was minuscule in comparison to the
entire cost of the liberation of that country, and it would be next to
impossible to arrive at a final figure anyway. In strategic terms, the
answer is no easier to find; if the fluttering of a butterfly's wings on one
side of an ocean can induce a tropical storm on the other, as some would
have us believe, then who is to say what effect the destruction of a dump
of supplies, the diversion of a specific unit of troops or even the death of
just one man may have had on the outcome of the war in Europe?

In real terms, we can be sure of one thing: the SAS Brigade, during
the summer of 1944, established enduring behind-the-lines operations
by organised bodies of troops as a legitimate feature of modern warfare,
and that, by any reckoning, was justification enough.

APPENDIX A

The Training and Equipment of the SAS Brigade

The SAS training regimen was defined in Training Instruction No. 1 of 24 March 1944. Basic training was based on improving physical fitness by the relatively simple expedient of loading the men like mules and running and marching them off their feet on a daily basis, combined with 'PT' (i.e. simple callisthenics) and regular trips to the assault course where they could practise such arcane but confidence-building skills as falling face-downward on barbed wire entanglements while their comrades used them as gangplanks.

More advanced training focused on specific types of sabotage targets – roads, railways (a section of branch line was set aside for the SAS's use, and was blown up and rebuilt on a regular basis), telecommunications, power stations, factories and even dockyards, including instruction in the use of the available sabotage weapons, notably plastic explosive (PE) and the devices developed to set it off – together with the approach to be taken in dealings with partisans (described, somewhat grandiloquently perhaps, as 'Raising the flag of revolt among the local inhabitants and [providing] assistance to existing resistance groups.') Concealment techniques were a major focus:

> All parties, whatever their role, must be prepared for their drop to be observed by the enemy, even at night, and for immediate search parties to be sent out. They must be trained so that they are not found by such search parties and can remain concealed in an area for up to 36 hours without being caught. Unit commanders will institute competitions between Sections and Troops and will frequently make use of search parties to locate and round up parties attempting to remain hidden.

The most unconventional elements of the training programme were the so-called 'initiative tests', which often involved penetrating a guarded area or making long cross-country journeys in all weathers, their participants instructed to adopt the mind-set of enemy parachutists. There were no restrictions placed on the troopers during these excursions, and the results, which displayed what one writer was moved to describe as 'the delightful element of mischief which characterised so many SAS operations' were perhaps predictable – farmers lost livestock, and householders vegetables from their kitchen gardens and milk from their doorsteps, while vehicles, both civilian and military (including an RAF truck, an Airborne Division rations truck and a police car, whose occupants, having tried to arrest the SAS soldiers, were left tied up), were freely 'requisitioned'. Needless to say, any man who failed any element of the course was liable to be returned to his unit (RTU'd), though some who failed the parachuting course stayed on as rear-echelon personnel.

It is clear from surviving junior officers' reminiscences that they later came to realise that the military (as opposed to fitness) training they and the men underwent in Scotland was actually woefully inadequate, and did little to equip them to carry out combat operations behind enemy lines, references to 'crack troops' notwithstanding. Youth and enthusiasm were to play a larger part than appropriate instruction, and the paucity of task-specific training may have been the reason why only relatively few men were actually allowed to participate in sabotage operations in the field. This is not to suggest that the programme was skimped or deficient; the men involved in planning it simply did not know any better – this was ground-breaking stuff, after all – and the lessons learned on the battlefield were to profit the SAS men of a later period. It is perhaps significant that returning party commanders were required to make a comprehensive report on their operation, to cover not just their doings and those of the enemy but also 'Comments on own equipment, tactics, training, and suggestions for improvement', as well as 'Comments on resupply; accuracy of dropping, organisation of DZs and reception, packing and stores supplied' and 'Any other 'lessons learnt' of value in planning, equipping or carrying out future operations.' Some of those lists of "lessons learnt" were long, and some were scathing in their criticism, sometimes of the party's own poor preparation but more frequently of the level of support they received from Headquarters. It is noteworthy, too, that advances in technology were vitally important to the success of the Brigade; even three years earlier it could not have carried out the missions it undertook in France in 1944, simply because the underpinning technological infrastructure did not exist.

Parachute insertion, though it was first practised on a meaningful scale as early as the mid-1930s, in the Soviet Union, is a case in point. Initial parachute instruction for those SAS personnel who were not already jump-qualified took place at Ringway, near Manchester, where No. 1 Parachute Training School was by now well established, and further practice jumps were made from Prestwick, on the Ayrshire coast. Here the men were introduced to the cumbersome (and unpopular) 'leg bags' – similar to a standard kitbag, some 30 inches in length and 12 inches in diameter; these were secured to the right leg with two quick-release straps retained by a single pin while the parachutist exited the aircraft and were then (at least, in theory) let down to hang on the end of a twenty-foot cord attached to the harness as he dropped. The extra weight – up to eighty pounds – thus hit the ground independently of the parachutist, lightening his impact. In the event, many men were to experience difficulties with the original arrangement when it came both to exiting the aircraft and actually reaching the quick-release pin, owing to the amount of equipment and clothing they were wearing and to the bags being insecurely fastened and sliding down the leg (the weight of the bags preventing them from lifting the leg), and in desperation, kicked the kitbag away, which was probably the most common cause of the cord retaining it breaking. A very necessary revision saw the bags carried across the chest instead, and one might suggest that the officer who wrote that 'If all the procedures were followed in the proper order, there was no reason for a leg bag to ever give problems', had probably never jumped out of an aircraft wearing one. The leg bags, though they were far from perfect and often malfunctioned, were nonetheless an improvement on the earlier system, which saw the men's kit packed into containers to be dropped with them; all too often the containers went astray, and occasionally the loadmasters neglected to push them out of the hatch of the aircraft; either way, the men were left without any of the resources they would need to sustain them in the field.

The containers used were of two basic types. Both types were designed to be suspended from the quick-release mechanism in the aircraft's bomb bay, and were fitted with a parachute (canopies were available in five sizes, from a diameter of 16 feet 6 inches to 32 feet) appropriate to the all-up weight. Each had a shock-absorbing 'percussion head' at the end opposite the parachute anchorage. The 'C' Type container was cylindrical, 68 inches long and 15 inches in diameter overall. It was hinged down its length and was not internally divided, though smaller cylindrical cells – actually, metal drums – 19 inches long, which fitted tightly inside the body, were available. The rather better 'H' Type container was actually a series of five smaller individual cylindrical cells, held together by two longitudinal tie rods into an ensemble just 2 inches shorter than the 'C' Type. The individual cells were 14 inches in diameter and 9 inches long, and were assembled with nose- and tail sections. The tie rods of the 'H' Type were fitted with quick-release catches, so that the ensemble could be quickly separated for ease of transportation after landing (a full 'C' Type container might weigh 500 pounds or more, and was thus a very unwieldy load, especially in difficult conditions); each was provided with a spade to allow the redundant fittings to be buried quickly, though much of the material was recycled instead.

'H' Type containers and 'C' Type cells were routinely packed with standard loads, designated by a four-letter code and with a simple marking stencilled on the outside (and some – those filled with petrol, for instance – were painted in distinctive colours). The SERA load, for example, comprised twenty pounds of plastic explosive, six Lewes bombs, fifteen assorted time pencils, two hundred feet of Cordtex fuze, thirty No. 27 detonators, thirty-six feet of Bickford safety fuze, thirty copper tube igniters, eight fog signals, three rolls of adhesive tape, three boxes of non-flaming fuzee matches, thirty primers, thirty fuze-sealing tubes, six percussion igniters, six tyre bursters and 'miscellaneous items', and was simply marked 'E', for Explosives. The JODI load, marked 'R 24' (for Rations, 24) comprised fourteen twenty-four-hour ration packs, seven tins of twenty cigarettes, two tins of water sterilising powder, two Hexamine cookers and fourteen fuel blocks, and fourteen books of matches, while the PAGI load, the other standard rations container, comprised one 14-pound tin of biscuits, one tin of boiled sweets, one tea ration, one tin of cigarettes, one bar of soap, one 1-pound tin of anything which came to hand and a quantity of latrine paper. One tin of chocolate, six 'large tins, various' and six '1lb tins, various' could be substituted for the tin of biscuits. These were marked R 14 A or B. It was common practice initially to pack loose items in a 'C' Type container – weapons, for example – with sandbags actually filled with sand, until someone pointed out quite what a waste of capacity this was! Better were the two proprietary materials used as shock-absorbant packing – 'Hairlok', which was rubberised hair preformed into sheets, and 'Koran', which was curled coir (coconut) fibre, available 'needled on canvas' to form sheets, or loose, but better still, according to the men on the ground, was absolutely anything which might have made a fairly hard life somewhat easier.

Both 'Hairlok' and 'Koran' were used widely with the 'Panniers, Wire' which were used as an alternative to containers for dropping items which would not fit inside them or which needed little protection – sleeping bags, clothing and boots, for example. The panniers, which fell free, were constructed of frames of spring steel wire to which a lattice-work of steel strips was fitted, and were then covered with canvas. They were available in three sizes: the 'A' Type, 22 x 16 x 16 inches; the 'B' Type, 24 x 18 x 20 inches and the 'C' Type, 29 x 18 x 13 inches. 'A' Type panniers were also available fitted with (internal) coiled wire spring shock-absorbers in the base. The panniers were very unpopular with the men on the ground. One officer was to sum up their shortcomings thus in his after-action report: 'Panniers were always a worry and we lost a high percentage. As they were pushed out of the hole [they were carried inside the aircraft, and had to be man-handled out, not dropped by remote control from the bomb bay] the time taken in getting them out represented a long way on the ground. They also drifted more than containers as they were usually lighter. It was quite common to find panniers two miles away and on one occasion twelve miles away.' [We should note that at an airspeed of 180 knots (335km/h, the aircraft covered almost a hundred metres in every second, and that panniers were inevitably dropped last]. Standard aircraft loads were up to twenty-four containers and ten panniers for a Stirling; a Halifax could carry fifteen containers.

The only commonly-issued weapons a parachutist could carry on his person, save for a pistol, were a submachine-gun (largely useless, except at close quarters, though they were effective noise-makers) or the folding-stock M1A1 version of the American .30-calibre carbine, chambered for an 'intermediate' round. Although 'valises' were developed to carry a Bren gun or Lee-Enfield rifle on the person, to be deployed in the same way as the leg bag, and these were routinely employed by airborne forces, few, if any, were issued to the SAS parties.

The M1A1 carbine was chosen to replace the standard .303-calibre Lee-Enfield No. 4 rifle for three basic reasons: it weighed little over half as much as the rifle at just over five and a half pounds as opposed to just over nine pounds and with the butt folded it was 26 inches instead of 46 inches long; it was semi-automatic, and thus the effective rate of fire which could be sustained was much greater, and a round of ammunition was less than half the size and weighed only slightly more than half as much as a standard .303in round, so the soldier could carry considerably more on his person (one hundred .30-calibre rounds weighed two and three-quarter pounds; one hundred .303 rounds weighed over five and quarter pounds). The intermediate round was much less powerful, of course, with a muzzle velocity of 1,900 feet per second against 2,395fps for the Lee-Enfield, and as a result the carbine was reckoned to be effective to something like one hundred yards in the hands of the average soldier instead of four times that or more; in fact, the effect of that degradation in combat was negligible, and the semi-automation more than made up for it. The .30-calibre carbine, designed by two young toolmakers at the Winchester Repeating Arms Co. in their spare time, was to become the most widely distributed weapon of World War Two.

The standard side arm the SAS troopers carried was of American origin, too, the .45-calibre Colt M1911 semi-automatic pistol replacing the Enfield, Webley and Smith and Wesson .38-calibre revolvers which were standard issue for British troops. They were popular before the troops went into the field, but in action their weight and inaccuracy were criticised. 9mm Browning 'Hi-Power' GP35 semi-automatic pistols were sometimes available, and were a great improvement. Other weapons were standard British issue – Sten and Thompson submachine-guns (and a few examples of the superior Patchett, conceived as a more reliable replacement for the Sten and the precursor of its eventual successor, the Sterling L2), Bren LMGs, the PIAT anti-tank weapon (which could also function as a mortar to a limited degree), and 2in and 3in mortars – though American Bazookas (i.e. Rocket Launchers, Mk 1) were sometimes available. Some captured German weapons, especially the MP38 and MP40, the 'Schmeisser' submachine-guns, chambered, like the Sten, for the 9mm Parabellum round, were much in demand; one SAS officer who was parachuted into France on D-Day soon obtained an MP38, which was the superior version, and carried it throughout the rest of the war.

And of course each man carried a 'Fighting Knife, Mark I' the famous and talismanic 'commando dagger', designed by William Fairbairn and Eric Sykes, two men who had served together for over two decades as police officers in the city of Shanghai, Fairbairn latterly as Assistant Commissioner, and head of the riot police, and Sykes as head of the sniper unit and chief firearms instructor. SOE had called them back to the UK early on, and employed them to turn lethal hand-to-hand combat into a formalised fighting skill, accessible to all. The knife they designed as a silent-killing weapon had a double-edged stiletto blade, just under 7 inches in length. Some 250,000 examples were to be produced before the war's end by Wilkinsons, sword-makers to the British Army, at a cost of thirteen shillings and sixpence (67.5p) each, including sheath, and a near-copy was manufactured in the United States as the V-42 by W.R. Case & Co. There was a 'Fighting Knife, Mark II' also, generally known as the Smachet, which resembled a heavy-bladed short sword. It was less popular than the dagger, though Fairbairn rated it more highly. A miniature version of the dagger, with a diminutive flat 'thumb and forefinger' grip and a blade 3 inches long, the sheath of which was to be concealed in the lapel of a jacket, was also developed for clandestine operatives, as was a robust 'flick-knife'. Fairbairn and Sykes had also been responsible for developing and teaching both armed and unarmed combat techniques including the ways of employing the dagger, such as the almost-certainly fatal method of severing the sub-clavian artery by means of a vertical stabbing stroke through the trapezius muscle at the base of the neck, behind the collar bone. Fairbairn says of this technique, in his *All-In Fighting*, published in 1942: 'This is not an easy artery to cut with a knife, but, once cut, your opponent will drop, and no tourniquet or any help of man can save him'. In all honesty, most FS knives were never used for the purpose for which they were designed; few men could stomach the thought, let alone the reality, which was 'extremely messy', as one man with personal experience put it, euphemistically. Among commandos, it was accepted that it usually took at least two men to subdue another with a knife, one to hold him, the other to wield the weapon. In the opinion of most World War Two-vintage Special Forces soldiers the fighting knives were best adapted to preparing food.

Grenades were important weapons in clandestine warfare, and as well as the standard No. 36 'Mills' bomb, the SAS used No. 82 'Gammon' bombs – simple yet powerful grenades which were no more than a canvas bag (various sizes were used) holding a quantity of PE connected to an all-ways fuze contained in a screw-on cap, which exploded (at least in theory) on impact, no matter at what angle it struck. A kilogramme of plastic explosive – the most common size – is a considerable charge, and users were advised to ensure that their mouths were open when the bombs went off, to avoid blowing out their eardrums. Users reported very good results against armour as well as soft-skinned vehicles; Operation Abel destroyed two Pz.Kpfw. IV medium tanks this way during the fighting in the mouth of the Belfort Gap. The Gammon grenade was often transformed into an anti-personnel weapon by adding objects – nuts and bolts, nails, scraps of wire; even small flints – to the explosive charge. Lewes bombs, named after David Stirling's original 2i/c in Egypt who devised them, were also widely used against vehicles; these were modified satchel charges which combined high explosive with diesel oil, and were effective incendiary devices.

Both chemical and mechanical time-delay fuzes were commonly used to set off explosive charges, but often the arrival of the target in proximity to the device was a far more appropriate trigger – employing the passage of a train to detonate a charge placed on the tracks, for example, rather than simply blowing the permanent way, presented the possibility that not only it, but also the passing locomotive and its rolling stock, along with whatever it was carrying, would be damaged. We may recall that disabling railways had always been an important part of the SAS's brief, and considerable efforts were made to develop a fool-proof (perhaps 'anxiety-proof' would be better), reliable detonator specifically for railway demolition. The device chosen was known as the fog signal, because it was so similar to the small explosive devices which railway employees placed on the track ahead of a train to supplement visual signals in bad visibility. The fog signal was a simple percussion-type igniter and detonator housed in a waterproof tin box attached to a primer by means of a length of Cordtex fuze. It was fitted with a pro-filed spring clip to allow it to grip the rail. The primer was buried in a suitably-sized chunk of PE, which was attached initially to the outside of the rail (this was found to be less efficient than attaching the PE to the underside of the rail, where it not only severed it, but also caused a crater in the roadbed, and the procedure was soon changed); multiple charges were generally used, placed ahead of the fog signal, and the ideal spacing between them was reckoned to be six feet more than the wheelbase of the locomotive, though this degree of accuracy was hard to achieve in the field. More sophisticated versions saw the percussion cap in the igniter activated remotely by the movement of an antenna, or a trip-wire acting on a pull-switch, which many believed to be the most reliable method of all, minimising the risk of a misfire caused by the locomotive's wheel cutting the fuze and also proof against the small blade-like scoop device the Germans took to fitting ahead of a locomotive's front wheels to dislodge the fog signals (though that measure could be circumvented, if one had time, by the addition of a simple anti-tamper device. The most basic of these consisted of a Mills bomb with the pin out, wired to the underside of the rail around the fog signal, with its time fuse taped to a detonator which was itself connected to the main charge via a length of Cordtex; if the grenade was dislodged it was detonated, setting off the main charge in the process).

Sabotage and ambush were to be the most effective offensive techniques and tactics employed by the SAS's combat parties in France. While much has been made of the use of armed jeeps as light assault vehicles, the damage they did in real terms was much less than that achieved with a few hundred well-placed kilogrammes of plastic explosive, and the vehicle-mounted Vickers K machine-guns were more often, although not exclusively, employed in the defensive role. The watchword of the operational credo, we should not forget, was stealth, at least up until the end of August. When all was said and done, up until that time the combat parties' prime concern – and their prime responsibility, although that was not always understood – was to remain undetected, and that was their best protection; if their presence came to the attention of the German forces of occupation, they faced annihilation.

At least as important as the all-round battle-fitness of the SAS troopers was the quality of the back-up logistical support they needed, both to insert them into their operational areas, and to keep them supplied while they were there. Responsibility for these vital aspects of the Brigade's operations were, of course, delegated to the Royal Air Force, and in particular to 38 Group, Transport Command, which had its headquarters, in mid-1944, at Netheravon in Wiltshire. 38 Group, which had responsibility for supporting all airborne forces operations, was equipped with converted Handley-Page Halifax and Short Stirling bombers, together with smaller Douglas Dakotas, Lockheed Hudsons and Armstrong-Whitworth Albemarles, and operated from Netheravon and Fairford, Keevil, Harwell, Brize Norton and Tarrant Rushton; the last, although it was a considerable way away from the supply dump, was the main base for resupply operations to the SAS parties in the field, and all the jeep drops were made from here, while the 'main force' SAS parachutists themselves were usually deployed from Fairford. The two-man reconnaissance parties, which were often inserted with Jedburgh teams, went by way of the base the SOE used, RAF Tempsford, in Bedfordshire, home of 138 and 161 'Special Duties' Squadrons with their Westland Lysanders, Halifaxes and Hudsons.

Other Jedburgh missions were launched either from Fairford (when they were inserted with SAS parties) or from the USAAF base at Harrington in Northamptonshire, some thirty miles away from Tempsford, the main base for the USAAF 801st (Provisional; later 492nd) Bomb Group's 'Carpetbagger' missions which supplied the Resistance with much of its weaponry. The Carpetbaggers' Consolidated B-24 Liberators also flew agent-insertion missions, sometimes out of Tempsford. Not all the aircraft employed by the RAF could be described as 'state-of-the-art' by any means; in particular the Hudsons and Albemarles were not well adapted to carrying parachutists and had basic flaws in the means by which the men exited the aircraft, while the Stirlings were definitely Bomber Command's third string. It is said that men from bomber squadrons equipped with Halifaxes and Avro Lancasters heaved a sigh of relief if they heard that Stirling-equipped squadrons were to be operating alongside them.

The task of co-ordinating insertion and particularly resupply missions, in a pre-computer age, was almost impossibly complex, even before the uncertainty of radio communications with combat teams already in the field, which relied completely on those drops of ammunition, fuel, rations and replacement equipment to remain operational, was factored in. Despite the manifold difficulties, on occasion the performance of the resupply system was very impressive – one oft-repeated story tells of an SAS party requesting a pair of shoes in a particular size and fitting, and receiving them the following day – but in general there were often shortages of common items, particularly 'comforts' such as cigarettes and chocolate, and somewhat surprisingly, tea was always in short supply.

Parenthetically, the problem of supplying the men with cigarettes (and small amounts of alcohol) was to be an on-going source of misery, as much as anything thanks to the attitude of HM Commissioners for Customs and Excise, who long insisted that 'duty-free' supplies could not be furnished to SAS combat parties in the field since they did not have an official Army Post Office address outside the United Kingdom! It was not until mid-September 1944 that Customs and Excise relented and permitted bulk stocks to be held at Station 1090 for issue to SAS parties at duty-free prices (100 cigarettes cost 3/4d [17p]; a bottle of whisky 8/6d [42.5p]), provided that returns of stock issued were made (in triplicate, of course) at the end of every month and that on no account were duty-free articles to be consumed in the UK.

Ian Wellsted, in his account of Operation Houndsworth, tells us that rum – 'Navy neaters', as issued aboard ship and sometimes to land forces on arduous duty, which was got up in gallon stone jars – was occasionally dropped in rations containers, and his commanding officer, Bill Fraser, said in his lengthy critique of operational methods and arrangements 'A liberal rum issue is essential, particularly in so wet a climate [as the Morvan area was that summer]'. Otherwise, there was usually wine to be had and no shortage of locally distilled eau-de-vie, to give it a polite name.

Resupply operations were relatively straightforward under ideal conditions, but that does not mean that they were risk free. As well as the known anti-aircraft batteries protecting specific locations, which could usually be circumvented, and the unpredictable, though small, chance of encountering a mobile battery, there was the ever-present danger of night-fighters, increasingly efficient by this time thanks to advances in radar technology. More real, though, were the risks which are always inherent in flying low over hilly country at night, especially when more than one aircraft was present in the same area. There were a number of very near misses reported, but there was one mid-air collision during a resupply mission over the Morvan on the night of 13 July. An RAF Halifax and a USAAF Liberator collided in mid-air almost directly over the village of Mazignien, close to which A Squadron, 1 SAS, part of the group engaged in Operation Houndsworth, had its HQ campsite. Indeed, the wreckage of the B-17 actually fell in and around the camp, and it was only by good fortune that there were no casualties on the ground. As it was, none of the crew of either aircraft survived. The report made by Capt Tom Moore, leader of the Phantom patrol which operated with the Houndsworth party, states that he believed the two aircraft were running in toward the same Eureka radar beacon (q.v.), ignorant of each other's presence, one aircraft on its dropping run, the other searching for the lights on the DZ; the RAF Halifax was said to have been carrying among its cargo some 60 million francs, destined for the Resistance, a substantial part of which was never recovered.

One of the innovations 1 SAS had made in North Africa was the employment of 'Trucks, Utility, 4x4, M38', having received a batch of them towards the end of June 1942. The M38 was designed as a general-purpose (or GP, hence 'jeep') vehicle, sturdy, light and manoeuvrable. It seemed almost purpose-built for Stirling's operations, and he lost no time in modifying three of them by the addition of pintle mounts for twin .303-calibre Vickers Type K machine-guns (see below), front and rear, while all received sun compasses, auxiliary fuel tanks, coolant condensers and sand planks – standard equipment for desert travel. Piled with stores and equipment, the jeeps would carry a crew of three (though were generally overloaded), and immediately proved their worth. One operational commander in France, Bill Fraser, suggested that Daimler Dingo scout cars, which were lightly armoured but had performance similar to the M38, would have been 'of the utmost assistance operating in conjunction with jeeps', but the suggestion was not taken up, presumably because the Dingo weighed in at around three tons, right at the upper limit of what could practically be dropped by parachute.

38 Group was presented with the problem of implementing a variety of completely new techniques, but by far the most spectacular of them involved delivering the jeeps by air, which involved slinging one (later, two) from the main support beam within the bomb-bay of a Halifax and dropping it, suspended from a cluster of four 60-foot-diameter parachutes, to a reception party waiting below. This entirely new method of delivering vehicles had worked well (or, more accurately, well *enough*, eventually; there is no record of how many jeeps were expended before the staff of the Airborne Forces Experimental Establishment, at Sherburn-in-Elmet, near Harrogate, where the system was developed, got it right) in training, but remained to be tested operationally. It was to work well enough under real conditions, too, though in some operations only fifty per cent of the vehicles delivered were actually useable; if all four parachutes did not deploy properly, usually because the jeep somersaulted on leaving the aircraft and snagged the rigging lines, the drop was doomed. The first vehicles dropped operationally were despatched to the Bulbasket and Dingson parties on 17 June.

Originally the jeep drops employed eight (and later up to a dozen) standard X-type 28-foot parachutes, with their rims stitched together where they met, to promote clustering, but it was found that the arrangement was very difficult to handle on the ground as well as increasing the likelihood of snagging on leaving the aircraft, and that in fact, the parachutes formed a natural cluster anyway. Further experimentation showed that four 60-foot 'chutes were adequate, though the protective cradles into which the jeeps were loaded were absolutely essential. The cradles consisted of a sub-frame upon which the jeep sat, with attachment points for steel suspension cables adjacent to each wheel; these cables were attached in pairs to a transverse beam from which the whole ensemble was suspended from the longitudinal beam in the aircraft's bomb bay, and which also provided an attachment point for a single cable, ten feet long, to which the parachute lines were in turn secured. The link was broken and the parachutes released by means of a small explosive device actuated on landing by impact. The vehicles' suspension was protected by the addition of two transverse crash pans, one for the front and one for the rear wheels; these were designed to deform and flatten on impact. Otherwise, preparation was minimal – the windshields were folded flat, and the machine guns with which they were to be armed, and the steering wheel, were stowed inside. The four parachutes were contained in a pair of valises stowed on the back seats of the vehicles; they were deployed by a small (12-foot) 'retarder' 'chute, which opened first by means of a static line, pulling the main 'chutes free of their valises, which then dropped free under the retarder and were recovered aboard the aircraft. The marginally heavier 6pdr anti-tank gun (it weighed 3,700 pounds with protection and parachutes), two of which were to be dropped to the Operation Houndsworth party, was fitted with a crash pan beneath the wheels and another under the limits of the trailing arms of the carriage, but no protective cradle; it too was suspended from four 60-foot 'chutes.

The jeeps were usually armed with Vickers Type K machine-guns–also known as the Vickers Gas-Operated, VGO, to differentiate it from the much more common recoil-operated Vickers Type C– the first examples of which David Stirling had procured for the SAS during the early days in the Western Desert. Produced as defensive armament for bomber and transport aircraft and introduced as recently as 1935, they were already obsolescent, thanks to the recent development of the powered gun turret, and Stirling got them by a 'back channel' from the RAF (the weapons stockpiled in Egypt were actually spares for Bristol Bombay and Vickers Wellesley bombers, the last of which were withdrawn from front-line service in 1941; the arrangement was later formalised, and the RAF handed over to the Army all its remaining stocks of the weapon). The design evolved from that of a light machine-gun produced in France by Adolph Berthier during World War One. Rights to manufacture this were acquired by Vickers, who hoped to produce a rival to the Bren, which, with its top-mounted, curved box magazine it closely resembled, both in appearance and in operation, in 1925. The Type K was a strengthened version, with modified furniture, intended for flexible mounting in the air gunner/observer's position in an aircraft, and its main virtues were a very high cyclical rate of fire –

marginally over 1,000 rounds per minute, achieved by the simple expedient of adopting a weaker buffer spring than that fitted to the
Vickers-Berthier – and its ammunition delivery system. The Type Ks
were fed from static, round, top-mounted pan magazines (much more
convenient for flexibly-mounted guns than cumbersome belts; they
were also fitted with bags to catch ejected cartridge cases and keep them
from underfoot), holding ninety-six rounds, normally a mixture of
tracer, standard ball and incendiary (resupply packages consisted of 288
tracer rounds and 144 each of ball and incendiary, compared with Bren
resupply packages, which contained 384 rounds of ball ammunition,
144 tracer and 48 incendiary). An unusual feature was the position of
the trigger mechanism, within the abbreviated spade grip which
replaced the conventional butt of the Vickers-Berthier; in twin installations, triggers were not cross-linked. The Type Ks were mounted in
pairs, one for the front-seat passenger and one in the rear (though some
vehicles mounted a pair in the front and a singleton at the rear). They
were to prove reliable and trustworthy weapons in general, but there
were always problems with the quality of the pintle mountings aboard
the SAS's vehicles, and as late as 1945, SAS jeep crews were still com-
plaining about a disturbing tendency they had to snap off altogether,
usually in the middle of a firefight, as well as poor stability which made
the guns inaccurate at anything other than short range. From late in
1944 some jeeps carried a single belt-fed .50-calibre Browning M 2
instead of the forward pair of Vickers guns, some replaced the rear-
facing Vickers with a Bren, and there were other variations including
the addition of a single Type K for the driver, mounted outboard. It is
reported that small numbers of Vickers Type Ks were still in action with
the SAS in a similar role as late as the 1970s.

As well as the gun mountings, from August 1944 jeeps were routinely
fitted with rudimentary armour plating, which consisted of a grill
mounted ahead of the radiator, a scuttle-mounted shield for the driver
and front-seat passenger, with an armoured windshield for the driver
and a windshield/gunshield for the passenger, a plate in front of the
battery and, for 1 SAS vehicles, a rear shield. Five clips to take Vickers
Type K magazines were provided on the bonnet, a luggage rack was
supplied, to be fitted to the rear of the vehicle, and a second additional
petrol tank was mounted under the front passenger's seat.

Communications were also vitally important, of course. It had long
been understood that without reliable radio the effectiveness of isolated
combat parties in the field for long periods would be much reduced, so

it was essential to maintain links between them and Brigade Tactical HQ at Moor Park. The BBC was responsible for the base installation there, which comprised five transmitter/receiver sets that were manned by personnel from the Royal Corps of Signals; they maintained two-way contact with the combat parties, each of which had its own organic signallers, via miniaturised self-contained transceivers known as Jedsets. The receiver component of the set, the MCR 1, was also distributed separately, allowing smaller, detached parties to receive (very simple) instructions directly, but also, of course, to listen in to the BBC's Forces Network, with its regular offerings of news and entertainment. Somewhat surprisingly, there was no provision made initially for direct voice communication between parties on the ground, even over short distances; if one wanted to pass a message to another, it had to do so via Moor Park, and that happened only infrequently. Various commanders in the field asked for No. 19, No. 22 or No. 38 sets (the two-way 'tactical' radios then commonly available to the British Army; they were cumbersome and delicate, and the US Army's SCR300 was reckoned to be vastly superior), but it was not until the long-range jeep operations commenced in mid-August that any were issued. They were No. 22 sets, and their effectiveness was found to be very patchy; Farran, in the report cited above, said: 'The tendency of No. 22 sets to wander off frequency made them useless for jeep intercommunication. I think a No. 19 set would have been better.'

There were never enough SAS signallers available save among the Belgians, and an addition to the SAS Brigade in the shape of a squadron from GHQ Liaison Regiment augmented its communications capability considerably. GHQ Liaison Regiment was the successor to an operational unit set up in 1940 to provide communications links between the British Expeditionary Force in Belgium and the Chiefs of Staff. It was re-formed after Dunkirk as No. 1 GHQ Reconnaissance Unit, and achieved regimental status on 31 January 1941; it was widely known as Phantom, and that name was generally used by its operating units. Its squadrons were divided into patrols, commanded by a captain, with a corporal and three men. At the time SAS Brigade was formed, the Phantom CO, Lt-Col Mackintosh, asked for volunteers to serve with it, and a new Squadron, F, was formed, under Major the Hon. JJ 'Jakie' Astor. In April, F Squadron was assigned to the SAS Brigade, two patrols to each of the British SAS regiments. It was envisaged that a Phantom patrol, or an element of one, would be attached to a squadron-strength SAS operation to act as its main communications channel, augmenting, rather than replacing, its organic signallers.

In what appears to be a throwback to an earlier era, the SAS combat parties also employed homing carrier pigeons as a one-way communications channel between parties in the field and Moor Park. Once again, reports on the effectiveness of the 'pigeon post' are very variable; some made it back to HQ with only minor delays, others seem not to have flown any further than the nearest tree. It is perhaps indicative of the esteem in which the birds were held that orders to some combat parties included a reminder that the pigeons were not to be regarded as a rations supplement.

APPENDIX B

Operations Mounted by the SAS Brigade in France, 1944

Code name	Mounted by	In	From	To
Titanic	1 SAS	Manche	6 June	Abortive
Bulbasket	1 SAS	Vienne	6 June	9 August
Dingson	4 SAS	Brittany	6 June	25 August
Samwest	4 SAS	Brittany	6 June	Consolidated into Dingson
Houndsworth	1 SAS	Côte-d'Or/ Nièvre/ Yonne	7 June	6 September
Cooney	4 SAS	Brittany	7 June	Consolidated into Dingson
Lost	4 SAS	Brittany	20 June	Consolidated into Dingson
Gain	1 SAS	Loiret	14 June	19 August
Haft	1 SAS	Mayenne	8 July	11 August
Dickens	3 SAS	Vendée	16 July	7 October
Defoe	2 SAS	Calvados/Orne	9 July	23 August
Gaff	2 SAS	Eure	26 July	late August
Hardy	2 SAS	Côte-d'Or	26 July	Precursor of Wallace
Chaucer	5 SAS	Mayenne	29 July	14 August
Shakespeare	5 SAS	Mayenne	1 August	12 August
Moses	3 SAS	Vienne/Indre/ Vendée	2 August	4 October
Dunhill	2 SAS	Mayenne	4 August	17 August
Rupert	2 SAS	Aisne/Ardennes	4 August	end August
Derry	3 SAS	Brittany	5 August	18 August
Bunyan	5 SAS	Eure-et-Loir	9 August	15 August

Haggard	1 SAS	Cher	10 August	9 September
Samson	3 SAS	Haute-Vienne/ Vendée	10 August	28 September
Marshall	3 SAS	Correze/Indre/ Vendée	11 August	12 October
Snelgrove	3 SAS	Creuse/Indre/ Vendée	13 August	12 October
Loyton	2 SAS	Vosges	13 August	October
Harrod	3 SAS	Saône-et-Loire	13 August	4 September
Barker	3 SAS	Saône-et-Loire	13 August	4 September
Kipling	1 SAS	Nièvre/Yonne	14 August	end September
Jockworth	3 SAS	Loire/Rhône	15 August	8 September
Trueform	2 SAS	Eure	17 August	22 August
Newton	3 SAS		18 August	Reinforcement operation
Wallace	2 SAS	Côte-d'Or/ Haute-Marne/ Haute-Saône	19 August	17 September
Spenser	4 SAS	Loire valley	26 August	mid September
Abel	3 SAS	Doubs	27 August	25 September
Wolsey	F Squadron, Phantom	Oise	27 August	1 September
Benson	5 SAS	Oise	28 August	1 September
Robey	2 SAS	Haute-Marne	31 August	13 September
Pistol	2 SAS	Meurthe-et-Moselle	6 September	early October

SOURCES

Much of the material concerning the activities of the SAS Brigade in France during 1944 held at the Public Record Office (PRO) at Kew in south-west London is contained in the War Diaries of the Brigade, to be found in the WO 171 series files and in the WO 218 series, specifically WO 218/114 and /115, which are those for HQ SAS Troops between February and December 1944. Other documents in the WO 218 series include Operations Reports and Operations Logs. Material generated by the Brigade's War Crimes Investigation Team is to be found in the WO 309 and WO 311 series.

There is some additional material to be found in the reports of the Jedburgh teams, which are held at Kew in the HS 6 series, specifically HS 6/471 to HS 6/564; those reports are largely duplicated in the holdings of the National Archives and Records Administration (NARA) at College Park, Maryland, near Washington DC, in the Office of Strategic Services' Special Operations Branch War Diary (OSS London SO War Diary).

INDEX

Primary references to individual SAS Operations are in **bold**
Map references are in *italic*